ENGLISH
IN THE
NEWS

ENGLISH IN THE NEWS

Éloi le Divenach

BELIN

8, rue Férou – 75278 PARIS CEDEX 06

© Éditions Belin 1997   ISSN 0769-3036   ISBN 2-7011-**2119**-1

Table des matières

Avant-propos

Cette troisième édition d'*English in the News*, comme les deux précédentes, est consacrée au vocabulaire anglais de l'actualité. Ce vocabulaire, organisé en séquences, fait appel au vocabulaire du contexte, c'est à dire aux termes habituellement associés à tout compte-rendu de l'événement ou de la situation. Par exemple, nous avons inclus dans *Space* les notions de retard, de report, d'annulation et d'expérimentation. Ce qui entraîne, en ne citant que les verbes, la présence de : *to delay, to postpone, to put off, to cancel, to carry out,* etc.

Nous avons profité de cette nouvelle édition pour effectuer une mise à jour approfondie du vocabulaire, en constante évolution. De nombreux mots nouvellement apparus dans l'usage, ou récemment poussés sur le devant de la scène, avec bien souvent de nouvelles acceptions, ont ainsi été inclus. Figurent dans ces catégories des termes comme : *sustainable, biodiversity (Environment), globalisation, convergence criteria (Economy), cloning, keyhole surgery (Medicine), sleaze, soundbite (Politics), digital TV, communication superhighways (Entertainment), electronic tagging (Crime), ethnic cleansing (Miscellaneous), road hump, car sharing (Travel),* etc., etc.

Notre souci d'étoffer le *Vocabulaire complémentaire* nous a, en fait, conduits à prendre en compte plusieurs centaines de mots supplémentaires. S'y ajoutent également de nouvelles formes d'exercices. *English in the News* s'est donc considérablement enrichi dans sa nouvelle édition.

Aux nouveaux utilisateurs, nous croyons utile de rappeler que, pour faciliter l'utilisation de l'ouvrage, le vocabulaire a été divisé en deux parties : le *Vocabulaire à haute fréquence* et le *Vocabulaire complémentaire*, séparées par un ensemble d'expressions et de locutions idiomatiques.

Chaque chapitre de vocabulaire est complété par deux articles (à l'exception du chapitre 24) tirés des meilleurs quotidiens et hebdomadaires britanniques et ces articles ont, naturellement, été entièrement renouvelés pour cette troisième édition. Ils sont suivis d'exercices qui permettent de pratiquer le vocabulaire acquis et de se familiariser avec la presse anglophone. L'utilisateur trouvera en fin d'ouvrage un corrigé. Celui-ci joue un rôle de guide sémantique, de test d'évaluation, de source d'information et il incite l'utilisateur à la recherche personnelle.

Conçu de cette manière, le livre permet l'acquisition systématique et graduée du vocabulaire de l'actualité. Pour tous ceux qui s'efforcent d'entretenir ou de perfectionner leur anglais, soit par un travail individuel, soit dans le cadre de cours de langues, *English in the News* devrait constituer un outil précieux.

Il s'adresse tout particulièrement aux étudiants des premières années de l'enseignement supérieur désireux d'acquérir une connaissance du vocabulaire anglais de l'actualité.

Conseils d'utilisation

Nous conseillons de commencer par le *Vocabulaire à haute fréquence* choisi dans un chapitre quelconque du livre, en fractionnant l'étude de ce vocabulaire selon les possibilités ou les disponibilités de chacun et de jeter un coup d'œil rapide au *Vocabulaire complémentaire* avant d'étudier les articles situés en fin de chapitre et de faire les exercices qui les accompagnent ; certains de ces exercices sont spécialement conçus pour obtenir une lecture attentive et précise. Enfin, vérifier le travail en le confrontant au corrigé situé à la fin de l'ouvrage. L'étude du *Vocabulaire complémentaire* peut ensuite être modulée selon l'objectif plus ou moins avancé poursuivi par l'utilisateur.

La lecture des journaux et des magazines, la compréhension des informations des média audio-visuels ainsi que l'expression orale et écrite seront sensiblement améliorées par une utilisation d'*English in the News*.

Afin d'enrichir le travail de préparation, nous suggérons que l'étudiant, pour chaque exercice du type QCM ou « vrai/faux » justifie sa réponse en se référant à l'article de journal concerné. Nous suggérons également l'entraînement à l'écoute de courts bulletins d'information, en se greffant sur l'actualité du moment, de préférence enregistrés. Cet exercice de compréhension et d'expression complétera de façon très profitable les exercices proposés dans *English in the News*.

Abréviations utilisées dans l'ouvrage

EU	The European Union	**UE**	l'Union Européenne
UK	the United Kingdom	**qch.**	quelque chose
sb.	somebody	**qn.**	quelqu'un
sth.	something	**fam.**	familier
US	The United States		

Signes phonétiques

Sons voyelles

about	[ə]	bird	[ɜ:]
b**a**g	[æ]	clock	[ɒ]
c**ar**	[ɑ:]	four	[ɔ:]
h**ea**d	[e]	put	[u]
s**ea**t	[i:]	moon	[u:]
sit	[ɪ]	bus	[ʌ]

Sons diphtongues

m**a**ke	[eɪ]	toy	[ɔɪ]
s**o**	[əu]	near	[ɪə]
f**i**ve	[aɪ]	ch**air**	[ɛə]
n**ow**	[au]	pure	[uə]

Sons triphtongues

pl**ayer**	[eɪə]	power	[auə]
f**ire**	[aɪə]		

Sons consonnes

book	[b]	**n**arrow	[n]
cap	[k]	**p**art	[p]
down	[d]	**r**iver	[r]
four	[f]	**s**imple	[s]
go	[g]	**t**op	[t]
hat	[h]	**v**ery	[v]
Jim	[dʒ]	**w**est	[w]
list	[l]	**y**es	[j]
mist	[m]	**z**oo	[z]
mea**s**ure	[ʒ]	**sh**op	[ʃ]
chicken	[tʃ]	lo**ng**	[ŋ]
think	[θ]	**th**is	[ð]

The Environment 1 L'environnement

VOCABULAIRE À HAUTE FRÉQUENCE

General Background	Contexte général
to pollute [pə'lu:t]	polluer
pollution	la pollution
environment [ɪn'vaɪərənmənt]	l'environnement
an environmentalist [ɪnˌvaɪərən'mentəlɪst]	un défenseur de l'environnement
nature conservation	la protection de la nature
a conservationist	un protecteur de la nature
to discharge	décharger, déverser
to dump	rejeter, déposer
to get rid of, to dispose of	se débarrasser de
disposal	la destruction, l'élimination
waste	les déchets
rubbish, refuse ['refju:s], trash, garbage (US)	les ordures
litter	les détritus
a tip, a dump	une décharge, un dépôt
to escape	s'échapper
to leak	fuir, s'échapper
a leakage	une fuite, une coulée
a sewer ['sju:ə]	un égout
sewage	les eaux usées
a sewage farm/plant	une station d'épuration
a sewage system	un réseau d'assainissement
to treat	traiter
treatment	le traitement
a standard	une norme
to recycle	recycler
recyclable	recyclable
biodegradable	biodégradable
the greenhouse effect	l'effet de serre
global warming	le réchauffement du globe
biodiversity	la biodiversité

Industry and Car Pollution
La pollution industrielle et automobile

chemistry ['kemıstrı]	la chimie
a chemical	un produit chimique
a gas	un gaz, une vapeur
exhaust fumes	les gaz d'échappement
to release	libérer, dégager
a release	un dégagement, une émanation
an emission	une émission, un rejet
nitrogen ['naɪtrədʒən]	l'azote
sulphur ['sʌlfə]	le soufre
mercury	le mercure
lead [led]	le plomb
lead-free, unleaded	sans plomb
acid rain	la pluie acide
the ozone layer	la couche d'ozone

Farm Pollution
La pollution agricole

pesticide	un pesticide
an insecticide	un insecticide
to spread	épandre
a fertiliser	un engrais
manure [mə'njuə]	le fumier
nitrates ['naɪtreɪts]	les nitrates
to spray	pulvériser
a spray	une pulvérisation
a crop	une récolte
intensive	intensif
factory farming	l'élevage hors-sol
farm produce	un produit agricole
organic farming	l'agriculture biologique

Oil Pollution
La pollution pétrolière

crude oil	le pétrole brut
an oil tanker	un pétrolier
a cargo	une cargaison
a tank	une cuve
to spill	(se) déverser
a spill	un déversement
an oil spill	une marée noire
a slick	une nappe

a detergent [dɪˈtɜːdʒənt]	un détersif
marine life	le milieu marin
oiled	mazouté
to soil, to foul [faul]	salir, souiller
to clean up	nettoyer

Nuclear Pollution — La pollution nucléaire

a power plant/station	une centrale
fuel	le combustible
enriched uranium	l'uranium enrichi
to cool	refroidir
a cooling system	un système de refroidissement
a breakdown	une panne
a fault	un défaut, une anomalie
faulty	défectueux
radiation [ˌreɪdɪˈeɪʃn]	les radiations
radioactivity	la radioactivité
radioactive	radioactif
a level	un niveau, une teneur
a reading	un relevé (de mesure)
a fall-out	une retombée
dust	la poussière
to process	traiter
to reprocess	retraiter
material	des matières
to bury	enfouir
burying	l'enfouissement
to store	stocker
storage	le stockage
a site	un emplacement, un site

Consequences — Les conséquences

to sustain	faire durer, maintenir
sustainable	durable, soutenable
a hazard	un risque
to affect, to hit	toucher, atteindre
to do harm to sth.	faire du mal à qch.
harmful	nuisible
safe, harmless	sans danger, inoffensif
noxious	nocif
to endanger	mettre en danger
to threaten [ˈθretn]	menacer
a threat	une menace

to poison	empoisonner
toxic, poisonous	toxique, empoisonné
a dose	une dose
a trace, a residue	une trace, un résidu
drinking water	l'eau potable
underground waters	les nappes souterraines
water supply	l'alimentation en eau
the food chain	la chaîne alimentaire
to damage	endommager
damage	les dégâts
to destroy	détruire
destruction	la destruction
a disaster	un désastre
a catastrophe [kə'tæstrəfɪ]	une catastrophe
to contaminate	contaminer
a contamination	une contamination
to compensate	indemniser
compensation	une indemnité

/// EXPRESSIONS

to deplete the ozone layer	appauvrir la couche d'ozone
to pose a threat	constituer une menace
dumping at sea	les décharges en mer
to break down a slick	réduire une nappe
the balance of nature	l'équilibre de la nature
environmentally friendly	respecte l'environnement

/// VOCABULAIRE COMPLÉMENTAIRE

General Background — Contexte général

the rainforest	la forêt tropicale
a pollutant	un polluant
ecology ['ɪkɒlədʒɪ]	l'écologie
an ecologist	un écologiste
ecological [i:kə'lɒdʒɪkl]	écologique
an ecosystem	un écosystème
a dustbin, a trash can (US)	une poubelle
a dustman	un éboueur
a landfill site	un site d'enfouissement
strewn/littered with	jonché de
a bottle bank	un conteneur de collecte du verre
sewage sludge	les boues d'épuration

Industry and Car Pollution
La pollution industrielle et automobile

to mix	(se) mélanger
a mixture	un mélange
an effluent	un effluent
sump oil	l'huile de vidange
carbon	le carbone
chlorofluorocarbons (CFCs)	les chlorofluorocarbones
a propellant	un propulseur
an aerosol	un aérosol
a substitute	un produit de substitution
an alternative	un produit de remplacement
depletion	l'appauvrissement
an oxide	un oxyde
a monoxide	un monoxyde
carbon dioxide	le gaz carbonique
catalytic	catalytique
asbestos	l'amiante
dioxin	la dioxine

Farm Pollution
La pollution agricole

a weedkiller	un désherbant
a herbicide	un herbicide
weeds	les mauvaises herbes
a fungicide	un fongicide
to apply	appliquer, mettre (sur)
an application	une application, un usage
slurry	le lisier
fish farming	l'élevage piscicole
a battery	une batterie (élevage)
animal feed	les aliments pour animaux
a hormone	une hormone
an additive	un additif
a preservative	un produit conservateur
a substance	une substance
anabolic steroids	les stéroïdes anabolisants

Oil and Nuclear Pollution
La pollution pétrolière et nucléaire

to flush, to swill tanks	dégazer
hydrocarbons	les hydrocarbures
the hull	la coque

the hold	la soute
an oil rig	une plate-forme de forage
to drill	forer
offshore	au large
to drift	dériver
ashore	vers la côte
a containment boom	un barrage flottant
a skimmer vessel	une barge de récupération
spent fuel	le combustible usé
to decommission	désaffecter
a reprocessing plant	une usine de retraitement
leukaemia [lu:'ki:mɪə]	la leucémie
caesium ['si:zɪəm]	le césium
iodine ['aɪədaɪn, 'aɪədi:n]	l'iode
a containment structure	une enceinte de confinement
the core	le cœur
a fast breeder	un surgénérateur
plutonium	le plutonium
to expose to	mettre en contact avec
exposure	l'exposition, la mise en contact

Consequences — Les conséquences

sustainability	la pérennité, la durabilité
to cull	éliminer, abattre
a cull	une élimination, un abattage
to concentrate	concentrer
a concentration	une concentration
to build up	accumuler
a build-up	une accumulation
a living tissue ['tɪʃu:]	un tissu vivant
cancer	le cancer
a carcinogen [kɑ:'sɪnədʒn]	un produit cancérigène
carcinogenic	cancérigène
wildlife	la faune et la flore
habitat	le biotope
long-term	à longue échéance
threatened species	les espèces menacées
endangered species	les espèces en voie de disparition
extinct	disparu
a strain	une souche (d'espèce)
resistant	insensible, résistant

15

The Birth of BSE

by Mark Watts

(...) It was in 1988, following a recommendation of the Southwood report on the implications of BSE[1], that the Government banned the feeding of ruminants to other ruminants. The report was categorical about the source of the disease: «This problem has arisen as a result of the practice of feeding ruminant materials to herbivores, which are thus exposed to infective risks against which they have not evolved* any defences. Such practices are a feature of modern intensive agriculture, but inevitably... they open up new pathways for infection to the farmed animals and potentially from them to man.»

Cows initially contracted BSE after eating sheep with scrapie*, according to the report. BSE then spread, it said, when cattle ate infected bovine products. Yet as we have seen, ruminants eating ruminants was not new. The trigger* for the outbreak of BSE was a change in the way the meat products fed to cattle were processed, or «rendered» by the animal feed industry.

Sir Richard Southwood, who headed the 1988 working party, explained last week: «During the 1970s this practice took place, but the rendering at that time was done by a process which involved hydrocarbon* solvents, and involved long periods at high temperatures. At that time, it didn't appear to cause diseases.»

But the use of solvents and high temperatures in the rendering of animal remnants was phased out* in the early 1980s – Dr Narang says it was for reasons of cost – and there is widespread agreement that these changes caused BSE to spread in cattle.

[1] Bovine Spongiform Encephalopathy

The Independent on Sunday,
March 31, 1996

---

1. **Choose the right explanation for each of the following words (with asterisks in the passage).**

1. *to evolve*
A. to develop   B. to destroy   C. to find

2. *scrapie*
A. a disease which makes sheep and goats change colour
B. a disease which makes sheep and goats put on weight
C. a disease which makes sheep and goats scratch themselves

3. *a trigger*
A. it brings about failure   B. it starts something off
C. it initiates a decline

4. *hydrocarbons*
A. a combination of carbon and oxygen
B. a combination of carbon and hydrogen
C. a combination of carbon and nitrogen

2. Say whether the following statements are true (T) or false (F).

1. The Southwood report was uncertain about the origin of the disease.

2. Cows contracted BSE after having been fed animal products.

3. The report didn't imagine BSE could spread to humans.

4. Giving meat products to cattle only became common practice in the early 1980s.

5. It is difficult to understand why the original process was safer.

6. Profit may have had something to do with the change in the way of processing meat products.

3. Fill in each blank with a word from the following list. Use each word once only. Verbs are given in the infinitive.

oil	to run	catastrophe	important
crude	supertanker	cargo	to offload

Salvage experts aboard a crippled ...(1)... struggled last night to prevent an environmental ...(2)... on the coast of West Wales.

As winds whipped a five-mile ...(3)... slick towards one of the most ...(4)... wildlife habitats in Britain, plans were in hand ...(5)... the remaining ...(6)... of 136,000 tonnes of light ...(7)... oil from the Liberian-registered Sea Empress, 24 hours after she ...(8)... on to rocks near Milford Haven.

The Times, February 7, 1993

4. BSE (Bovine Spongiform Encephalopathy) is the English for ESB (Encéphalite spongiforme bovine). Give the English equivalents for the following acronyms and phrases.

1. OTAN (Organisation du traité de l'Atlantique nord)

2. ONU (Organisation des nations unies)

3. PAC (Politique agricole commune)

4. FMI (Fonds monétaire international)

5. PIB (Produit intérieur brut)

6. OMS (Organisation mondiale de la santé)

Not quite as organic as it seems

by Steve Connor, Science Correspondent

Organic vegetables are not as organic as you are led to believe. They grow with the help of substantial amounts of chemical fertiliser that literally rains down from the sky.

Atmospheric pollution is now so bad that practically every farm in Britain, whether organic or intensive, benefits from huge quantities of free artificial fertiliser deposited from above.

Scientists calculate that a typical organic farm receives an extra helping of nitrogen fertiliser from the atmosphere equivalent to about 8,000 cowpats[1] falling on each hectare of land every year.

This is equivalent to 40-45kg – about a quarter of the amount of chemical fertiliser typically used on intensive farms.

"It really is quite significant," said Keith Goulding, a soil chemist at the Rothamstead Experimental Station in Hertfordshire, where the oldest field experiment in the world has helped to estimate how much airborne nitrogen is falling on Britain.

A field at Rothamstead has been cultivated with cereals every year since 1843, and the amount of added nitrogen fertiliser carefully monitored on individual plots. Water running off in a drain is monitored for nitrogen.

Rothamstead scientists have also kept records of nitrogen in rainwater since 1853. They have found that over the past 150 years the nitrogen content of rainwater has increased by about three times as a result of pollution from cars, power stations, farm animals and the increased use of chemical fertilisers that can be blown away.

[1] A cow's excretions on the ground.

The Independent on Sunday,
March 21, 1993

1. Choose the appropriate endings for the following sentences.

1. Organic vegetables are not really organic because
A. farmers spray chemicals to fertilise them.
B. chemical fertilisers, carried in the atmosphere, fall to the ground.
C. they are grown according to intensive farming methods.

2. For organic farmers, chemical fertilisers falling from the sky are
A. useless.
B. a benefit.
C. a nuisance.

3. When compared to organic farms, the soil on intensive farms receives about
A. four times the amount of fertiliser.
B. three times the amount of fertiliser.
C. twice the amount of fertiliser.

4. Keith Goulding works in
A. a chemist's.   B. a laboratory.   C. a power station.

5. Water running off in a drain gives information about the amount of nitrogen
A. in rainwater.   B. washed away.   C. in the air.

6. The situation described in the article is
A. really amusing.
B. rather intriguing.
C. deeply worrying.

2. "Organic" and "atmospheric" are examples of adjectives ending in "-ic". Use the definitions to find eight other adjectives with the same ending.

1. These missiles end in a free fall.   B☐☐☐☐☐☐IC
2. Results like these mean a remedy has to be found.   C☐☐☐☐☐☐☐☐☐IC
3. These flights do not leave the country.   D☐☐☐☐☐IC
4. In these regimes, power comes from the citizens.   D☐☐☐☐☐☐☐IC
5. Eruptions like these can be very destructive.   V☐☐☐☐☐IC
6. This type of surgery improves a person's look. C☐☐☐☐☐IC
7. The same as number 6.   P☐☐☐☐IC
8. These tests may be used to solve a crime.   F☐☐☐☐☐IC

3. Fill in the nine lines across the grid with translations of the corresponding French words. This will give you the answer to number 10 in column D.

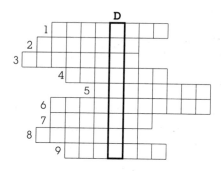

1. norme   2. poubelle   3. inoffensif   4. traiter   5. menacer
6. durable, soutenable   7. détruire   8. stockage   9. dégager
10. déverser

The Economy I $\boxed{2}$ L'économie I

///VOCABULAIRE À HAUTE FRÉQUENCE

Variations and Assessment	Variations et évaluation
to go up, to rise	monter
a rise in prices	une hausse des prix
inflation	l'inflation
inflationary	inflationniste
to drop, to fall, to come down	baisser, diminuer
a fall/drop in prices	une baisse des prix
expensive, dear	cher
to cost	coûter
the cost	le coût
costly	coûteux
cheap	bon marché
worth	la valeur
to be worth	valoir
a profit	un bénéfice
profit	le profit
profitable, economic	rentable
a benefit	un avantage, une allocation, une prestation
to gain	gagner
a gain	un gain, une plus-value
a loss	une perte
loss-making, unprofitable, uneconomic	non rentable
economical	économique, économe
to survey	étudier
a survey	une étude, une enquête
a price index	un indice des prix
to assess, to estimate	évaluer
an assessment, an estimate	une évaluation

20

to value	évaluer, apprécier
the face value	la valeur nominale
a figure	un chiffre
a billion	un milliard
to exceed	dépasser
a trend	une tendance
to grow	croître
growth	la croissance
a rate	un taux
to expand	(se) développer
expansion	l'expansion
to thrive, to prosper	prospérer
thriving, prosperous	prospère
prosperity	la prospérité
a boom	une vague de prospérité
to decline	décliner
a decline	un déclin, une baisse
a crisis	une crise
a recession	une récession
to improve	(s')améliorer
an improvement	une amélioration
to recover	reprendre, se rétablir
recovery	la reprise, le rétablissement

Measures — Les mesures

a policy	une politique
to increase, to raise	augmenter
an increase	une augmentation
to bring down	abaisser, diminuer
to reduce, to cut back	réduire
a reduction, a cut-back	une réduction
to curb	juguler, maîtriser
a curb	un frein
austerity	l'austérité
to restrict	restreindre
a restriction	une restriction
to devalue	dévaluer
a devaluation	une dévaluation
to subsidise	subventionner
a subsidy	une subvention
to boost	doper, relancer
a boost	une relance

Taxes | Les impôts

to tax	taxer, imposer
taxation	l'imposition, la taxation
income tax	l'impôt sur le revenu
a taxpayer	un contribuable
the council tax	les impôts locaux
to collect	lever, recouvrer
collection	le recouvrement
a tax collector	un percepteur, un receveur

Money | L'argent

cash	les espèces, le numéraire
a banknote, a bill (US)	un billet de banque
a coin	une pièce
currency	les devises, la monnaie
to earn	gagner
earnings	les gains
to spend	dépenser
spending	les dépenses
expenses	les dépenses, les frais
to owe money	devoir de l'argent
to save	économiser
savings	l'épargne, les économies
to invest	investir
an investment	un investissement
an investor	un investisseur
a sum	une somme
an amount	un montant
to amount to	s'élever à, revenir à

Production | La production

to produce	produire
a product	un produit
production, output	la production
productivity	la productivité
farm produce	les produits agricoles
to manufacture	fabriquer
a manufactured product	un produit fabriqué
goods, wares	les marchandises
a warehouse	un entrepôt

a commodity	une marchandise primaire
supply	l'offre
demand	la demande
to consume	consommer
consumption	la consommation
a grade	une catégorie

Trade and the EU

Le commerce et l'UE

business	les affaires
a customer	un client
to sell retail	vendre au détail
a sale	une vente
to buy wholesale	acheter en gros
to purchase	acheter, acquérir
a purchase	un achat, une acquisition
to order	commander
an order	une commande
to supply/provide sb. with sth.	fournir qch. à qn.
to charge	faire payer
a charge	les frais, un prix à payer
an invoice	une facture —
a bill, a check *(US)*	une note, une addition
to bargain	marchander, négocier
a bargain	une (bonne) affaire
a (clearance) sale	les ventes de soldes
an auction	une vente aux enchères
to trade	faire du commerce
a market	un marché
to advertise	faire de la publicité
advertising	la publicité
an advertisement [əd'vɜːtɪsmənt]	une publicité
an adman	un publicitaire
to import [ɪm'pɔːt]	importer
an import ['ɪmpɔːt]	une importation
to export [eks'pɔːt]	exporter
an export ['ekspɔːt]	une exportation
home trade	le commerce intérieur
foreign/overseas trade	le commerce exterleur
to globalise	mondialiser
globalisation	la mondialisation
to share	partager
a share	une part
a trade gap	un déficit commercial

a deficit	un déficit
a surplus	un excédent
an outlet	un débouché, un point de vente
to compete with sb.	concurrencer qn.
competition	la concurrence
competitive	compétitif
competitiveness	la compétitivité
to protect	protéger
protectionism	le protectionnisme
a protectionist	un protectionniste
customs	la douane
a duty	un droit
a tariff	un tarif douanier
a barrier	une barrière
a quota ['kwəutə]	un quota
free trade	le libre-échange
a free trader	un libre-échangiste
to join sth.	adhérer à qch.
a summit	un sommet
a directive	une directive
a single market	un marché unique
a single currency	une monnaie unique
to veto sth.	opposer son veto à qch.
a veto	un veto
the qualified majority	la majorité qualifiée
convergence criteria	les critères de convergence
the stability pact	le pacte de stabilité
an opt-out (clause)	une clause d'exemption

/// EXPRESSIONS

it's worth trying	cela mérite d'être essayé
it sells well	cela se vend bien
to sustain/suffer a loss	subir une perte
to recoup ones losses	récupérer ses pertes
to plough back profits	réinvestir les bénéfices
to get value for money	en avoir pour son argent
to hit the jackpot	gagner le pactole
to earn one's living	gagner sa vie
the standard of living	le niveau de vie
the cost of living	le coût de la vie
to fetch a high price	atteindre un prix élevé

to sell at a premium	(se) vendre au-dessus du cours
to foot the bill	payer la note, régler l'addition
to pick up the tab	payer l'addition
the retail price index	l'indice des prix de détail
the consumer price index	l'indice des prix à la consommation
a package of measures	un ensemble de mesures
to kickstart the economy	faire démarrer l'économie
pay as you earn (PAYE)	le prélèvement à la source
value added tax (VAT)	la taxe à la valeur ajoutée (TVA)
to put out to tender	lancer un appel d'offres
to drive a hard bargain	ne pas faire de cadeau, être dur en affaires
to cut corners	rogner sur les coûts
the Gross National Product	le produit national brut
the Gross Domestic Product	le produit intérieur brut
the Balance of Trade	la balance commerciale
the Balance of Payments	la balance des paiements
a current account deficit	un déficit de la balance des paiements courants
the Exchange Rate Mechanism	le Mécanisme des changes
the European Monetary System (EMS)	le Système monétaire européen
the European Monetary Union (EMU)	l'Union monétaire européenne
a European Member of Parliament	un député européen

/// VOCABULAIRE COMPLÉMENTAIRE

Variations and Assessment	Variations et évaluation
a profit margin	une marge bénéficiaire
cost effective	rentable, d'un bon rapport coût-performance
dirt cheap	très bon marché
to stagnate	stagner
stagnation	la stagnation
to slacken, to slow down	ralentir
a slack, a slow-down	un ralentissement
to dip	fléchir, baisser

a dip	un fléchissement
to slump	baisser brutalement
a slump	une chute brutale, un marasme
to plummet	dégringoler
to collapse	s'effondrer
a collapse	un effondrement
a setback	un revers, une déconvenue
a recession	une récession
to look up, to pick up	se redresser
an upturn, an upswing	un redressement
a downturn, a downswing	un fléchissement
to flourish	prospérer
flourishing	florissant, prospère
to overheat	surchauffer
to soar	s'envoler
to shoot up	monter en flèche
to revive	se rétablir
a revival	une rétablissement
to make up for sth.	compenser qch.
to offset	contrebalancer, compenser
in real terms	en argent constant
a spin-off	une retombée
an analyst	un analyste, conjoncturiste
a pundit	un expert
a prospect	une perspective
to forecast	prévoir
a forecast, an outlook	une prévision

Measures and Taxes — Les mesures et les impôts

the Budget	le budget
public expenditure	les dépenses publiques
monetary	monétaire
monetarism	le monétarisme
deflation	la déflation
deflationary	déflationniste
to levy	percevoir, prélever
a levy	un prélèvement, une taxe
a fee	un droit, une redevance
to squeeze	comprimer
a squeeze	une compression, une rigueur
to bite	faire de l'effet
to nationalise	nationaliser

nationalisation	la nationalisation
to privatise	privatiser
privatisation	la privatisation
regulation	la réglementation
deregulation	la déréglementation
an incentive	une mesure d'incitation
to stimulate	stimuler
to grant	accorder
a grant	une aide financière
to finance, to fund	financer
funds	les fonds
to slash	réduire radicalement
a slash	une réduction radicale
to jack up	relever (les prix)
to hike prices *(US)*	relever les prix
a price hike *(US)*	une augmentation des prix
to index	indexer
index-linked	indexé
a tax haven	un paradis fiscal
tax relief	un dégrèvement fiscal
a tax allowance	un abattement fiscal
a tax break	une réduction d'impôt
tax evasion	la fraude fiscale
to cap taxes	fixer un plafond à l'impôt
revenue	les rentrées fiscales
the tax burden	le poids des impôts
inheritance tax	les droits de succession

Money / L'argent

a hard currency	une devise forte
to waste	gaspiller
waste, wastage	le gaspillage
to squander	dilapider, gaspiller
to skimp	lésiner, économiser
thrift	l'épargne
thrifty	économe
a spendthrift	un panier percé
extravagant, profligate	dépensier, prodigue
extravagance, profligacy	la prodigalité
a windfall	une aubaine, un pactole
a godsend	un don du ciel, une manne
a money-spinner	une mine d'or, un filon

27

Production

Production	La production
just-in-time production, zero stock production	la production à flux tendu
a shortage	une pénurie
a shortfall	une insuffisance, un manque
a glut	un engorgement
to contract	s'engager par contrat
a contract	un contrat
a contractor	un entrepreneur
an entrepreneur	un chef d'entreprise
enterprise	l'esprit d'entreprise
to subcontract	sous-traiter
a subcontractor	un sous-traitant
a tender	une soumission
to exhaust	épuiser
exhaustion	l'épuisement
a brand	une marque commerciale
a make	une marque, une fabrication
to target	cibler
a target	une cible
custom-made	fait sur commande

Trade and the EU — Le commerce et l'UE

Trade and the EU	Le commerce et l'UE
a niche	un créneau, un marché
a shopper	un client de magasin
a patron	un client fidèle
a punter	un chaland
a good buy	un bon achat
barter	le troc
to haggle	marchander
to shop around	comparer les prix
to refund	restituer de l'argent
a refund	une restitution d'argent
a discount	une remise
a rebate	un rabais
into the bargain	par-dessus le marché
hard sell	l'agressivité de vente
a hoarding, a billboard (US)	un panneau publicitaire
to undercut, to undersell	vendre moins cher que
to net	empocher, engranger
proceeds	le produit, les recettes
consumer goods	les biens de consommation

capital goods	les biens d'équipement
business premises	les locaux commerciaux
mail-order	l'achat par correspondance
a middleman	un intermédiaire
to insure	assurer
insurance	l'assurance
to underwrite	souscrire
a policy	une police
a premium	une cotisation, une prime
a claim	une demande d'indemnisation
invisibles	les exportations et les importations invisibles
an imbalance	un déséquilibre
to corner	accaparer
to fix prices	s'entendre sur les prix
price-fixing	l'entente illicite
a contribution	une contribution, une cotisation
an MEP, a Euro MP	un député européen
a commissioner	un commissaire
subsidiarity	la subsidiarité
the social charter	la charte sociale
the social chapter	le chapitre social
set-aside land	les terres incultes, gelées

'I don't think the dustmen liked those new Euro notes you gave them for Christmas'

29

Primera absorbs Nissan's profit

by Roland Gribben

Nissan Motor Manufacturers will struggle to stay in profit this year following the launch of the new Primera model. Ian Gibson, chief executive, said yesterday the company would be "hard put" to repeat last year's net profit of £10m.

Profits will be hit by the first tranche of the £340m costs of the new car. About £250m of the total has been spent on retooling at the Sunderland factory to accommodate the Primera, the fourth model to be produced at the plant.

Local management are hailing* the car as the "coming of age"* for Nissan in Europe because it is the first of the Sunderland-built range designed at the company's engineering base in Cranfield, Bedfordshire. It will be officially launched in Britain at the Birmingham motor show on October 16. Nissan is aiming to increase production to 120,000 next year, about half the ultimate total.

Overall output this year is expected to show little change on last year's figure of 217,000 because of the model change-over and difficulties in Continental markets. Demands for the Micra during the rest of the year will dictate whether Nissan stays in the black this year.

The company plans to export the Sunderland-built Primera to 58 countries, including Japan, and says 44 British-based suppliers have benefited from the development programme.

The Daily Telegraph, August 6, 1996

1. Choose the right explanation for each of the following words (with asterisks in the passage).

1. *to hail*
A. to criticise   B. to condemn   C. to salute

2. *to come of age*
A. to become adult   B. to be getting old
C. to be too young

2. Choose the appropriate endings for the following sentences.

1. Compared to 1995, Nissan's 1996 profits looked like being
A. higher.   B. not so high.   C. the same.

2. Taking the 1995 profits into account, it is apparent that launching a new model is
A. a small investment.
B. a moderate investment.
C. a huge investment.

3. Sunderland is located in the
A. north-west of England.
B. north-east of England.
C. south-west of England.

4. The European division of Nissan seems to be gaining
A. more independence.
B. less independence.
C. no independence.

5. Ultimately, output at the Sunderland plant will be
A. maintained.   B. reduced.   C. increased.

6. The opposite of "to stay in the black" is "to stay
A. in the red".   B. in the white".   C. in the green".

3. Which of the words in each list is not synonymous with the first one?

1. to struggle, to strive, to endeavour, to manage.
2. to stay, to remain, to delay, to continue.
3. a show, a saloon, an exhibition, a display.
4. a factory, a plant, a branch, a works.

Will Europe's unemployed pay the price of a single currency?

Tony Barber

(...) EU leaders, already worried that Europe's economic difficulties may force a postponement of the Euro's planned launch in January 1999, accept that public support for monetary union is essential if the project is to succeed. This, in turn, requires governments to show their electorates that they can deliver more jobs in the next three years despite the rigid Maastricht conditions.

If they fail to do so, it is quite conceivable that the Euro will not get off the ground. Lamberto Dini, Italy's outgoing Prime Minister, puts it bluntly*: as long as unemployment is so high, monetary union is "unthinkable".

To qualify for the single currency, governments must bring their budget deficits down to 3 per cent or less of gross domestic product and public debts to 60 per cent or less. They must also meet strict targets on low inflation, low interest rates and exchange rate stability.

It is the deficit and debt criteria that are proving hardest for governments to fulfil* – so hard that at the moment only Luxembourg, which contains 0.1 per cent of the EU's population, meets all Maastricht's conditions. But no EU member-state (except, it seems, Britain once again) is happy at the prospect of being left out in 1999, and so most governments have embarked on the unpopular course of squeezing public spending and pruning* their welfare systems.

But it would be unfair to blame Maastricht for everything. Whether or not the treaty existed, EU governments would need to reduce their deficits and reform their social security systems, some of which, like France's, would otherwise simply go bust.

The Independent on Sunday,
February 4, 1996

1. **Choose the right explanation for each of the following words (with asterisks in the passage).**

1. *bluntly*
A. rather carefully   B. somewhat brutally   C. very politely

2. *to fulfil*
A. to satisfy   B. to ignore   C. to destroy

3. *to prune*
A. to develop   B. to establish   C. to cut back

2. **Say whether the following statements are true (T) or false (F).**

1. Governments can be content with satisfying the Maastricht conditions.
2. Cutting down on unemployment is a key factor.
3. Lamberto Dini played down the importance of unemployment.
4. The convergence criteria are clearly summed up in the article.
5. The gross domestic product plays a major part in the conditions.
6. The measures adopted to meet the conditions seem to vary greatly from country to country.
7. Maastricht is likely to be used as a scapegoat.

3. **Read the article again and find the following:**

1. Three adjectives showing that meeting Maastricht's conditions is no easy task.
2. Two adverbs, used together, revealing that Britain often stands out on its own in the EU.
3. One adjective which is in sharp contradiction with "public support".

4. **Relative value can be shown by a percentage (e.g. 3 per cent) or by a fraction (e.g. a quarter, three-fifths). Using the smallest possible numerator, write down in full the fractions corresponding to the following percentages.**

1. 5%   2. 10%   3. 20%   4. 33%   5. 40%
6. 50%   7. 60%   8. 66%   9. 80%

VOCABULAIRE À HAUTE FRÉQUENCE

Real Estate	Les biens immobiliers
to own	posséder
ownership	la propriété
property	les biens
a landlord	un propriétaire immobilier
a tenant	un locataire
to let	donner en location
to rent	prendre en location
rent	le loyer
a flat, an apartment (US)	un appartement
an estate agent, a realtor (US)	agent immobilier
housing	le logement
a council house	une HLM

Wealth and Poverty	La richesse et la pauvreté
rich, wealthy	riche
well-off	aisé, bien nanti
poor	pauvre
the poverty line	le seuil de pauvreté
hard up, broke	fauché
a need	un besoin
the needy	les nécessiteux
misery	la misère
hardship	les difficultés matérielles
to beg	mendier
a beggar	un mendiant
destitute	sans ressources, démuni
destitution	l'indigence

deprived	déshérité
deprivation	le dénuement
underprivileged	défavorisé
to assist	assister, aider
assistance, welfare	l'assistance, l'aide
the welfare system	l'aide sociale
the welfare state	l'État providence

Banking / Les banques

a bank	une banque
an account	un compte
a balance	un solde
a cheque book	un carnet de chèques
to draw money	tirer de l'argent
a draft	un retrait
to overdraw	tirer à découvert
an overdraft	un découvert
to borrow	emprunter
to lend	prêter
a loan	un prêt, un emprunt
a mortgage ['mɔːgɪdʒ]	un prêt immobilier
a debt	une dette
a debtor	un débiteur
credit	le crédit
a creditor	un créancier
to pay back, to repay	rembourser
a payment	un paiement, versement
repayment	le remboursement
to settle	régler
a settlement	un règlement
overdue	en retard, échu
interest	l'intérêt
the exchange rate	le taux de change

Businesses / Les entreprises

to set up	(s')établir
to establish	fonder
a firm, a business	une firme, une affaire
a multinational	une multinationale
to manage, to run	diriger, gérer
management	la direction, la gestion
a partner	un associé

a partnership	une société de personnes
a company, a corporation (US)	une société commerciale
a joint-stock company	une société par actions
the head office, the headquarters	le siège social
capital	le capital
a stake, a holding	une participation au capital
a chairman, a president (US)	un président
a managing director, a chief executive officer (CEO)	un directeur général
a chief executive	un président délégué
a director	un administrateur
a board of directors	un conseil d'administration
an executive	un cadre
an annual report	un rapport d'activité
a general meeting	une assemblée générale
an agenda	un ordre du jour
turnover	le chiffre d'affaires
a dividend	un dividende
to bid for	faire une offre pour
a bid	une offre d'achat
to take-over	racheter, prendre le contrôle de
a takeover	un rachat, une prise de contrôle
a take-over bid	une offre publique d'achat

Ailing Companies — Les sociétés en difficulté

running costs	les frais de fonctionnement
overheads, fixed costs	les frais généraux
assets	l'actif
liabilities	le passif
cash flow	le flux de liquidités
a lame duck	un canard boiteux
to prop up	soutenir, étayer
to bail out	renflouer
mismanagement	la mauvaise gestion
to fail, to go bust, to go bankrupt, to go under, to collapse	faire faillite
a failure, a bankruptcy	une faillite
a receiver	un administrateur judiciaire
to wind up, to liquidate	liquider
liquidation	la liquidation

The Stock Exchange — La Bourse des valeurs

The Stock Exchange	La Bourse des valeurs
stock, securities	les valeurs, les titres
a share	une action
a bond	une obligation
to subscribe	souscrire
a deal	une transaction
a dealer	un opérateur
a bearer	un porteur
a stockbroker	un agent de change
to quote	coter
a quotation	une cote, un cours
to close	clôturer
close [kləuz]	la clôture
to open up	ouvrir en hausse
to close down	clôturer en baisse
to yield	rapporter
a yield	un rapport

Market fluctuations — Les fluctuations du marché

Market fluctuations	Les fluctuations du marché
steady	stable
firm	ferme
dull	inactif, maussade
volatile	nerveux, fébrile
to slide	baisser
a slide	une baisse
to crumble	s'effriter
to fall back	se replier
a fall-back	un repli
a crash	un krach
to rally	se raffermir
a rally	un raffermissement
to level off	se stabiliser
to ease	se détendre
buoyant ['bɔɪənt]	soutenu, bien orienté
brisk	actif, animé

/// EXPRESSIONS

to go on welfare	s'inscrire à l'aide sociale
to feel the pinch	sentir les effets de la rigueur
to tighten one's belt	se serrer la ceinture

to make ends meet	joindre les deux bouts
a balance of account	un solde de compte
a statement of account	un relevé de compte
to be in the red	être à découvert, en déficit
to be in the black	être créditeur
to break even	équilibrer les comptes
to go public	introduire en Bourse
to dabble on the Stock Exchange	boursicoter
to buy forward	acheter à terme
to sell short	vendre à terme, vendre au rabais, sous-évaluer
an all-time high	un record à la hausse
an all-time low	un record à la baisse
the Securities and Investment Board (UK), the Securities and Exchange Commission (US)	la Commission des opérations de Bourse
to mount a take-over bid	lancer une OPA
to drive out of business	contraindre à la fermeture
to go out of business	cesser son activité
to go to the wall	aller à sa perte
to file for bankrutcy, to file under chapter 11 (US)	déposer son bilan
to go belly up (US)	faire faillite
to go into administration	être mis en redressement judiciaire
to be placed into receivership, to go into liquidation	entrer en liquidation

VOCABULAIRE COMPLÉMENTAIRE

Wealth, Poverty and Housing	La richesse, la pauvreté et le logement
affluent	fortuné
affluence	l'abondance, l'opulence
means	les moyens
means testing	l'évaluation des ressources
purchasing power	le pouvoir d'achat
a breadwinner	un soutien de famille
down and out	sans le sou
bread (fam.)	le fric, l'oseille
National Insurance	la Sécurité sociale
social security	l'aide sociale
food stamps (US)	les bons de nourriture

a bread line, a soup kitchen	une soupe populaire, un resto du cœur
to lease	prendre, donner en location
a lease	un bail
a housing estate	un lotissement
a council estate	une cité HLM
a slum	un taudis
homeless	sans logis
to sleep rough	dormir dehors
housing benefit	l'allocation de logement
child benefit	les allocations familiales
planning permission	le permis de construire
town planning	l'urbanisme
a property developer	un promoteur immobilier
to repossess	saisir pour non-paiement
repossession	saisie pour non-paiement
to evict	expulser
eviction	expulsion

Banking / Les banques

the base rate	le taux de base
the discount rate	le taux d'escompte
the lending rate	le taux de l'argent
a flat rate	un taux uniforme
a composite rate	un taux composé
a merchant bank	une banque d'affaires
a building society	une mutuelle d'épargne-logement
a blank cheque	un chèque en blanc
a bounced cheque	un chèque refusé
a dud/rubber cheque	un chèque sans provision
to default	ne pas honorer, se dérober
a cash point	un distributeur de billets
a credit card	une carte de crédit
direct debit	le prélèvement direct
a quid (fam. UK)	une livre sterling
a buck (fam. US)	un dollar
to loan	prêter
a loan shark	un usurier
a bad debt	une créance impayée
arrears |əˈrɪəz|	les arriérés
money supply	la masse monétaire

Businesses | Les entreprises

Businesses	Les entreprises
a concern	une entreprise, une firme
to undertake	entreprendre
an undertaking	une opération entreprise
a limited partnership	une société en commandite
a private company	une société à responsabilité limitée
a public company	une société anonyme
a parent company	une société mère
a sister company	une société du même groupe
a holding company	une société de portefeuille, un holding
an offshoot	une branche
a subsidiary	une filiale
a joint venture	une société commune
a front company	une société écran
a deputy chairman, a vice-president (US)	un vice président
a non-executive director	un administrateur extérieur à la société
working capital	les fonds de roulement
returns, proceeds	les recettes, les rentrées
corporate tax	l'impôt sur les sociétés
pre-tax profits	les bénéfices avant impôt
a balance sheet	un bilan comptable
provisions	les provisions
the bottom line	le résultat final
an auditor	un commissaire aux comptes
to issue shares	émettre des actions
a share issue	une émission d'actions
a rights issue	une émission de droits d'attribution
a golden share	une action à droit particulier
to allot	attribuer
an allotment	une attribution
to float	lancer (une société, des actions)
a flotation	une émission financière
a high flier	une personne de haut vol
a Yuppie	un jeune cadre dynamique
a tycoon, a magnate	un magnat
a mogul	un nabab

Companies as Targets

to amalgamate, to merge	fusionner
an amalgamation, a merger	une fusion
a management buy-out	un rachat par les cadres
a leveraged buy-out	un rachat avec emprunt
a war chest	un trésor de guerre
a bidder	un repreneur
a predator	un rapace boursier
a raider	un assaillant
a raid	une attaque, un assaut
a white knight	un chevalier blanc
a (friendly) suitor	un repreneur amical
a sweetener	une douceur, une sucrette
an insider	un initié
insider dealing/trading	le délit d'initié
a watchdog	un organisme de surveillance

Les sociétés pour cible

The Stock Exchange

a stock market	une place boursière
a portfolio	un portefeuille (valeurs)
equities	les actions ordinaires
gilt-edged securities	les valeurs sans risque (obligations d'État)
blue chips	les actions des grandes sociétés
junk bonds	obligations de pacotille
a bull	un spéculateur à la hausse
a bear	un spéculateur à la baisse
the spot market	le marché au comptant
the futures market	le marché à terme
to hedge	se couvrir (risque)
the Mercantile Exchange	la Bourse des marchandises

La Bourse des valeurs

Banks throw Eurotunnel a £4.7bn lifeline

by Jonathan Prynn and Marianne Curphey

A £4.7 billion agreement to rebuild Eurotunnel's shattered finances was unveiled yesterday, ending a traumatic year during which the company tottered* on the brink of insolvency.

The deal, thrashed out in a marathon round of talks between bankers and the two co-chairmen of the Channel tunnel operator, paves the way for Eurotunnel shares to resume trading today, after an eight-day suspension.

Unveiling the agreement, Sir Alistair Morton, the co-chairman of Eurotunnel who retires at the end of the month, described it as "fair and robust" and said that it had averted the "Domesday* scenario" of administration.

Under its terms, the banks have agreed to cut £4.7 billion of high interest borrowing from the company's £9 billion debt mountain in return for a minimum 45.5 per cent share of the company's equity*.

The banks can take a majority share of up to 60 per cent by 2003 if the company performs badly. In the event of Eurotunnel once again facing insolvency, the banks could end up with around 75 per cent early in the next century.

Sir Alistair said that the deal made the payment of dividends a possibility from 2005. "The restructuring plan provides Eurotunnel with the medium-term stability to allow it to consolidate its substantial commercial achievements and develop its operations," he said.

It still has to win approval from 75 per cent of UK shareholders and two thirds of the more militant French shareholders.

The Times, October 10, 1996

1. Choose the right explanation for each of the following words (with asterisks in the passage).

1. *to totter*
A. to walk at a brisk pace
B. to walk with a firm step
C. to walk as if about to fall

2. *Domesday*
A. implying disaster
B. implying a happy ending
C. implying huge profits

3. *equity*
A. the total value of the dividends
B. the total value of the debt
C. the total value of the shares

2. Say whether the following statements are true (T) or false (F).

1. Eurotunnel had cash flow problems in 1996.
2. The company would have gone into administration if no deal had been reached.
3. The banks have given Eurotunnel a new loan.
4. The stake held by the banks in the company will be reduced if Eurotunnel does not do well.
5. No significant profits are likely to be made in the next few years.
6. Eurotunnel cannot boast success in its operations.
7. Small shareholders are likely to be worse off after the agreement.

3. Read the article again and find the following:

1. A noun showing Eurotunnel could no longer meet its liabilities.
2. A verb revealing that negotiations had been strenuous.
3. A noun implying that Eurotunnel is a Franco-British joint venture.
4. A compound noun defining what Eurotunnel is.
5. Synonyms for each of the following verbs:
A. to stagger   B. to restart
B. to disclose   D. to avoid.

4. The noun "insolvency" is made up of the adjective "insolvent" and the ending "-cy". Use the definitions to find eight other nouns with the same ending.

1. It has to do with crime.   D☐☐☐☐☐☐☐☐☐CY
2. Connected with time and repetition.   F☐☐☐☐☐☐☐CY
3. Not showing enough severity.   L☐☐☐☐☐☐CY
4. Being full of self-satisfaction.   C☐☐☐☐☐☐☐☐☐CY
5. Being at ease in a foreign language.   F☐☐☐☐CY

Boeing in "historic" $13 bn merger

by Charles Pretzlik in New York

Boeing yesterday announced a $13.3 billion merger with McDonnell Douglas, which will create the largest aerospace group in the world.

Announcing the deal, Boeing's president and chief executive, Philip Condit, said it was "an historic moment in aviation and aerospace." McDonnell Douglas's chairman, John McDonnell, said the new company will be the "largest, strongest, broadest, most admired aerospace corporation in the world and by far the largest US exporter."

If the deal is approved by anti-trust regulators, the takeover will reduce the number of major commercial jet makers in the world from three to two. Industry analysts said that could pose a serious competitive threat to Airbus Industrie, the four-nation European consortium which is the world's second largest commercial jet maker.

Mr Condit said he did not expect regulatory approval to be "a big issue".

Although both companies characterised the deal as a merger, the company will retain the Boeing name and be based at Boeing's headquarters in Seattle, Washington. Two thirds of the board directors will be from Boeing.

Boeing's $28 billion annual sales exceed McDonnell's $20 billion. Mr Condit will remain chief executive and assume the chairmanship, and McDonnell's chief executive Harry Stonecipher will become president and chief operating officer. The chairmen of both companies, Mr McDonnell and Boeing's Frank Shrontz, said they will retire next year.

The Daily Telegraph,
December 12, 1996

1. Choose the appropriate endings for the following sentences.

1. When compared to that of the chairman of McDonnell Douglas, the president of Boeing's comment showed
A. as much restraint.
B. more restraint.
C. less restraint.

2. For European jet makers, the merger is
A. rather good news.
B. no news.
C. rather bad news.

3. Regulatory approval is needed to avoid
A. Stock Exchange speculation.
B. a monopoly situation.
C. labour tension.

4. The merger seemed to be
A. with one dominant company.
B. on equal terms.
C. against the will of one company.

5. It seems to appear in the article that the chairman (in this particular case) is
A. above the president.
B. on the same level as the president.
C. below the president.

2. The noun "takeover" is made up of the verb "take" and the adverb "over". Use the definitions to find eight other nouns constructed in the same way.

1. An escape, usually by criminals.　　　　　GⵧⵧAⵧⵧⵧ
2. A confrontation, often seen in westerns.　　SⵧⵧⵧDⵧⵧⵧ
3. An attempt to conceal something.　　　　　Cⵧⵧⵧⵧ-Uⵧ
4. Troops leaving an area.　　　　　　　　　Pⵧⵧ-Oⵧⵧ
5. The volume of business done.　　　　　　　TⵧⵧⵧOⵧⵧⵧ
6. A reorganisation, of a cabinet for example.　Sⵧⵧⵧ-Uⵧ
7. A gun battle (cowboys, gangsters, etc.).　　Sⵧⵧⵧ-Oⵧⵧ
8. Land kept out of cultivation　　　　　　　Sⵧ-Aⵧⵧⵧⵧ
in the European Union.

3. Fill in the ten lines across the grid with translations of the corresponding French words. This will give you the answer to number 11 in column D.

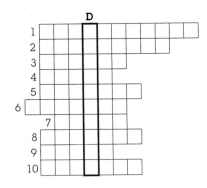

1. le passif
2. remboursement
3. ordre du jour
4. participation
5. en retard, échu
6. compte
7. rembourser
8. associé (n.)
9. valeurs, titres
10. soutenu
11. faillite

The Third World **4** Le Tiers - Monde

/// VOCABULAIRE
À HAUTE FREQUENCE

Development and Population	Le développement et la population
to develop	(se) développer
under-developed	sous-développé
developing	en voie de développement
a native	un indigène, un autochtone
industrialised	industrialisé
to settle	s'installer
a settlement	un peuplement, une colonie
a refugee [refju:'dʒi:]	un réfugié
a camp	un camp
literacy	l'alphabétisation
illiteracy	l'analphabétisation
literate	alphabétisé
illiterate	analphabète

Production	La production
to feed on, to live on	se nourrir de, vivre de
to supply/provide sb. with sth.	fournir qch. à qn.
a supply	un approvisionnement
rainfall	les précipitations
a pump	une pompe
a well	un puits
to drill, to bore	forer
to irrigate	irriguer
irrigation	l'irrigation
to grow, to cultivate	faire pousser, cultiver
to produce [prə'dju:s]	produire
farm produce ['prɒdju:s]	les produits agricoles
farming	l'agriculture

45

to farm	cultiver
to plough	labourer
to sow	semer
seeds	les semences
a crop	une récolte
a harvest	une moisson
livestock	le cheptel
to breed, to rear, to raise	élever
a flock of sheep	un troupeau de moutons
a herd of cattle	un troupeau de bétail
to graze	paître
grazing land, pasture land	les pâturages
self-sufficient	auto-suffisant
self-sufficiency	l'auto-suffisance
raw materials	les matières premières
a commodity	une marchandise primaire

Famine — La famine

a desert	un désert
drought [draut]	la sécheresse
a shortfall	une insuffisance
a shortage	une pénurie
a lack	un manque
scarce	rare, peu abondant
scarcity	la rareté, la disette
hunger	la faim
hungry	affamé
underfed	sous-alimenté
malnutrition	la malnutrition
malnourished	malnutri
to starve	manquer de nourriture
starvation	le manque de nourriture
an area	une zone, une région

Aid — L'aide

funds	les fonds
to collect, to raise	recueillir, collecter
relief	les secours
relief workers	les équipes de secours
a charity	une organisation caritative
a voluntary agency	une agence bénévole
a voluntary organisation	une organisation humanitaire

a relief organisation	une organisation d'aide
relief aid, humanitarian aid	l'aide humanitaire
to donate	faire don
a donation	un don
a donor	un donateur
a consignment, a shipment	un envoi
to deliver	livrer
a delivery	une livraison
a tool	un outil
equipment	l'équipement
a project, a scheme |ski:m|	un projet
to advise	conseiller

EXPRESSIONS

to wear out the soil	épuiser le sol
the standard of living	le niveau de vie
the poverty line	le seuil de pauvreté
help with no strings attached	l'aide sans contrepartie

VOCABULAIRE COMPLÉMENTAIRE

Population / La population

a census	un recensement
a nomad	un nomade
nomadic	nomade (adj.)
a hut	une hutte
a cabin	une case
a shack	une cabane
a shanty town	un bidonville
forced resettlement	l'exode forcé
an influx	un afflux
an exodus	un exode

Production / La production

famished	affamé
a protein |'prəuti:n|	une protéine
a deficiency	une carence
topsoil	la terre végétale
to erode	éroder

erosion	l'érosion
staple food	la nourriture de base
food crops	les cultures vivrières
cash crops	les cultures de rente
a swarm of locusts	un essaim de criquets
to plague	tourmenter, affliger
a plague, a scourge [skɜːdʒ]	un fléau
fallow land	la terre en jachère
to exploit	exploiter
exploitation	l'exploitation
deforestation	le déboisement
to fell, to chop down, to log	abattre
logging	l'abattage
reforestation	le reboisement
barren	stérile, aride
parched	desséché
to desertify	désertifier
desertification	la désertification
a resource [rɪˈzɔːs, rɪˈsɔːs, ˈriːsɔːs]	une ressource
soya bean, soybean (US)	le soja
cocoa	le cacao
sugar cane	la canne à sucre
manioc, cassava	le manioc
to plunder	piller
plunder	le pillage

Outside Aid | L'aide extérieure

to appeal to	faire appel à
an appeal	un appel
a campaign	une campagne
a volunteer [vɒlənˈtɪə]	un volontaire
a convoy	un convoi
a humanitarian corridor	un couloir humanitaire
a hand-out	une aumône
to grant	accorder
a grant	une aide financière
tied aid	l'aide liée
untied aid	l'aide non liée
a string	une contrepartie
to pay back, to repay	rembourser
repayment	le remboursement
to reschedule	rééchelonner
to write off, to cancel	annuler

to cooperate	coopérer
cooperation	la coopération
self-help	l'auto-assistance

Specific Diseases — Les maladies spécifiques

sanitation	les installations sanitaires
rampant	très répandu
cholera	le choléra
malaria [mə'lɛərɪə]	la malaria, le paludisme
typhus ['taɪfəs]	le typhus
leprosy	la lèpre
a leper ['lepə]	un lépreux

Export drive could help poor nations' development, says UN

by Frances Williams in Geneva

Developing countries can repeat the economic miracle of the east Asian "tigers", according to the United Nations Conference on Trade and Development.

Unctad's latest Trade and Development Report published today says the policies that produced rapid export-led growth in South Korea, Taiwan, Hong Kong and Singapore can be applied elsewhere, though for the strategy to succeed fully, the rich North must keep its markets open.

Many developing countries have scope* to boost* exports of labour-intensive manufactures, Unctad says. It estimates that, in the textile and clothing sector alone, poor countries could triple their exports to the North over the next ten years if import quotas are phased out under World Trade Organisation rules.

This would raise their market share in the North from one quarter today to about three-quarters, giving them an extra $175bn of exports a year.

However, the report says that if too many countries simultaneously expand exports of low-skill products, they will flood the market and weaken prices. This will in turn reinforce a long-term downward trend in relative price for low-skill manufactures.

The report thus recommends setting up an international "marketing-cum-information agency" such as the Japanese External Trade Organisation to give developing countries early warning of impending market gluts*.

Unctad acknowledges that a huge export drive by the South could create serious dislocations* in the North, even though new markets would be opened up in developing countries for the North's more sophisticated manufactures, capital goods and services.

The Financial Times,
September 19, 1996

1. Choose the right explanation for each of the following words (with asterisks in the passage).

1. *scope*
A. funds
B. restrictions
C. opportunities

2. *to boost*
A. to increase
B. to reduce
C. to maintain

3. *a glut*
A. a result of overconsumption.
B. a result of overpopulation.
C. a result of overproduction

4. *dislocations*
A. improvements
B. difficulties
C. profits

2. Say whether the following statements are true (T) or false (F).

1. We are given no clues as to who the east Asian "tigers" are.
2. The cost of labour would play a major part in development.
3. Import quotas existed in the North in 1996.
4. The law of supply and demand is not alluded to in the article.
5. For the North, the only result of this development would be keener competition.
6. The article gives two examples of policies to be followed.

3. Find the words.

1. "To triple" means to multiply by three. Express the same idea in two different ways:
A. to increase three☐☐☐d
B. to increase three ☐☐☐☐s.

2. Use the definitions to find words ending in "-ward", like "downward". (The first four often end in "-wards".)

A. coming later	☐☐☐☐☐WARD
B. towards the exterior	☐☐☐WARD
C. towards the interior	☐☐WARD
D. towards the place where one lives	☐☐☐☐WARD
E. whose reactions cannot be predicted	☐☐☐WARD

Town's hunger is worst of war

The skeletal, swollen-bellied children discovered in the western Liberian town of Tubmanburg show some of the worst symptoms of malnutrition seen in almost seven years of civil war, aid workers say.

The children, 150 of whom have been evacuated to a special feeding centre in the capital, Monrovia, were among thousands of starving civilians discovered by aid workers in the town, which had been cut off by the civil war since February. Food is now being shuttled in by road.

"This is the worst thing we have seen in the seven-year history of the war in Liberia," one worker with the United Nations children's fund (Unicef) said.

The precise death toll is unclear but locals speak of up to 16 people dying each day before help arrived.

Aid workers, who estimate that more than 80 per cent of the 35,000 population is seriously malnourished, say hundreds of hungry civilians have emerged from the forest looking for food as word of the relief operation has spread.

Workers expect to find more pockets of hunger in the isolated parts of the country.

Reuter, September 12, 1996

1. Choose the appropriate endings for the following statements.

1. The town of Tubmanburg had been isolated for about
A. seven years.
B. seven months.
C. seven weeks.

2. Hunger in the Liberian town resulted from
A. fighting.
B. bad weather.
C. crop disease.

3. The victims of starvation were
A. only children.
B. only adults.
C. both children and adults.

4. It seems that when aid workers reached the town, they
A. felt helpless.
B. acted efficiently.
C. acted slowly.

5. It can be added that, in Third World countries, such a situation
A. often occurs.
B. seldom occurs.
C. always occurs.

2. Read the article again and find the following:

1. Five words implying a lack of food.
2. Two words that are synonyms for help.
3. Four verbs expressing movement, either of things or of persons.

3. One sentence has been cut up into parts and the parts scrambled. Put them back into the right order. (Punctuation and the capital letter at the beginning of the sentence have been removed.)

many peoples around the world/increase during this decade/the UN Secretary General said/where poverty was expected to/that while conditions were improving for/Africa was the only region

EC urged to curtail toxic waste exports from UK

The British Government's attempt to by-pass a proposed EC ban on exporting toxic waste to the Third World was condemned as shameful yesterday by Mr Ken Collins, chairman of the European Parliament's influential environment committee.

Mr Collins, Euro-MP for Strathclyde East, said the Parliament's legal committee supported action against the EC Council of Ministers to enforce the ban. A case is expected to be heard in the European Court of Justice in Luxembourg in the summer...

The Herald, March 20, 1993

Employment **5** L'emploi

(voir Variations et évaluation p. 25)

/// VOCABULAIRE À HAUTE FRÉQUENCE

Industries and Workplaces — Les industries et les lieux de travail

to employ	employer
a firm, a business	une entreprise
a plant, a factory	une usine
a steelworks	une aciérie
coal-mining	les charbonnages
shipbuilding	la construction navale
a shipyard	un chantier naval
management	la direction, la gestion
to manage, to run	diriger, gérer

Employment and Employees — L'emploi et les employés

to train	former
vocational training	la formation professionnelle
skilled	qualifié
unskilled	non qualifié
labour	la main-d'œuvre
to qualify for	(se) rendre apte à
qualifications	les qualifications
a workman, a worker	un ouvrier
the labour force, the workforce, the staff	le personnel
a blue collar worker	un ouvrier
a white collar worker	un employé
a technician	un technicien
an engineer [endʒɪ'nɪə]	un ingénieur
an executive	un cadre
a job	un emploi
wages	les salaires hebdomadaires

a salary	un salaire mensuel
pay	la paie, le salaire
a pay packet, a paycheck (US)	une fiche de paie, une paie
a bonus	une prime
working conditions	les conditions de travail
the working population	la population active
a job centre	une agence pour l'emploi
a situation, a post	une situation, un poste
a vacancy	une offre d'emploi
job-seeking, job-hunting	la recherche d'un emploi
to apply for	être candidat à
an application	une demande
a C.V.	un C.V.
to interview	recevoir
an interview	un entretien
a self-employed worker	un travailleur indépendant
self-employment	le travail indépendant
to retire [rɪ'taɪə]	prendre sa retraite
retirement	la retraite
early retirement	la retraite anticipée
a pension	une pension, une retraite
a pensioner	un retraité

Ups and Downs — Les variations

advanced technology, high technology	la technologie avancée
an order	une commande
an order book	un carnet de commandes
a robot ['rəubɒt]	un robot
productive	productif
productivity	la productivité
to compete with sb.	concurrencer qn.
competition	la concurrence
competitive	compétitif, concurrentiel
competitiveness	la compétitivité
overtime	les heures supplémentaires
short-time working	le chômage partiel
part-time working	le travail à temps partiel
temporary employment	le travail intérimaire

Consequences — Les conséquences

a job loss	une perte d'emploi
to axe/shed (jobs)	supprimer (des emplois)

redundant	licencié
to make redundant, to lay off	licencier
a redundancy, a lay-off	un licenciement
a redundancy payment	une indemnité de licenciement
a closure, a shut-down	une fermeture
to create	créer
a creation	une création

Unemployment — le chômage

unemployed, on the dole	au chômage
out of work, jobless	sans emploi
to register	s'inscrire
to be eligible for, to be entitled to	avoir droit à
to claim sth.	percevoir qch.
a claimant	un bénéficiaire
unemployment benefit	l'allocation de chômage
income support	l'allocation complémentaire
a job seeker's allowance	une allocation de recherche d'emploi
a school-leaver	un jeune sorti de l'école
to issue figures	publier des chiffres
to adjust	corriger
an adjustment	une correction
seasonal distortion	les variations saisonnières
to retrain	(se) reconvertir
retraining	la reconversion
a scheme [ski:m]	un plan
a course	un stage

/// EXPRESSIONS

a low-paid job	un emploi mal rétribué
a dead-end job	un emploi sans avenir
to work overtime	faire des heures supplémentaires
performance-related pay	le salaire au mérite
to go out of business	cesser son activité, fermer
driven out of business	contraint à la fermeture
to give notice to sb.	donner son préavis à qn.
to give a new job to sb.	reclasser qn.
a temporary employment agency	une agence de travail intérimaire
a seasonally-adjusted figure	un chiffre corrigé des variations saisonnières

to massage figures	triturer les chiffres
to attend a crash course	suivre un stage intensif
on-the-job training	la formation permanente

/// VOCABULAIRE COMPLÉMENTAIRE

Employment and Employees
L'emploi et les employés

an apprentice	un apprenti
apprenticeship	l'apprentissage
a craftsman	un artisan
a workshop	un atelier
an industrial estate	une zone industrielle
a factory hand	un ouvrier
a casual worker	un ouvrier intérimaire
the labour market	le marché de l'emploi
a graduate	un diplômé universitaire
a skill	une compétence technique
a shift	une équipe de travail
to engage, to take on, to hire	engager, embaucher
a prospect	une perspective
a career [kə'rɪə]	une carrière
secure	stable, sûr
job security	la sécurité de l'emploi
fringe benefits	les avantages divers
perks	les à-côtés
a share option	une option de souscription d'actions, une stock option
profit-sharing	la participation aux bénéfices
flexible	flexible
flexibility	la flexibilité
a workaholic	un bourreau de travail
to skive	tirer au flanc
moonlighting	le travail au noir

Ups and Downs
Les variations

work-sharing	le partage du travail
turnover	la rotation
natural wastage	les départs en retraite et les départs volontaires
voluntary redundancies	les départs volontaires
compulsory redundancies	les licenciements secs
to refurbish, to revamp	rénover, remettre en état

a refurbishment, a revamp	une rénovation, une remise en état
to computerise	informatiser
computerisation	l'informatisation
to automate	automatiser
automation	l'automatisation
robotisation	la robotisation
to relocate	délocaliser
relocation	la délocalisation

Consequences — Les conséquences

to restructure	restructurer
restructuring	la restructuration
manning levels	les effectifs
overmanning	le sureffectif
to run down	réduire l'activité
a run-down	une réduction d'activité
to streamline, to slim down	dégraisser
a pay-off	une indemnité de départ
a development area	une zone de conversion

Barclays set to shed 1,000 jobs

by Helen Dunne, Banking Correspondent

Barclays Bank, which unveiled record pre-tax profits of £2.08 billion last month, is expected to announce today plans to shed about 1,000 branch managerial and clerical* jobs through voluntary redundancy. A week ago, it said that 500 jobs were to be cut in its 12 regional offices – about one in four.

Branch managers are expected to issue "personal invitations" to staff in back-office functions to join a "voluntary early-leavers' scheme". It is understood that the bank does not expect compulsory redundancies.

About two-thirds of the job losses are likely to be among administrative and secretarial staff. The rest will involve managerial positions. Nearly all the losses are due to technology.

UNIFI, the staff union, is expected to react angrily if it thinks specific staff are being targeted. It is also likely to contrast the job losses with record profits and may ask Barclays to carry out an overtime survey to ensure that staff do not work excessive hours.

Barclays has shed 18,500 jobs since 1990 as technological advances meant that some functions could be carried out more efficiently with fewer staff.

It now employs 66,000 in branch banking and recently rewarded them with one-off* bonuses averaging £1,400 in recognition of their part in its profit-making.

The Daily Telegraph,
March 25, 1996

1. Choose the right explanation for each of the following words (with asterisks in the passage).

1. *clerical*
A. in the office   B. in the Church   C. in the sales department

2. *one-off*
A. unreasonable   B. exceptional   C. regular

2. Say whether the following statements are true (T) or false (F).

1. It was a bad year for Barclays.
2. There is a sharp contrast mentioned in paragraph one.
3. Compulsory redundancies are usually looked upon as the better solution.
4. Most of those leaving back-office jobs will end up in retirement.
5. The reason behind the decision is clearly stated.
6. The staff union thought a number of jobs could be saved.
7. Barclays has reduced its workforce by more than a quarter since 1990.

3. The words in italics have been scrambled. Put the letters back into the right order.

Philips, the troubled Dutch electronics giant is *tugnict* up to 15,000 jobs in its second big restructuring this decade. The *pourg*, which has been forced to set *daise* 1.2bn guilders (£459M) to cover the restructuring *tocss*, blamed its problems on the unexpected depth of the recession.

Jan Timmer, Philips' *dinrespet*, who took over three years ago to implement an initial restructuring involving the *sols* of more than 45,000 jobs, said renewed cuts were *anceysers*.

The Independent, March 5, 1993

4. Fill in the eleven lines across the grid with translations of the corresponding French words. This will give you the answer to number 12 in column D.

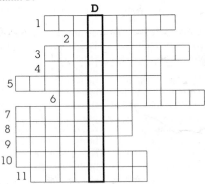

1. cadre 2. prime 3. sans emploi 4. chantier naval 5. direction
6. retraite 7. heures supplémentaires 8. s'inscrire 9. allocation
10. personnel 11. ingénieur 12. concurrence

"I can't afford to lose my job. Others would take it."

by Jojo Moyes

Dean Smith, 31, earns £3.20 an hour. This is 20p more than when he started at his company nearly three years ago – and 70p and hour more than many of the jobs advertised where he lives.

Mr Smith is a security guard at a leisure complex outside Manchester. He gets no overtime and works up to 60 hours a week, mostly evenings. "I've been doing mainly unskilled jobs since I left school. I'm married with three children and this fits in with the childcare," he said.

He recently escaped a mass redundancy of employees who had been with the company for less than two years by threatening to go to an industrial tribunal. "I can't afford to lose my job. There's always plenty of people out there who would take it."

Although Mr Smith lives in Manchester, he is often sent to other complexes at Preston or Chester. He is given an extra hour's pay, but no travelling expenses. In his last pay cheque, he took home £93 after tax for 34.5 hours. Money is deducted for his 15-minute tea break.

"The worst thing about the job is the unsocial hours. I have to work every weekend. The other day they made me come all the way in to show this lad around on my night off – they paid me for one hour at £3.20. But if I say anything they'll just cut my hours down," he said.

(Mr Smith asked that his real name not be used because he feared it would affect his job.)

The Independent, September 9, 1996

1. Choose the appropriate endings for the following statements.

1. Bearing in mind the local employment market, it could be said that, when he started at his company, Dean Smith was
A. really well-paid.
B. badly paid.
C. comparatively well-paid.

2. Dean Smith had been doing unskilled jobs for
A. a long time.
B. a short time.
C. three years.

3. Because of the hours he had to work, Dean's children
A. didn't see him.
B. saw little of him.
C. spent a lot of time with him.

4. When there was a mass redundancy in his company, Dean Smith
A. put up a fight for himself.
B. accepted it.
C. wasn't concerned.

5. His employers
A. had to take strict regulations into account.
B. could easily make life difficult for Dean Smith.
C. didn't take advantage of the situation.

2. Complete the words in the following sentences. Each box represents one letter.

1. Earning only £3.20 an hour, Dean Smith had a ☐O☐-☐☐☐☐ job.

2. He received 20p more than when he started, which means he had had an ☐N☐☐☐☐☐☐ (or a ☐I☐☐) in his wages.

3. Jobs are sometimes advertised in newspapers. They are to be found in the ☐L☐☐☐☐☐☐☐☐ ads.

4. Overtime is usually paid over and above the normal ☐A☐☐ for the job.

5. If an employee feels he can lose his job from one day to the next, it means he has no job ☐E☐☐☐☐☐☐.

6. The time Dean Smith spent on his tea break was not ☐N☐☐☐☐☐☐ in his paid working hours.

7. To combat low wages, some people campaign for the introduction of a ☐I☐☐☐☐☐ wage.

3. Which of the words in each list is synonymous with the first one?

1. to earn, to save, to take home, to spend.

2. nearly, hardly, almost, approximately.

3. leisure, business, outdoor, free time.

4. mass, large scale, total, limited.

5. extra, excellent, unusual, additional.

6. to cut down, to reduce, to destroy, to cancel.

Disputes and Tension 6 Conflits et tensions

(voir Variations et évaluation p. 23)

/// VOCABULAIRE À HAUTE FRÉQUENCE

The World of Labour — Le monde du travail

a wage earner	un salarié
a trade union, a labor union (US)	un syndicat ouvrier
a member	un adhérent
a trade unionist	un syndicaliste
a local branch	une section locale
a shop steward	un délégué syndical
the management	la direction
a pay claim	une revendication salariale
a mass meeting	une assemblée générale
a rally	un rassemblement
to ballot	consulter par vote
a ballot	une consultation

International Tension — La tension internationale

tense, strained	tendu
a relationship, a relation	une relation
a chill	un refroidissement
a strain	une tension
to deteriorate	se dégrader
a deterioration	une dégradation
detente	la détente
to ease	se détendre
a summit	un sommet
a conference	une conférence
a bloc	un bloc
a pact	un pacte

to violate	violer
a violation	une violation
to impose	imposer
a sanction	une sanction
a boycott	un boycott
an embargo [em'bɑ:gəu]	un embargo
a ban	une interdiction

Negotiations — Les négociations

a delegate	un délégué
an official	un responsable
to talk	s'entretenir, discuter
a talk	un entretien, une discussion
to claim	revendiquer, affirmer
a claim	une revendication, une affirmation
to demand	exiger
a demand	une exigence
to organise, to stage	organiser
to consider	examiner, étudier
a consideration	un examen, une étude
to bargain, to negotiate	négocier
the bargaining/negotiating table	la table des négociations
an agenda	un ordre du jour
an issue	une question, un problème
to propose	proposer
a proposal	une proposition
to offer	offrir
an offer	une offre
a step	une mesure, une disposition
a move	une décision, une initiative
a gesture	un geste
a formula ['fɔ:mjulə]	une formule

Disagreement — Le désaccord

to reject, to turn down	rejeter, décliner
a rejection	un rejet
to refuse	refuser
a refusal	un refus
a stalemate, a deadlock	une impasse, un blocage
an obstacle, a hurdle	un obstacle

to disagree	être en désaccord
to warn	avertir, mettre en garde
a warning	un avertissement
to threaten ['θretn]	menacer
a threat	une menace
to break off	rompre
to break down	(se) rompre, échouer
to walk out	quitter la salle
a walk-out	une sortie, un départ
to fail to	ne pas réussir à
a failure	un échec
a crisis ['kraisis]	une crise

Industrial Disputes — Les conflits sociaux

to walk out	débrayer
a walk-out	un débrayage
to stop work	cesser le travail
a work stoppage	un arrêt du travail
to strike, to go on strike	se mettre en grève
a strike	une grève
a non-striker	un non-gréviste
a scab	un jaune
to disrupt	perturber
a disruption	une perturbation
a picket	un piquet (de grève)
to picket	installer un piquet
to suspend	mettre à pied, suspendre
a suspension	une mise à pied
to dismiss, to sack	renvoyer, limoger
a dismissal, a sacking	un renvoi

A Settlement — Un règlement

to resume	reprendre
a resumption	une reprise
to compromise	transiger
a compromise	un compromis
to give in, to yield	céder
to back down	renoncer, abandonner sa position
to grant	accorder
to draw up, to work out	établir, élaborer
a breakthrough	une avancée

a term	une condition
to accept	accepter
an acceptance	une acceptation
to agree	être d'accord
an agreement, a deal	un accord
to manage to, to succeed in	réussir à
to solve, to resolve	résoudre, solutionner
to overcome	surmonter
a difference	une divergence, un différend
to settle	régler
a spokesperson	un(e) porte-parole
a statement	une déclaration

Ending a Strike — La fin d'une grève

a peace formula	une formule d'apaisement
a peace process	un processus de paix
a pay settlement, a pay deal	un accord salarial
a pay award	une augmentation de salaire
to call off a strike	terminer/annuler une grève

/// EXPRESSIONS

Trades Union Congress	la Fédération des syndicats
to press a claim	déposer
to lodge a claim	une revendication
to come to a halt	s'arrêter (production)
to come to a standstill	être paralysé
to refer to arbitration	soumettre à l'arbitrage
to take industrial action	entamer une action revendicative
to cross the picket line	franchir le piquet de grève
to call out a strike	appeler à la grève
the strike won't go ahead	la grève n'aura pas lieu
to fight to the bitter end	lutter jusqu'au bout
to enter into negotiations	entamer des négociations
a round of talks	une série d'entretiens
to come to a deadlock	aboutir à une impasse
to break the deadlock/stalemate	débloquer la situation, sortir de l'impasse
to pave the way	préparer la voie
to prepare the ground	préparer le terrain
to strike a deal	conclure un accord

to come to/reach (an) agreement	parvenir à un accord
an across-the-board increase	une augmentation générale uniforme
to put to a vote	soumettre au vote
to report for work, to turn up for work	se présenter à l'embauche
to be back to normal	être de retour à la normale
to break off diplomatic links	rompre les liens diplomatiques
to sever diplomatic ties	rompre les relations diplomatiques
a show of strength	une démonstration de force
a trial/test of strength	une épreuve de force
gunboat diplomacy	la diplomatie de la canonnière
to make representations	élever une protestation
to issue a statement	publier une déclaration
to get the sack	se faire virer

VOCABULAIRE COMPLÉMENTAIRE

The World of Labour / Le monde du travail

collective bargaining	la négociation collective
the shopfloor	les ouvriers, la base
rank and file	la base
an official	un responsable
closed shop	le monopole de l'embauche
organised labour	les ouvriers syndiqués
a pay packet	une enveloppe de paie
a pay check (US)	une paie, un salaire
working conditions	les conditions de travail
working hours, the working week	la durée du travail
work patterns	les tableaux de service
safety standards	les normes de sécurité

International Tension / La tension internationale

to go sour	se gâter
to escalate	monter, faire monter
escalation	l'escalade
a breach	une rupture
a diplomat ['dɪpləmæt]	un diplomate

diplomacy	la diplomatie
diplomatic [dɪplə'mætɪk]	diplomatique
an embassy	une ambassade
an ambassador [æm'bæsədə]	un ambassadeur
at large, roving	itinérant
a hot line	un numéro spécial
to normalise	normaliser
normalisation	la normalisation
an envoy	un envoyé, un émissaire
an emissary	un émissaire
a counterpart, an opposite number	un homologue
the West Bank	La Cisjordanie
the Gaza Strip	la bande de Gaza
the Near East	le Proche-Orient
the Middle East	le Moyen-Orient

Negotiations — Les négociations

a stand, a stance	une attitude, une position
to founder	achopper
a sticking point, a stumbling block	un point de désaccord, une pierre d'achoppement
to be bogged down, to be mired down	s'enliser
a log jam	un blocage, une impasse
a stand-off	un face-à-face
a counterproposal	une contre-proposition
a row [rau]	une querelle
a pre-condition	un préalable
to thrash out	élaborer par discussion
a draft	un projet
a draft agreement	un protocole d'accord
a framework	un cadre
a showdown	un bras de fer
confrontation	l'affrontement
a deadline	une limite de temps, une date butoir
behind the scenes, backstage	dans les coulisses
to attempt to	tenter de
an attempt	une tentative
to mediate	servir d'intermédiaire
a mediator	un médiateur
to defuse	désamorcer
to placate, to appease	apaiser

an appeasement	un apaisement
to conciliate	concilier
conciliation	la conciliation
conciliatory [kən'sılıətrı]	conciliant
to trade off for	échanger contre
a trade-off	un échange, une contre-partie
a bargaining chip	une monnaie d'échange
an accord	un accord

Industrial Disputes — Les conflits sociaux

a grievance ['gri:vəns]	une doléance
pace	les cadences
working practices	l'organisation du travail
job demarcation	le domaine de compétence
to consult	consulter
a consultation	une consultation
strike pay	l'allocation de grève
a blackleg	un jaune
a strike breaker	un briseur de grève
a lightning strike	une grève éclair
a selective strike	une grève limitée, ponctuelle
an all-out strike	une grève totale
a token strike	une grève d'avertissement
a go-slow, a work-to-rule	une grève du zèle
a sympathy strike	une grève de solidarité
a sit-down strike	une grève avec occupation
an official strike	une grève préparée, légale
an unofficial strike	une grève spontanée
a wildcat strike	une grève sauvage
a rolling strike	une grève tournante
an indefinite strike	une grève illimitée
a hunger strike	une grève de la faim

Consequences — Les conséquences

to cripple, to paralyse	paralyser
to lay off	mettre en chômage technique
lay-off	le chômage technique
to black	mettre sur la liste noire
a court ruling	une décision de justice
to discipline	punir, sanctionner

to fire	virer
an industrial tribunal	un Conseil de prud'hommes
unfair dismissal	le licenciement abusif
to reinstate	réintégrer
reinstatement	la réintégration

Ending a Strike / La fin d'une grève

to crumble	s'effriter
to drift back	retourner progressivement
a drift-back	un retour

Postal strike looms

A postal strike looked "almost inevitable" yesterday after a union decided to ballot 140,000 Royal Mail workers on industrial action in a dispute over hours and working practices.

The Communication Workers' Union announced the move after the breakdown of talks over a five-day week and reduced working time.

Voting will begin on May 13 and if the strike goes ahead it will be the first national mail stoppage for almost a decade.

The union has been seeking a reduction in the 41 1/2-hour, six-day working week, while the Royal Mail wants to introduce greater flexibility through "team working".

Alan Johnson, the union's joint general secretary, said: "Our members have created the most efficient, profitable, and productive postal service in the world. Meanwhile, 86 per cent of postmen and women work a six-day week for a basic wage of less than £10,000 a year."

Brian Thomson, Royal Mail personnel director, said the proposed package offered better pay, a shorter working week and a commitment to job security in return for greater flexibility.

The Daily Telegraph, May 3, 1996

1. Say whether the following statements are true (T) or false (F).

1. The headline suggests an idea of a threat.
2. It seems that, in Britain, trade union members have to vote before unions can call a strike.
3. There had been negotiations before the decision was taken to hold a ballot .
4. Such a ballot can be carried out almost from one day to the next.
5. Postal workers seemed prone to take industrial action.
6. Postal workers have a long working week.
7. Pay seemed to be the central issue.
8. The spokesman for the union sounded proud of his members' record.
9. Job security would reduce the number of accidents at work.
10. No keyword related to working patterns is used twice in the article.

2. The word "stoppage" in the article is made up of the verb "stop" and the ending "-age". Use the definitions to find words constructed in a similar way.

1. The escape of liquid or of information.   L☐☐☐☐☐☐

2. Keeping goods in a place such
as a warehouse until they are delivered.   S☐☐☐☐☐☐

3. The amount paid for sending letters
or parcels.   P☐☐☐☐☐☐

4. The remains of a car, a plane
or a boat after a disaster   W☐☐☐☐☐☐☐

5. It allows excess water to be taken
away from land.   D☐☐☐☐☐☐☐

6. The way in which things are used,
particularly words in certain contexts.   U☐☐☐☐

3. "Breakdown" is a compound noun made up of the verb "break" and an adverb. Use the definitions to find more compound nouns with "break".

1. Significant progress or an important discovery.
2. The division or separation of things or of people that were united, by marriage for example.
3. The way a burglar often enters a building.
4. An escape from prison.

Clinton scrabbles* to save crisis summit

Martin Walker in Washington

Bill Clinton announced yesterday that Israel's prime minister, Binyamin Netanyahu, and the Palestinian leader, Yasser Arafat, have agreed to resume immediate talks on the Israeli withdrawal from the flash-point* West Bank city of Hebron.

The United States president said talks on Hebron would begin on Sunday at the Erez border point between Israel and the Gaza Strip – but could not conceal the fact that no progress had been reached on the main issues underlying the crisis, which had left at least 70 dead and hundreds wounded over the past week.

"The problems are still there, the differences are still there," Mr Clinton said. "They were not able to resolve their differences here."

He was speaking as a last chance negotiating session over lunch at the White House failed to break the deadlock between the two sides.

Earlier, after morning talks had ended without result, one Palestinian official said: "It's finished – we could not agree on a single thing."

The sticking point was the Palestinian demand that Israel set a firm date for withdrawing its troops from Hebron, as agreed by the former Israeli government.

Mr Netanyahu said this was impossible without agreed security arrangements for Israeli settlers in the city. Instead, he offered only a date for the end of talks on Hebron.

"The demands of the Palestinians are for an immediate redeployment from Hebron without any security arrangements anywhere else," an Israeli spokesman said.

The Guardian, October 3, 1996

1. Choose the right explanation for each of the following words (with asterisks in the passage).

1. *to scrabble*
A. to make a clever attempt
B. to make a laborious attempt
C. to make a brief attempt

2. *a flash-point*
A. a state likely to lead to peace
B. a state likely to lead to reconciliation
C. a state likely to lead to violence

2. Bearing the whole extract in mind, choose the appropriate endings for the following sentences.

1. After the 1967 war, Israel occupied former Palestinian territories and the article mentions
A. one of them.   B. two of them.   C. none of them.

2. After reading the article, we can pick out
A. none of the main issues.
B. one of the main issues.
C. two of the main issues.

3. At the end of the summit, Bill Clinton was
A. very optimistic.
B. left with some hope.
C. totally disheartened.

4. It is evident that, at the summit, the Israeli settlements
A. were an obstacle to an agreement.
B. were no obstacle to an agreement
C. were left out.

3. Complete the missing words.

1. The Israelis were not prepared to P☐☐☐ ☐☐T their troops from the West Bank city of Hebron.

2. As the two sides were unable to resolve their differences, there was no B☐☐☐☐☐☐☐☐☐☐H at the summit.

3. Setting a firm date for the Israeli withdrawal from Hebron was the main S☐☐☐☐☐☐☐☐ ☐☐☐☐K in the negotiations.

4. In trying to save the summit, President Clinton also wanted to preserve the P☐☐☐☐ ☐☐☐☐☐☐S established by the Oslo accord.

5. The Palestinians insisted that Israel had B☐☐☐☐N its promise.

Nationwide strike threat as Ford cuts 1,300 jobs

Ford was facing the threat of strike action throughout its British operations last night after announcing that 1,300 jobs would go at its Halewood plant and the phasing out of production of the Escort.

Proposals for strike ballots will be put to mass meetings being called by union leaders amid fears that further cuts are planned at other plants.

The Weekly Telegraph, January 8, 1997.

Medicine 7 La médecine

Health and Disease	La santé et la maladie
ill, sick	malade
an illness, a sickness, a disease	une maladie, un mal
to suffer from	souffrir de
pain	la douleur
painful	douloureux
sore	endolori
a sore throat	un mal de gorge
a headache	une migraine
to hurt	faire mal
temperature, fever	la fièvre
a fit	un accès, une attaque
a fit of coughing	une quinte de toux
critical	critique
a condition	un état
healthy	bien portant
a virus ['vaɪrəs]	un virus
bacteria [bæk'tɪərɪə]	les bactéries
contagious, infectious, catching	contagieux
to pass on, to transmit	transmettre
to develop, to contract	attraper contracter
an outbreak	un début d'épidémie
an epidemic	une épidémie
a case	un cas
a cold	un rhume
measles [mi:zlz]	la rougeole
chicken pox	la varicelle
flu, influenza [ɪnflu:'enzə]	la grippe
to spread	se répandre, s'étendre
to infect	infecter
an infection	une infection

to contaminate	contaminer
contamination	la contamination
to incubate	incuber
incubation	l'incubation
a carrier	un porteur
benign [bɪ'naɪn]	bénin
a malignant tumour	une tumeur maligne
cancer	le cancer
leukaemia [luː'kiːmɪə]	la leucémie
Aids	le sida
an Aids sufferer	un malade du sida
HIV positive	séropositif
the immune system	le système immunitaire
to faint, to pass out	s'évanouir
to come to	reprendre connaissance
disabled	handicapé
a heart attack	une crise cardiaque
a heart failure	une défaillance cardiaque
a nervous breakdown	une dépression nerveuse
a victim	une victime
mentally handicapped	handicapé mental
life expectancy	l'espérance de vie
euthanasia [juːθə'neɪzɪə]	l'euthanasie

Organs and Tissues — Les organes et les tissus

blood	le sang
a cell	une cellule
a blood cell	un globule
a blood sample	une prise de sang
blood pressure	la tension artérielle
a kidney	un rein
the liver	le foie
a breast	un sein
a lung	un poumon
the brain	le cerveau
the womb [wuːm]	l'utérus
a nerve	un nerf
a chromosome ['krəuməzəun]	un chromosome
a gene [dʒiːn]	un gène
genetic engineering	le génie génétique
to clone	cloner
a clone	un clone
cloning	le clonage

Health Service and Treatment
Les services de santé et le traitement

a general practitioner	un médecin généraliste
a surgeon	un chirurgien
surgery hours	les heures de consultation
a surgery	un cabinet médical
a chemist, a pharmacist	un pharmacien
a hospital	un hôpital
a nurse	une infirmière
an outpatient	un malade de jour
a ward	une salle, un service
an emergency	une urgence
to examine	examiner
an examination	un examen
to check	vérifier
a check-up	un contrôle
to diagnose ['daɪəgnəuz]	diagnostiquer
a diagnosis	un diagnostic
a test	une analyse
to detect	déceler, dépister
detection	le dépistage
to screen	examiner pour dépister
screening	examen de dépistage
to prescribe	prescrire
a prescription	une ordonnance
a medicine, a drug	un médicament
a pill	une pilule
a tablet	un comprimé, un cachet
a tranquilliser	un tranquillisant
to treat	traiter, soigner
to respond	réagir
efficient	efficace
a side effect	un effet secondaire
to relieve	soulager
a relief	un soulagement
to cure	guérir
a cure	une guérison, un remède
a remedy	un remède
incurable	incurable
to save	sauver
to recover	se rétablir
a recovery	un rétablissement
a diet	un régime
a slimming diet	un régime amincissant

Operations | Les opérations

surgery	une intervention
to perform	effectuer
to undergo	subir
an operating theatre	une salle d'opération
intensive care	les soins intensifs
a transfusion	une transfusion
to remove	enlever
a removal	une ablation
to transplant [trænsˈplɑːnt]	transplanter
a transplant [ˈtrænsplɑːnt]	une transplantation
to donate	faire un don
a donor	un donneur
a recipient	un receveur
to reject	rejeter
a rejection	un rejet

Research | La recherche

a survey	une étude, une enquête
to research	faire de la recherche
a scientist	un scientifique
a laboratory	un laboratoire
to carry out	effectuer
an experiment	une expérience
to discover	découvrir
a discovery	une découverte
findings	les résultats (recherche)
to develop	mettre au point
development	la mise au point
a breakthrough	une percée, une avancée

Childbearing | La maternité

sterile, infertile	stérile
childless	sans enfant
to fertilise	féconder
in vitro fertilisation	la fécondation in vitro
a test tube	une éprouvette
sperm	le sperme
to inseminate	inséminer
insemination	l'insémination
an embryo [ˈembrɪəu]	un embryon

pregnant	enceinte
a pregnancy	une grossesse
a foetus ['fiːtəs]	un fœtus
to deliver	accoucher
a delivery	un accouchement

/// EXPRESSIONS

to be on a diet	suivre un régime
to be confined to bed	être cloué au lit
to take a sample	faire un prélèvement
a sexually transmitted disease	une maladie sexuellement transmissible
to have an X-ray	passer une radio
to be operated on	subir une opération
to be on a life support machine	être sous assistance respiratoire
he is making good progress	son état s'améliore
to be doing well	être en bonne voie
to nurse a cold	soigner un rhume
to have a heart condition	avoir une affection cardiaque
to take to hospital	transporter à l'hôpital

/// VOCABULAIRE COMPLÉMENTAIRE

Health and Disease	La santé et la maladie
sound	sain
a deficiency	une carence
stamina	le tonus
a complaint	une affection
acute	aigu
chronic	chronique
a germ	un germe
a microbe ['maɪkrəub]	un microbe
a bug	un microbe, un virus
a strain	une souche
an enzyme	une enzyme
bronchitis	la bronchite
pneumonia	la pneumonie
hepatitis [hepə'taɪtɪs]	l'hépatite
jaundice	la jaunisse

cystic fibrosis	la mucoviscidose
muscular dystrophy	la myopathie
diabetes [daɪə'biːtiːz, daɪə'biːtɪz]	le diabète
asthma ['æsmə]	l'asthme
arthritis [ɑːθ'raɪtɪs]	l'arthrite
rheumatism ['ruːmətɪzm]	le rhumatisme
multiple sclerosis	la sclérose en plaques
meningitis [menɪn'dʒaɪtɪs]	la méningite
rabies ['reɪbiːz]	la rage
angina [æn'dʒaɪnə]	l'angine de poitrine
a stroke	une attaque cérébrale
cholesterol	le cholestérol
a symptom	un symptôme
a sick note	un certificat de maladie
sick leave	un congé de maladie
a growth, a lump	une grosseur, une tumeur
cancerous	cancéreux
a stage	un stade
mercy killing	l'euthanasie
a hæmophiliac [hiːmə'fɪliæk]	un hémophile
food poisoning	l'intoxication alimentaire
salmonella	la salmonellose
listeria	la listeriose

Organs and Tissues — Les organes et les tissus

a vessel	un vaisseau
a vein	une veine
an artery	une artère
coronary	coronaire, coronarien
a blood clot	un caillot de sang
the belly, the tummy	le ventre
the bladder	la vessie
bone marrow	la moëlle des os
the uterus	l'utérus
an intestine	un intestin
the bowels	les entrailles
the cervix	le col de l'utérus
cervical	du col de l'utérus
a gland	une glande
a mole	un grain de beauté
a boil	un furoncle

Health Service and treatment

Les services de santé et le traitement

a physician	un médecin
a consultant, a specialist	un spécialiste
a junior doctor	un interne
a sister	une infirmière chef
a unit	un service
to hospitalise	hospitaliser
a clinic	une clinique, un service de consultation
a nursing home	une maison de santé
a mental hospital	un hôpital psychiatrique
terminal care, palliative care	les soins palliatifs
antibiotics [æntɪbaɪˈɒtɪks]	les antibiotiques
a painkiller	un analgésique
a geneticist	un généticien
the genetic fingerprint	l'empreinte génétique
gene therapy	la thérapie génique
to vaccinate	vacciner
a vaccine	un vaccin
to immunise	immuniser
immunisation	l'immunisation
to eradicate	éradiquer
eradication	l'éradication
a smear [smiːə]	un frottis (vaginal)
a biopsy [baɪˈɒpsɪ]	une biopsie
chemotherapy	la chimiothérapie
radiation therapy	radiothérapie
metastasis	les métastases
a serum	un sérum
a report, a bulletin	un bulletin
to pull through	s'en sortir
sickness leave	congé de maladie

Operations

Les opérations

surgical	chirurgical
cosmetic/plastic surgery	la chirurgie esthétique
keyhole surgery	la chirurgie mini invasive, la vidéo chirurgie
under anaesthetic	sous anesthésie
a bypass	un pontage
to implant	implanter

an implant	un implant
a pioneer |paɪəˈnɪə|	un pionnier
to graft	greffer
cross-species	inter-espèces
a graft	une greffe
a pacemaker	un stimulateur
a respirator	un respirateur
a dialysis machine	un rein artificiel

Childbearing / La maternité

to conceive	concevoir
conception	la conception
an ovary |ˈəuvərɪ|	un ovaire
ovulation	l'ovulation
Fallopian tubes	les trompes
periods	les règles
semen |ˈsiːmən|	la semence
a miscarriage	une fausse couche
stillborn	mort-né
newborn	nouveau-né
a surrogate mother	une mère porteuse
surrogacy |ˈsʌrəgəsɪ|	la substitution
Caesarian section	une césarienne
an offspring	un descendant
to breastfeed	nourrir au sein
to bring up	élever
premature	prématuré
cot death	la mort subite du nourrisson
twins	des jumeaux
triplets	des triplés
quadruplets	des quadruplés
abnormal	anormal
malformed	malformé
malformation	la malformation
a disability	un handicap
a wheelchair	un fauteuil roulant

Baby to get first gene transplant

Celia Hall, Medical Editor

A baby girl will today make British medical history when doctors begin the first gene transplant designed to cure a deficiency which, untreated, could lead to her death.

Carly Todd, aged eight months, from Lennoxtown, near Glasgow, has the same immune system deficiency which killed her 14-month-old brother four days before she was born.

Children with this rare condition do not make an enzyme called Adenosine Deaminase, or ADA, which is necessary for the immune system to develop properly. Without ADA, Carly is vulnerable to any infection which a baby with normal cells would be able to fight.

Doctors at Great Ormond Street hospital, London, working with scientists at the University of Leiden in the Netherlands, plan to reprogramme Carly's cells so that she can protect herself from infection.

A copy of the ADA gene will be inserted into the cells of Carly's bone marrow* which are responsible for making the cells of the immune system.

Dr Gareth Morgan, senior lecturer in immunology, described Carly as a delightful and responsive* baby. He said he was "cautiously optimistic" of success.

One Italian and two American children with ADA deficiency have been treated with a different type of gene therapy, aimed mostly at mature* cells, but its effect is short lived as the cells have a limited life and the treatment has to be repeated...

The Independent,
March 18, 1993

1. Choose the right explanation for each of the following words (with asterisks in the passage).

1. *bone marrow*
A. the hard part of the bone
B. the soft substance inside the bone
C. the joint between two bones

2. *responsive*
A. reacting badly
B. reacting well
C. reacting slowly

3. *mature*
A. adult
B. undeveloped
C. elderly

2. Say whether the following statements are true (T) or false (F).

1. This could be called a pioneering operation.
2. They could have waited for a year or more to carry out the operation.
3. Carly was taken to hospital near her home town.
4. We are told about the role of bone marrow cells.
5. Dr Gareth Morgan described her medical condition in detail.
6. The operation may cure Carly completely.
7. This deficiency has nothing in common with Aids.
8. The journalist has paid great attention to giving a step-by-step description.

3. Rebuild the compound nouns from the article by matching words from each list.

1. immune system	A. girl
2. bone	B. transplant
3. baby	C. deficiency
4. gene (two nouns)	D. therapy
	E. marrow

4. The word "infection" is used twice in the article. The corresponding verb is "to infect". Find the verbs corresponding to the nouns below.

1. contamination   2. examination   3. fertilisation
4. prescription   5. transmission   6. conception
7. explanation   8. recognition   9. description
10. production

5. Fill in each blank with a word from the following list. Use each word once only. Verbs are given in the infinitive.

quiet   operation   alone   to undergo   breast
media   singer   surgery   lump   to recuperate

Linda Mc Cartney has ...(1)... an operation after a ...(2)... cancer scare, her ...(3)... husband revealed yesterday. The mother of four, 53, underwent ...(4)... in London last week after a small ...(5)... was found in her breast. In a statement, Paul McCartney said: "The ...(6)... was a complete success. Linda is now ...(7)... and I personally would put in a request to the ...(8)... to leave her ...(9)... to do this and to give her and our family the peace and ...(10)... we need so she can recover."

The Independent on Sunday, December 17, 1995

New infection linked to mad cow disease

by Philip Webster and Jeremy Laurence

The Government admitted for the first time yesterday that "mad cow disease" could be transmitted to people.

A new strain* of the human form of the disease has been identified and the Government's chief adviser on the subject has said that it could turn into an epidemic.

The new findings, which relate to ten people suffering from a form of Creutzfeldt-Jakob Disease, were reported to ministers this week, prompting* tighter controls on slaughtering cattle and a call for urgent guidance on whether children can safely eat beef.

CJD, which usually affects the elderly is similar to Bovine Spongiform Encephalopathy (BSE), or "mad cow "disease, but for the past decade, the Government has refused to accept that it could be triggered* by BSE.

Now, however, research into the ten cases has suggested a link and raised the prospect that the variant may be a wholly new disease. The patients were all under 42 and their symptoms were different from those of typical CJD.

Government experts said there was no way of telling how virulent the new condition would be or how many people would be susceptible*. Dr John Pattison, chairman of the committee advising the Government on BSE, said that he had never seen the variant before. "It is totally unpredictable, but at one extreme there is a risk of an epidemic."

The Times, March 21, 1996

---

1. **Choose the right explanation for each of the following words (with asterisks in the passage).**

1. *a strain*
A. a type   B. a return   C. a case

2. *to prompt*
A. to make it impossible
B. to cause a delay
C. to be the source of

3. *to trigger*
A. to bring to an end
B. to make worse
C. to cause to start

4. *susceptible*
A. easily irritated
B. likely to develop
C. totally immunised

2. Say whether the following statements are true (T) or false (F).

1. Establishing whether a link existed between BSE and the new strain of CJD was an essential point.

2. The Government had never denied such a link existed.

3. CJD did not occur before "mad cow" disease appeared.

4. It seemed certain an epidemic would break out.

5. The findings could have huge economic repercussions.

3. Complete the missing words.

1. Scientists thought "mad cow" disease could be transmitted to humans because some people had ☐E☐☐☐☐☐☐☐ a new strain of CJD.

2. To identify the new strain was an important step. Indeed it could be called a ☐R☐☐☐☐☐☐☐☐☐H

3. If it turned into an epidemic, the disease would ☐P☐☐☐☐ all over the country.

4. Some people were infected because BSE entered the ☐O☐☐ ☐☐☐☐N through the sale of meat.

MATT

PIG ORGAN
TRANSPLANT
TRIALS

'Scalpel, swab, apple sauce...

Space 8 L'espace

VOCABULAIRE
À HAUTE FRÉQUENCE

Getting Ready	Les préparatifs
a rocket	une fusée
a spacecraft, a spaceship	un vaisseau spacial
a shuttle	une navette
on board, aboard	à bord
a cabin	une cabine
a spaceman	un spationaute
an astronaut	un astronaute
a spacesuit	un scaphandre
a crew	un équipage
a manned flight	un vol habité
to check	vérifier
the countdown	le compte à rebours
a computer	un ordinateur
a schedule ['ʃedjuːl, 'skedjuːl]	un horaire
on schedule	comme prévu
to delay	retarder
a delay	un retard
to put off, to postpone	reporter, ajourner
a postponement	un ajournement
to cancel	annuler
a cancellation	une annulation
a fault	un défaut, une anomalie
defective, faulty	défectueux
to work	marcher, fonctionner

Lift-off	Le décollage
to ignite	allumer, mettre à feu
ignition	l'allumage, la mise à feu
to launch	lancer

a launch	un lancement, un tir
a launching-pad	un pas de tir
to blast off, to lift off	décoller
a blast-off, a lift-off	un décollage, un envol
fuel	le carburant
a tank	un réservoir
a booster	un propulseur d'appoint
to soar	s'élever, s'élancer
a stage	un étage
to separate	se séparer
to fall off	se détacher
to orbit	tourner en orbite
an orbit	une orbite
to monitor, to track	suivre la trace de

In space / Dans l'espace

a stage	une étape
a flightpath	une trajectoire de vol
to dock (with)	accoster, (s')arrimer (à)
to link up	(se) relier, (se) rattacher
a docking, a link-up	un amarrage, un arrimage
to latch on to	(s')accrocher, (s')attacher à
a weather satellite	un satellite météo
a spy satellite	un satellite espion
weightlessness	l'apesanteur
a pull	une attraction
a laboratory	un laboratoire
to carry out	effectuer
an experiment	une expérience
a process ['prəuses]	un procédé, une méthode
a cargo	une cargaison
a payload	une charge utile
a pay-off, a spin-off	une récompense, une retombée
a drug	un médicament
the cargo bay, the hold	la soute
a panel	un panneau
a device	un dispositif
to retrieve, to recover	récupérer, reprendre
retrieval, recovery	la récupération
a spacewalk	une sortie dans l'espace
a spacewalker	un piéton de l'espace
a lifeline	un filin, une ligne de vie

a backpack	un fauteuil de l'espace
to steer [stɪə]	diriger, gouverner
to manoeuvre [məˈnuːvə]	manœuvrer
a manoeuvre	une manœuvre

Return	Le retour
to complete	terminer
to re-enter	rentrer
re-entry	la rentrée
the atmosphere	l'atmosphère
to land	atterrir
landing	l'atterrissage
a base	une base

/// EXPRESSIONS

to be behind schedule	être en retard
to be out of order	être en panne
there was something wrong with ...	il y avait quelque chose qui n'allait pas dans ...
they had some trouble with...	ils ont des ennuis avec...
to go off without a hitch	se dérouler sans anicroche
to go into orbit	se mettre en orbite
to put something right	remédier à quelque chose

/// VOCABULAIRE COMPLÉMENTAIRE

Flight	Le vol
space sickness	le mal de l'espace
lunar	lunaire
a module	un module
a capsule	une capsule
a retro-rocket	une rétrofusée
a rendez-vous	un rendez-vous
to team up	s'assembler
a back-up system	un système de secours
remote control	le contrôle à distance
an orbiting station	une station orbitale
a tracking station	une station de repérage
a meteorite [ˈmiːtɪəraɪt]	un météorite

Missions / Les missions

Missions	Les missions
geostationary	géostationnaire
to relay	relayer
to beam back	renvoyer, réfléchir
a telescope	un télescope
to probe	sonder
a probe	une sonde
an antenna [æn'tenə]	une antenne
outer space	le cosmos
a planet	une planète
a galaxy	une galaxie
the solar system	le système solaire
gravitation	la gravitation
gravity	la pesanteur
vacuum	le vide

Space rescue turns into race against time

by Nick Nuttal, Technology correspondent

With only seven days left to get the job done, unforeseen snags*, including jammed maintenance doors and a badly bent solar panel, are plaguing* the mission to rectify a string of faults in the Hubble space telescope.

Nasa officials fear the additional work needed to overcome the unexpected faults could make it impossible to correct all the craft's manufacturing defects on the five space walks planned during the 11-day mission. *Endeavour*, more than 360 miles above Earth, is travelling further than any previous shuttle, making fuel conservation vital if the mission is to be fully successful.

Despite this, it was decided late yesterday to expend fuel this morning to jettison* the bent 40ft solar array* in space rather than risk bringing it back. The solar panel retracted only about 30 per cent of the way in response to radioed commands from ground controllers in Houston, Texas, whereas it needed to roll up completely, like a window-blind, to fit in *Endeavour*'s cargo bay for the trip home.

Perched on the shuttle's robot arm, Dr Kathy Thornton, 41, a spacewalking veteran, was asked to uncouple the bent array from Hubble as *Endeavour* drew back to prevent the panel damaging it or the telescope. The astronauts, too, are at a constant risk of a piece of metal slicing through their spacesuits.

The Times, December 6, 1993

1. Choose the right explanation for each of the following words (with asterisks in the passage).

1. *a snag*
A. an order   B. a difficulty   C. a loss

2. *to plague*
A. to make things easier
B. to make things more pleasant
C. to make things more difficult

3. *a string*
A. a series
B. a rope
C. a report

4. *to jettison*
A. to keep
B. to repair
C. to throw away

5. *an array*
A. elements forming a unit
B. elements forming a dial
C. parts of a window pane

2. Choose the appropriate endings for the following sentences.

1. The shuttle had been in space for
A. seven days.
B. four days.
C. one day.

2. The mission turned out to be
A. easier than expected.
B. shorter than expected.
C. more difficult than expected.

3. One additional problem was created by
A. the weather
B. the distance.
C. the cost.

4. Once in space they decided to
A. change their plans.
B. keep strictly to their plans.
C. forget about their plans.

5. Because of its defect, the solar panel was
A. too heavy to handle.
B. too hot to handle.
C. too awkward to handle.

6. Separating the panel from the telescope involved
A. a single risk.
B. a double risk.
C. a triple risk.

3. Read the article again and find the following:

1. Two different nouns used for spacemen.
2. A verb revealing the telescope had been faulty right from the start.
3. An adjective underlining the importance of fuel conservation.
4. A verb showing that little attention is paid to litter in space.
5. A detail showing the spacewalker was a woman.

4. Which of the four words in each list should not be associated with the others.

1. to repair, to mix, to put right, to fix.
2. additional, extra, extreme, further.
3. fault, defect, flaw, decrease.
4. to suit, to fit, to agree, to mend.
5. to tell, to hamper, to thwart, to prevent.

Third time lucky for Mir space docking

Susan Watts, Technology Correspondent

A Russian cosmonaut secured* the future of a series of multi-million dollar international space missions yesterday by linking a cargo craft carrying fresh food, fuel and supplies with the Mir space station.

The successful manoeuvre followed two failed attempts late last month, when the Progress M-24 supply craft approached Mir under automatic computer guidance. The failed dockings had cast a shadow over the future of the Russian space programme, and over joint missions planned with Germany next month and later with the United States. These first two embarrassing attempts ended with the cargo craft bumping into the 130-tonne space station then sliding gently past.

Food supplies on board Mir had fallen so low that the cosmonauts could stay on board for only a few more weeks.

Since no back-up* space ship was ready, yesterday's delicate manual procedure had saved the three-strong Russian team on board from being sent home. This would have dashed the hopes of Valery Polyakov, a Russian doctor, who aims to break the 12-month space endurance record – extending this to 18 months. He has been in Mir since January.

Progress slid into place just after 2.40 pm BST[1] yesterday. It is carrying a number of scientific experiments that are the key to several planned joint space missions. One, a collaborative project with the European Space Agency (ESA), involves a German astronaut who hopes to join the Mir team next month.

[1] British Summer Time

The Independent, October 3, 1994

1. Choose the right explanation for each of the following words (with asterisks in the passage).

1. *to secure*
A. to endanger   B. to delay   C. to guarantee

2. *back-up*
A. substitute   B. return   C. jumbo

2. Say whether the following statements are true (T) or false (F).

1. The headline contains a saying which seems to be in contradiction with a French one.
2. No important developments depended on the success of the flight.
3. They adopted new tactics for the third approach.
4. The first two attempts could have damaged the craft or the space station.
5. The cosmonauts on board would have starved to death if the attempt had failed.
6. Valery Polyakov had been in space for 12 months.
7. No other flight to the space station was planned in the near future.
8. After reading the article we feel that international cooperation will play a major part in future space flights.

3. Which of the words in each list is synonymous with the first word (taken from the article)?

1. cargo, price, value, capital, freight.
2. attempt, perspective, bid, success, achievement.
3. to stay, to remain, to locate, to place, to set up.
4. to break (a record), to fight, to hit, to beat, to strike.

4. Fill in the ten lines across the grid with translations of the corresponding French words. This will give you the answer to number 11 in column D.

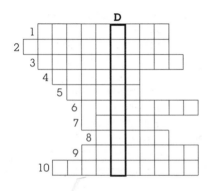

1. scaphandre
2. trajectoire de vol
3. laboratoire
4. dispositif
5. piloter, gouverner
6. fauteuil de l'espace
7. cargaison
8. panneau
9. filin
10. compte à rebours
11. vaisseau spatial

Voir p.113 pour les résultats des élections britanniques de 1997.

VOCABULAIRE
À HAUTE FRÉQUENCE

Political Parties | Les partis politiques

to join sth.	adhérer à qch.
a member	un adhérent, un membre
membership	les adhérents, l'adhésion
a policy	une politique
a politician	un homme politique
radical	radical, maximaliste
extreme [ɪks'triːm]	extrême
an extremist	un extrémiste
moderate	modéré
left-wing, leftist	de gauche
right-wing, rightist	de droite
Tory, Conservative	conservateur
Labour	travailliste
a programme	un programme
a view, an opinion	une opinion
a coalition	une coalition

Before the Election | Avant l'élection

an opinion poll	un sondage d'opinion
to publish	publier
to survey	interroger (échantillon)
a survey	une enquête, une étude
a figure	un chiffre
a rating	une cote, un score
a lead [liːd]	une avance
to trail	avoir du retard
a margin	une marge
popular	populaire
popularity	la popularité

dissatisfaction	le mécontentement
a referendum	un référendum
local	locale, municipale
general, legislative	législative
presidential	présidentielle
an election	une élection
a by-election	une élection partielle
to fight	disputer
to stand for, to run for	se présenter à, être candidat à
a candidate	un candidat
the front-runner	le mieux placé
a constituency	une circonscription
a deposit	une caution
a campaign	une campagne
to promise	promettre
a promise	une promesse
to pledge	promettre, s'engager
a pledge	une promesse, un engagement

Elections / Les élections

a ballot	un scrutin
a ballot paper	un bulletin de vote
polling day	le jour des élections
a polling station	un bureau de vote
a ballot box	une urne
to vote	voter
a vote	une voix, un suffrage
a voter	un électeur
the voters, the electorate	l'électorat
a round	un tour (de scrutin)
turn-out, polling	la participation
to count	dépouiller
counting	le dépouillement
a seat	un siège
to elect	élire
to win, to carry	remporter, enlever
a win, a victory	une victoire
overwhelming	écrasant
close	serré
to retain	conserver
a defeat	une défaite
an overall majority	une majorité absolue
to swing	faire pencher, basculer

a swing	un basculement, un transfert
to shift	changer, se déplacer
a shift	un changement, un déplacement
results	les résultats
the outcome	le résultat, la conclusion

The United States — Les États-Unis

a primary	une primaire
a caucus	un comité de primaire
a convention	une convention
a delegate	un délégué
nomination	la désignation
Congress	le Congrès
a congressman	un membre du Congrès
the Senate	le Sénat
a senator	un sénateur
the House of Representatives	la Chambre des représentants
a representative	un représentant
to inaugurate	investir
inauguration	l'investiture

EXPRESSIONS

to be in the lead	être en tête
they are 2 points ahead	ils ont 2 points d'avance
the run-up to an election	la période pré-électorale
to call an election	provoquer une élection
to hold an election	procéder à une élection
to go to the country	en appeler aux électeurs
to field a candidate	présenter un candidat
to jump on the bandwagon	prendre le train en marche
to hit the campaign trail, to go barnstorming (US)	se lancer dans la campagne électorale
to press the flesh	serrer les mains
to be a vote winner	attirer les suffrages
to go to the polls	aller aux urnes
to cast a vote	déposer un bulletin
to concede defeat	admettre la victoire
to hold the balance of power	détenir la minorité de blocage
to be sworn in	prêter serment

/// VOCABULAIRE COMPLÉMENTAIRE

Political Parties — Les partis politiques

the leading role	le rôle dirigeant
an apparatus	un appareil
the political spectrum	l'éventail politique
the rank and file, the grass roots	la base
an activist	un militant
influential	influent
reactionary	réactionnaire
progressive	progressiste
a hardliner, a diehard	un dur
a conference	un congrès
an umbrella organisation	un collectif, une fédération
to chair	présider
a rival	un rival
rivalry	la rivalité
a split	une division, un désaccord
a rift	un fossé, une faille
in-fighting	les luttes internes
a tendency	une tendance
to fall apart	éclater, se séparer
to break away	se détacher
a breakaway group	un groupe dissident
a fringe party	un groupuscule
the far right	l'extrême droite

Before the Election — Avant l'élection

a pollster, a poll taker	un sondeur
the don't knows	les indécis
the floating vote	l'électorat instable, mouvant
to conduct	organiser
a straw poll	une consultation improvisée
a standing	une position, un classement
a showing	une performance, une prestation
to lag	être à la traîne
neck and neck	au coude à coude
a constituent	un électeur (circonscription)
proportional representation	la représentation proportionnelle
an election manifesto	un manifeste électoral
a platform	une plate-forme

a feel-good factor	un sentiment de confiance, une impression d'optimisme
bread and butter issues	les questions matérielles
on the hustings, on the stumps(US)	en campagne
an electioneering promise	une promesse électorale
to canvass	faire du porte à porte
a rostrum	une tribune
to heckle	harceler
a soundbite	une petite phrase, une formule
to smear [smɪə]	diffamer
a smear campaign	une campagne de diffamation
character assassination	atteinte à la réputation
mudslinging	les coups bas
dirty tricks	les coups tordus
gerrymandering [dʒerɪˈmændərɪŋ]	les tripatouillages
to stand against sb.	se présenter contre qn.
to contend, to contest	disputer
a contest	une compétition, une lutte
a contender, a contestant	un concurrent
a safe seat	un siège sûr
a marginal seat	un siège menacé
a stronghold	un bastion, un fief
to commit	engager
a commitment, an undertaking	un engagement
to vow to [vau]	s'engager à
propaganda [prɒpəˈgændə]	la propagande
a constituency	une clientèle électorale
a ward	une circonscription (élections locales)
an image	une image

Elections — Les élections

a snap election, an early election	une élection anticipée
a run-off election	un deuxième tour avec deux candidats
to register	s'inscrire
to poll	recueillir
the poll	les suffrages
a polling-booth	un isoloir
an exit poll	un sondage à la sortie
returns	les résultats partiels

a tally	un décompte
to recount	recompter
a recount	un nouveau décompte
to declare	proclamer (résultats)
a declaration	une proclamation
an absolute majority	une majorité absolue
a landslide victory	une victoire écrasante
a rout, a drubbing	une déroute, une raclée
to trounce, to thrash	écraser
a groundswell	une lame de fond
a share of the vote	un pourcentage de voix
a protest vote	un vote sanction
a hung Parliament	un Parlement sans majorité
a mandate	un mandat (contrat)
a term	un mandat (durée)
the wilderness, limbo	le désert (politique)
fraud	la fraude
to rig	truquer
ballot rigging	le trucage électoral

The United States / Les États-Unis

the presidency	la présidence
the incumbent president	le président en exercice
the outgoing president	le président sortant
the president elect	le président élu
a ticket	un ticket électoral
an elector	un grand électeur

Clinton surges* to victory

*Martin Walker in Washington
and Jonathan Freedland in Little Rock*

President Bill Clinton was last night heading back to the White House and into history as the first Democrat to win re-election in the post-war era.

But although early exit polls gave Mr Clinton a comfortable majority in the electoral college, he was falling just short of his desired moral mandate of half or more of the popular vote – with 49 per cent to Republican Bob Dole's 42 per cent.

The exit polls also suggested that he will once again face a Congress with a narrow but hostile Republican majority in both House and Senate.

Mr Clinton was winning with a huge 26-point lead in California and easily in New York, Massachusetts, Pennsylvania and Illinois, and was ahead in the battleground state of Florida. But Mr Dole was comfortably holding the Republican strongholds of the South and West, and was ahead in Texas by 10 points on morning polling which showed an unusually heavy male vote.

A spirited* Republican recovery in the South, and the strenuous* Get Out The Vote efforts on its behalf by the Christian Coalition, appeared to have forestalled* a Clinton landslide in the popular vote and saved his exhausted Republican opponent from humiliation.

According to the early exit polls, Mr Dole appeared likely to carry at least 12 states, a far better performance than the wipeouts inflicted on the Democrats in the last landslide elections of 1972 and 1984.

The Guardian, November 6, 1996

1. Choose the right explanation for each of the following words (with asterisks in the passage).

1. *to surge*
A. to move slowly
B. to move hesitatingly
C. to move irresistibly

2. *spirited*
A. full of doubt   B. full of energy   C. full of regret

3. *strenuous*
A. relaxed   B. feeble   C. intense

4. *to forestall*
A. to prevent   B. to cause   C. to support

2. Say whether the following statements are true (T) or false (F).

1. For a time, Bill Clinton would be both the incumbent President and the President elect.
2. Bill Clinton was the first President to be re-elected since the war.
3. The two voting systems in the American presidential election are alluded to.
4. Bill Clinton was going to both win the election and reach the target he had set himself.
5. Facing a hostile Congress would be a new situation for President Clinton.
6. Groups of neighbouring states often seem to vote the same way.
7. In 1972 and 1984, the Republicans carried more than 38 states.

3. Test your knowledge and say whether the statements are true (T) or false (F).

1. Bob Dole finally won 19 states in the 1996 presidential election.
2. To be elected president, a candidate has to win the popular vote.
3. The number of senators per state depends on population size.
4. Senators and representatives are both elected for 4 years.
5. The Democratic candidates in the 1972 and 1984 presidential elections were George McGovern and Walter Mondale respectively.

4. To describe an election, reporters often borrow words usually associated with other topics. Read the article again and find the following:

1. Two words associated with natural phenomena.
2. One word associated with health and disease.
3. Two words associated with war.

Labour 18 points ahead, says poll

by George Jones, Political Editor

Labour enters election year with an 18-point lead over the Conservatives, according to the latest Gallup poll published in The Daily Telegraph today.

The poll puts Labour on 50 1/2 per cent, the Conservatives on 32 1/2 and the Liberal Democrats on 10 1/2.

At this point before the 1992 general election, the Tories had a 5 1/2-point lead over Labour.

Gallup's December voting intention figures are based on a new methodology which was designed to improve the poll's accuracy. Interviews have been conducted by telephone, reaching every part of the country.

Previous Gallup surveys have been based on face-to-face interviews conducted on the street and in people's homes. In future, where respondents are "shy" of* giving their intention, the new procedure considers other factors, such as support for John Major or Tony Blair.

The "new" results have been compared with previous adjusted Gallup results to avoid distortion.

The poll indicates that the Tories have got the best of "the unofficial" election campaign that has been raging since the start of the year.

When the new poll is compared with the adjusted figures for early December, it shows that the Labour lead has fallen from 24 points to 18.

The poll suggests the Conservatives are beginning to make inroads* into Labour's record poll lead as a result of their high-profile campaigning on tax – the issue which has been central at the last two general elections.

Labour is now seen as a party most likely to raise taxes if it wins the election.

The Daily Telegraph, January 17, 1997

1. Choose the right explanation for the following expression (with an asterisk in the passage).

1. *shy of*
A. willing to   B. unwilling to   C. frightened of

2. *to make inroads*
A. to take away part of
B. to make larger
C. to cause to vanish

2. Say whether the following statements are true (T) or false (F).

1. Members of Parliament are elected for a maximum of 5 years.

2. In comparison with the same period in 1992, the Conservatives' position, in relation to Labour's, has worsened by 23 points.

3. Pollsters seem to have been somewhat disappointed with some of their previous forecasts.

4. Pollsters make no allowance for a change in voters' intentions.

5. With an 18-point lead in December, Labour had no reason to worry.

6. The Conservatives have apparently adopted new tactics during this election.

7. The leaders of the three main parties are mentioned in the article.

3. Both the verb "to lead" and the noun "lead" appear in the article. Find the nouns corresponding to the following verbs from the passage.

1. to enter   2. to publish   3. to design   4. to improve
5. to conduct   6. to consider   7. to compare   8. to avoid
9. to indicate   10. to adjust

4. Fill in the twelve lines across the grid with translations of the corresponding French words. This will give you the answer to number 13 in column D.

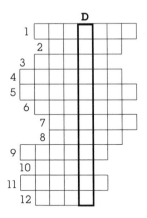

1. résultat
2. serré
3. se présenter
4. caution
5. dépouillement
6. cote
7. conserver (*siège*)
8. tour (*de scrutin*)
9. étude, enquête
10. adhérer
11. (une) politique
12. Conservateur
13. circonscription

Politics II **10** La politique II

VOCABULAIRE
À HAUTE FRÉQUENCE

Power	Le pouvoir
to set up, to establish	établir, installer
a regime	un régime
a dictator	un dictateur
a dictatorship	une dictature
to liberalise	libéraliser
liberalisation	la libéralisation
a say	une voix au chapitre
a status	un statut
a constitution	une constitution
constitutional	constitutionnel
democracy [dɪ'mɒkrəsɪ]	la démocratie
democratic [demə'krætɪk]	démocratique
a republic	une république
office	les fonctions
powerful	puissant
to rule	diriger, gouverner
the ruling party	le parti au pouvoir
rule	l'autorité, l'administration
majority rule	le gouvernement de la majorité
self-rule	l'autonomie
a state	un État
a statesman	un homme d'État
to corrupt	corrompre
corrupt	corrompu
corruption	la corruption
to bribe	soudoyer
a bribe	un pot de vin
bribery	la corruption
sleaze	les pratiques douteuses, la corruption

Parliament — Le Parlement

a Member of Parliament (MP)	un député
the House of Commons	la Chambre des députés
the House of Lords	la Chambre des lords
a committee	une commission
to sit	siéger
a sitting	une séance
to put forward	proposer, soumettre
to table	déposer
a motion	une motion
a bill	un projet de loi
a private member's bill	une proposition de loi
to amend	amender
an amendment	un amendement
to reject	rejeter
a rejection	un rejet
to rule out	exclure la possibilité de
to abolish	abolir
abolition	l'abolition
to carry	faire passer
to defeat	repousser
to adopt	adopter
an adoption	une adoption
a law	une loi

Debate — Les débats

to debate	débattre
an issue	une question, un problème
to propose	proposer
a proposal	une proposition
to discuss	discuter
a discussion	une discussion
to approve of sth.	approuver qch.
approval	l'approbation
to praise sth.	faire l'éloge de qch.
to criticise	critiquer
criticism	la critique
to argue	argumenter, faire valoir
to state	déclarer
a statement	une déclaration
to advocate	prôner
an advocate	un défenseur, un partisan
to support, to back	soutenir

support, backing	le soutien
to favour	être partisan de
confidence	la confiance
to agree to sth.	consentir à qch.
to agree with sb.	être d'accord avec qn.
an agreement	un accord
to disagree with sb.	être en désaccord avec qn.
a disagreement	un désaccord
a difference	une divergence
to explain	expliquer
an explanation	une explication
to contradict	contredire
a contradiction	une contradiction
to deny	nier
a denial	un démenti
to claim	affirmer
a claim	une affirmation
to maintain	continuer d'affirmer
to complain	se plaindre
a complaint	une plainte, une réclamation
to advise	conseiller
advice	les conseils
to press sb. to	pousser qn. à
pressure	la pression
to urge	exhorter
to blame sb. for sth.	reprocher qch. à qn.
to blame sth. on sb.	rendre qn. responsable de qch.
blame	la responsabilité
to protest [prə'test]	protester
a protest ['prəutest]	une protestation
a controversy	une polémique
controversial	controversé, polémique
to contest	contester
to oppose sth.	s'opposer à qch.
an opponent	un opposant
opposition	l'opposition
to challenge	défier
a challenge	un défi
to denounce	dénoncer
denunciation	la dénonciation
to accuse	accuser
an accusation	une accusation
to condemn	condamner

a condemnation	une condamnation
to outrage	provoquer l'indignation de
an outrage	un scandale
a row [rau]	une querelle, une dispute
a crisis ['kraɪsɪs]	une crise
a division	un vote au Parlement
to abstain	s'abstenir
abstention	l'abstention

Government — Le gouvernement

to govern	gouverner
to appoint	nommer
an appointment	une nomination
a (senior) minister	un ministre
a minister of state	un sous-secrétaire d'État
a junior minister	un secrétaire d'Etat, un ministre délégué
the Prime Minister	le Premier ministre
a cabinet	un cabinet
to deal with sth.	s'occuper de qch.
to tackle sth.	s'attaquer à qch.
to handle sth.	traiter, gérer qch.
to implement	mettre en œuvre
an implementation	une mise en œuvre
a move	une démarche, une initiative
a step	une disposition, une mesure
a stand, a stance	une position
an objective	un objectif
an aim	un but
to back down	faire marche arrière
to climb down	faire des concessions
a climb-down	une reculade
to yield, to give in	céder
to reform	réformer
a reform	une réforme
to reshuffle	remanier
a reshuffle	un remaniement
a setback	un revers, une déconvenue
to bring down	faire chuter
to overthrow, to topple	renverser
an overthrow	un renversement
the downfall	la chute
to resign [rɪ'zaɪn]	démissionner

the resignation	la démission
to hand in	remettre
the former Prime Minister	l'ancien Premier ministre

EXPRESSIONS

to take office	entrer en fonction
to remove from office	démettre de ses fonctions
the ousted president	le président déchu
to go to the vote	être soumis au vote
to put to the vote	soumettre au vote
to come to power	accéder au pouvoir
to bring into force	mettre en application
to come under pressure	subir des pressions
to bow to pressure	céder aux pressions
to address an issue	aborder un problème
to make political capital out of	exploiter politiquement
to take issue with sb.	engager une controverse avec qn.
to be critical of	trouver à redire à
to take sb. to task	prendre qn. à partie
to level a charge at sb.	lancer une accusation contre qn.
to be at loggerheads	être en conflit
to come under fire	être vivement critiqué
to pour scorn on	tourner en dérision
to resign the whip	démissionner d'un groupe parlementaire
to carry a lot of clout	avoir beaucoup d'influence

VOCABULAIRE COMPLÉMENTAIRE

Power	Le pouvoir
dictatorial	dictatorial
parliamentary	parlementaire
a junta ['dʒʌntə]	une junte
tyranny	la tyrannie
a tyrant	un tyran
a despot	un despote
despotism	le despotisme
totalitarian	totalitaire

to purge	purger
a purge	une épuration, une purge
a monarchy	une monarchie
a monarch ['mɒnək]	un monarque
influence peddling	le trafic d'influence
a kickback, a backhander	un pot de vin, un backchich

Parliament — Le Parlement

a session	une session
the Speaker	le Président de la Chambre
a whip	un chef de groupe
a front-bencher	un député porte-parole
a back-bencher	un député de la base
question time	la séance des questions
to sponsor	présenter (une proposition)
the sponsor	l'auteur (d'une proposition)
to endorse	appuyer, approuver, donner son aval
an endorsement	un soutien, une approbation
to legislate	légiférer
legislation	la législation
a framework	un cadre (de discussion)
a draft	une ébauche, un avant-projet
a loophole	une faille, une lacune
to outlaw	mettre hors la loi
an Act	une loi
to lobby	chercher à influencer
a lobby	un groupe d'intérêts
a surgery	une permanence (de député)
a deputy	un député (à l'étranger)

Debate — Les débats

to stress sth., to insist upon sth.	insister sur qch.
to emphasise	bien préciser
to underline	souligner
to highlight	mettre en valeur
to prop up	étayer, soutenir
to vindicate	justifier, donner raison à
vindication	confirmation du bien-fondé
to placate	apaiser
unanimous	unanime
unanimity	l'unanimité
consensus	le consensus

to alter	modifier
an alteration	une modification
to repeal	abroger
a repeal	une abrogation
to antagonise sb.	provoquer l'hostilité de
to incense	mettre en fureur
an outcry	un tollé
an uproar	un tapage
turmoil	les remous, la tourmente
to barrack	chahuter
to castigate	critiquer, fustiger
to deride	railler, se moquer (de)
to lambast	éreinter, fustiger
a scathing attack	une attaque cinglante
a stooge	un fantoche
a puppet	un pantin
a pawn	un pion
to filibuster	faire de l'obstruction
a guillotine	une limitation des débats
to rescind	révoquer, résilier
a turning-point, a watershed	un tournant, un virage
a milestone, a landmark	un moment décisif, un jalon
to turn around/about	faire volte-face
a turn-around, an about-turn, a U-turn	une volte-face
to stifle	étouffer
to cover up	camoufler, étouffer
a cover-up	un étouffement (scandale)
the Dispatch Box	la tribune du gouvernement
a White Paper	un avant-projet de loi
to censure	censurer
censure	la censure parlementaire
a no-confidence motion	une motion de censure
to defeat	mettre en minorité
a split vote	un vote sans majorité
a casting vote	une voix prépondérante
to assemble	se réunir
to adjourn	suspendre, reporter
an adjournment	une suspension, un report
to convene [kən'viːn]	convoquer (parlement)
recess ['riːses, rɪ'ses]	les vacances parlementaires
to re-assemble	rentrer (parlementaires)
to dissolve [dɪ'zɒlv]	dissoudre
dissolution	la dissolution

The United States — Les États-Unis

an aide	un collaborateur
bipartisan	bipartite
to veto sth. ['viːtəʊ]	opposer son veto à qch.
a veto	un veto
to override sth.	passer outre à qch.
to overrule sth.	annuler, casser qch.
to impeach	mettre en accusation
an impeachment	une procédure de destitution
the State Department	le ministère des Affaires étrangères
the Secretary of State	le ministre des Affaires étrangères
the Attorney General	le ministre de la Justice
the Supreme Court	la Cour suprême

Government — Le gouvernement

the Queen's speech	le discours du Trône
provisional	provisoire
interim	intérimaire
caretaker	chargé des affaires courantes
to cohabit	cohabiter
cohabitation	la cohabitation
a portfolio	un portefeuille
to shake up	réaménager, remodeler
a shake-up	un réaménagement
a decree	un décret, une ordonnance
a by(e)law	un arrêté municipal
a package of measures	un ensemble de mesures
to review	réexaminer
a review	un réexamen
a body	un organisme
a watchdog	un comité de surveillance, un « gendarme »
an ombudsman	un médiateur
a quango	un organisme paragouvernemental
a record	un bilan
to achieve	accomplir
an achievement	une réalisation
to mishandle sth.	se montrer maladroit
to scrap	mettre au rebut
to phase in	introduire progressivement

to phase out	abandonner progressivement
to undermine	saper, affaiblir
to step down	se désister
to stand down	se démettre
devolution	l'autonomie régionale
a Cabinet meeting	un conseil de cabinet
the Shadow Cabinet	le contre-gouvernement
the Lord Chancellor	le ministre de la Justice
the Home Secretary	le ministre de l'Intérieur
the Education Secretary	le ministre de l'Éducation
the Foreign Secretary	le ministre des Affaires étrangères
the Foreign Office	le ministère des Affaires étrangères
the Treasury	le ministère du Budget
the Statute Book	le Registre des lois

I'm a republican, says rebel shadow minister

by David Wastell and Julie Kirkbride

Ron Davies, the shadow Welsh Secretary, was embroiled* in fresh controversy over his views on the Royal family last night after *The Sunday Telegraph* established that further personal criticisms of the Prince of Wales were edited* out of the Welsh television programme broadcast by the BBC on Friday evening.

Sources at BBC Wales have described Mr Davies's contribution to the programme as "10 minutes of undiluted republican analysis of why the Prince of Wales should not be king".

Among the lengthy remarks which were not broadcast, Mr Davies declared: "I am a republican," adding that he believed most people shared his view that the monarchy had become a discredited institution. He also embellished* his view that the breakdown of Prince Charles's marriage and his hypocrisy over wildlife disqualified him from succeeding to the throne.

He said that Prince Charles could not be king and "live in sin" with Camilla Parker Bowles, and neither could he perform his constitutional duty as the Defender of the Faith if he were to marry his long-term mistress.

The fresh revelation will add to the Labour leadership's discomfort, proving that the remarks were part of a considered contribution rather than an off-the-cuff* observation on the prerecorded programme. It will also increase pressure on Mr Davies to resign his front-bench post.

The Sunday Telegraph,
March 3, 1996

1. Choose the right explanation for each of the following words (with asterisks in the passage).

1. *embroiled*
A. involved   B. praised   C. disappointed

2. *edited*
A. discovered   B. printed   C. cut out

3. *to embellish*
A. to give no details
B. to give fewer details
C. to give more details

4. *off-the-cuff*
A. planned   B. improvised   C. prepared

2. Choose the appropriate endings for the following sentences.

1. The controversy arose
A. only over what had been broadcast.
B. only over what had been edited out.
C. both over what had been broadcast and what had been edited out.

2. The decision was made to edit some out remarks because it was thought
A. the programme would be too long.
B. the remarks would shock some of the viewers.
C. the programme would be too expensive.

3. Ron Davies criticised
A. only the Prince's private life.
B. only the Prince's character.
C. both his private life and his character.

4. In his attacks on the Prince of Wales, Ron Davies
A. also included religion.
B. made no mention of religion.
C. put religion first.

5. We know that Ron Davies was a front-bencher
A. from the beginning of the extract.
B. half way through the extract.
C. only at the end of the extract.

6. At the time, the leader of the Labour Party was
A. John Smith.   B. Tony Blair.   C. Paddy Ashdown.

3. Fill in each blank with a word from the following list. Use each word once only.

contender   neck   new   rival   close   polls

Colombians voted for a ...(1)... president yesterday in a ...(2)... race. Opinion ...(3)... put the Liberal Party ...(4)... , Ernesto Samper, neck and ...(5)... with his conservative ...(6)... , Andres Pastrana.

Reuter, June 20, 1994

Matt

*'We've been here ages –
do you think there's any
hope that we've missed
the general election?'*

Bid to limit ban on guns abandoned

by George Jones and Joy Copley

Attempts by Conservative MPs to water down tough new curbs* on handguns proposed by the Government in the wake of the Dunblane massacre collapsed in the House of Commons last night. Faced with the prospect of overwhelming defeat, the pro-shooting MPs did not push to a vote a series of amendments aimed at allowing larger calibre, single shot pistols to escape the ban.

Parents and relatives of the 17 victims of the shooting at Dunblane primary school eight months ago were in the public gallery as MPs began debating the Firearms (Amendment) Bill that proposes to outlaw all but smaller calibre .22 pistols used for target shooting.

There were angry protests from several Tory MPs over the way the curbs were being rushed through Parliament, with a guillotine* intended to prevent any attempt to delay the Bill from becoming law before Christmas.

Nicholas Budgen, MP for Woverhampton South West, accused Parliament of behaving like a "lynch mob", taking away the rights of an honourable minority of shooting enthusiasts without proper consideration.

He said that compensation for gun owners who would have to hand over their weapons for destruction could cost between £500 million and £1 billion.

The unsuccessful attempt to exempt single shot pistols larger than .22 calibre for sporting purposes was led by Sir Jerry Wiggin, Tory MP for Weston-super-Mare. He said that the Bill was being dragged through the House with "indecent speed".

The Daily Telegraph,
November 19, 1996

1. Choose the right explanation for each of the following words (with asterisks in the passage).

1. *a curb*
A. an improvement
B. a restriction
C. an increase

2. *a guillotine*
A. an extension of a debate
B. an absence of debate
C. a limitation of a debate

2. Say whether the following statements are true (T) or false (F)

1. The Conservative MPs mentioned wanted tougher restrictions than those proposed by the Government.

2. We are made aware of the way an amendment can be adopted in the House of Commons.

3. MPs were under public pressure while discussing the Bill.

4. The word "shooting" refers to the killing of birds and animals.

5. It is difficult to see the difference between a Bill and a law.

6. The Conservative MPs mentioned thought it was wrong to legislate under pressure.

3. Read the article again and find the following:

1. A synonym for "a bid".

2. Two essential words to explain the meaning of ".22".

3. A noun showing what would happen to the weapons handed in.

4. Two words (both functioning as adjectives), describing non-automatic, less dangerous pistols.

4. "Government" and "amendment" can be divided into two parts: (a) the verb, and (b) the suffix "-ment". Use the definitions to find 8 other nouns of a similar construction.

1. Putting money into a business.	I▢▢▢▢▢▢MENT
2. Making larger.	E▢▢▢▢▢▢▢MENT
3. A turn for the better.	I▢▢▢▢▢▢MENT
4. Often made by a spokesman.	S▢▢▢▢MENT
5. A train leaving the track.	D▢▢▢▢▢▢MENT
6. Establishing oneself in a place.	S▢▢▢▢▢▢MENT
7. Annoying someone, often used with the adjective "sexual".	H▢▢▢▢▢MENT
8. This may lead to the downfall of a US president.	I▢▢▢▢▢▢▢MENT

The 1997 UK election results

	Seats	Gains	Losses	%
Labour	418	148	0	43
Conservative	165	0	78	31
Liberal Democrat	46	30	2	17
Ulster Unionist	10	1	0	-
Scottish Nationalist	6	3	0	-
Plaid Cymru	4	0	0	-
SDLP	3	0	1	-
Sinn Fein	2	2	0	-
Democratic Unionist	2	0	2	-
UKU	1	1	0	-
Independent	1	1	0	-
Speaker	1	1	0	-

Labour majority   179
Swing to Labour   10.5%
Turnout   71%
Total vote   31,372,549

The 1997 UK government

The Cabinet

Prime Minister	Tony Blair, 44
Deputy Prime Minister; Environment, Regions and Transport Secretary	John Prescott, 58
Chancellor of the Exchequer	Gordon Brown, 46
Foreign Secretary	Robin Cook, 51
Home Secretary	Jack Straw, 50
Lord Chancellor	Lord Irvine, 58
President of the Board of Trade	Margaret Beckett, 54
Education and Employment Secretary	David Blunkett, 49
Health Secretary	Frank Dobson, 57
Secretary for Scotland	Donald Dewar, 59
Defence Secretary	George Robertson, 51
Secretary for Northern Ireland	Marjorie Mowlam, 47
Agriculture Minister	Jack Cunningham, 57

Secretary for Wales	Ron Davies, 50
National Heritage Secretary	Chris Smith, 45
International Development Secretary	Clare Short, 51
Chief Secretary, Treasury	Alistair Darling, 43
Leader of the Commons	Ann Taylor, 49
Leader of the Lords	Lord Richard, 64
Duchy of Lancaster	David Clark, 57
Transport Secretary	Gavin Strang, 53

Non-Cabinet posts announced on May 5 1997[1]

Minister Without Portfolio	Peter Mandelson, 43
Minister for Europe	Doug Henderson, 47
Paymaster General	Geoffrey Robinson, 58
Ministers of State at Treasury	Helen Liddel, 46; Dawn Primarolo, 42
Chief Whip	Nick Brown, 46
Social Security Minister	Frank Field, 54
Environment Minister	Michael Meacher, 57
Heritage Minister	Tom Clarke, 56
Public Service Minister	Derek Foster, 59
Education and Employment Minister	Andrew Smith, 46

[1] More junior minister were appointed later.

Religion **11** La religion

VOCABULAIRE À HAUTE FRÉQUENCE

Religions	Les religions
religious [rɪ'lɪdʒəs]	religieux
a Jew	un juif
Jewish	juif
a Christian	un chrétien
a Roman Catholic	un catholique
a Protestant	un protestant
Islam ['ɪzlɑ:m]	l'islam
a Moslem, a Muslim	un musulman
a Sikh	un sikh
a god	un dieu
a goddess	une déesse
faith	la foi
faithful	fidèle
to obey sb.	obéir à qn.
obedience	l'obéissance
to worship	adorer, vénérer
a worshipper	un fidèle
to follow	suivre
a follower	un adepte
to believe	croire
a belief	une croyance
a creed	un credo, les principes
a dogma	un dogme
a verse	un verset
a doctrine	une doctrine
to endoctrinate	endoctriner
endoctrination	l'endoctrinement
a denomination	une confession religieuse
a non-believer	un incroyant
an atheist	un athée
a pagan, a heathen ['hi:ðən]	un païen

an idol ['aɪdl]	une idole
supernatural	surnaturel
to save	sauver
salvation	le salut
tolerance	la tolérance
tolerant	tolérant
intolerance	l'intolérance
intolerant	intolérant
to persecute	persécuter
persecution	la persécution
a fundamentalist	un intégriste
fundamentalism	l'intégrisme

Worship / La pratique religieuse

a cathedral [kə'θiːdrəl]	une cathédrale
a churchgoer	un pratiquant
an abbey	une abbaye
a mosque [mɒsk]	une mosquée
a temple	un temple
a chapel	une chapelle, un temple
a sanctuary	un sanctuaire
to pray	prier
a prayer	une prière
to celebrate	célébrer
a celebration	une célébration
mass	la messe
a service	un office
to bless	bénir
a blessing	une bénédiction
the congregation	l'assemblée des fidèles
the choir [kwaɪə]	le chœur
a hymn	un cantique
to preach	prêcher
a sermon	un sermon
the pulpit	la chaire
a saint	un saint
holy	saint
evil ['iːvəl]	le mal
to sin	pécher
a sin	un péché
blasphemy	le blasphème
a soul	une âme
to convert	convertir
a conversion	une conversion

a convert	un converti
a disciple	un disciple

Christianity — Le christianisme

Christ [kraɪst]	le Christ
the Lord	le Seigneur
the Holy Spirit	le Saint-Esprit
the Blessed Virgin	la Sainte Vierge
the Bible	la Bible
the Gospel	l'Évangile
Good Friday	le Vendredi saint
Easter	Pâques
Whitsun	la Pentecôte
Anglican	anglican
an angel	un ange
to damn	damner
a devil	un diable
Satan ['seɪtən]	Satan
heaven	le ciel
hell	l'enfer
a cross	une croix
to cross oneself	se signer

The servants — Les serviteurs

an ayatollah [aɪə'tɒlə]	un ayatollah
a rabbi ['ræbaɪ]	un rabbin
clergy	le clergé
a clergyman	un ecclésiastique
a priest	un prêtre
a vicar	un curé
a parish	une paroisse
a parishioner	un paroissien
a parson, a minister, a pastor	un pasteur
the ministry	le ministère religieux, le sacerdoce
a deacon	un diacre
a bishop	un évêque
an archbishop	un archevêque
a cardinal	un cardinal
the Pope	le pape
to ordain	ordonner
an ordination	une ordination

Cults — Les sectes

to join sth.	adhérer à qch.
a cult	une secte, un culte
a sect	une secte
a member	un membre, un adhérent
membership	les adhérents
a Freemason	un franc-maçon
Freemasonry	la franc-maçonnerie
a Jehovah's Witness	un Témoin de Jéhovah
to recruit [rɪ'kruːt]	recruter
a recruit	une recrue
recruitment	le recrutement

/// EXPRESSIONS

a born-again Christian	un chrétien régénéré
a place of worship	un lieu de culte
the Established Church	l'Église officielle
to take vows	prononcer des vœux

/// VOCABULAIRE COMPLÉMENTAIRE

Religions and cults — Les religions et les sectes

the Koran	le Coran
Muhammad, Mohammed	Mahomet
a Shiite, a Shiah, a Shia	un chiite
a Druse	un druze
a Sunni	un sunnite
Mecca	la Mecque
Buddha	Bouddha
Buddhism	le bouddhisme
a Buddhist	un bouddhiste
Hinduism	l'hindouisme
a Hindu	un hindouiste
a guru ['guruː]	un gourou
a prophet	un prophète
a prophecy	une prophétie
prophetic	prophétique
a martyr	un martyr
martyrdom	le martyre
a saviour	un sauveur

a miracle	un miracle
miraculous	miraculeux
a godsend	un don du ciel
devout [dɪ'vaut]	dévot
a persuasion	une confession, religion
a devotee	un fervent, un adepte
to lapse	ne plus pratiquer
to curse	maudir
a curse	une malédiction
mass suicide	le suicide collectif

Worship — La pratique religieuse

to practise	pratiquer
practice	la pratique
a synagogue ['sɪnəgɒg]	une synagogue
a shrine	un lieu saint
a rite	un rite
a sacrament	un sacrement
sacramental	sacramentel
a pilgrim	un pèlerin
a pilgrimage	un pèlerinage
an altar	un autel
an address	une allocution
to fast	jeûner
Ramadan ['ræmədæn]	le ramadan
to swear	jurer
a swear-word, an oath	un juron
to tempt	tenter
temptation	la tentation
sacrilege	un sacrilège
a zealot ['zelət]	un fervent, un ultra
to consecrate	consacrer
a consecration	une consécration
to desecrate	profaner
desecration	la profanation
a crusade	une croisade
sectarian	sectaire, confessionnel

Christianity — Le christianisme

the Messiah [mɪ'saɪə]	le Messie
the Almighty	le Tout-Puissant
the Scriptures	les Écritures

a lesson	une lecture des Écritures
a Testament	un Testament
the Apostles	les apôtres
Christendom	la chrétienté
celibacy	le célibat
a diocese ['daɪəsɪs]	un diocèse
the Holy See	le Saint-Siège
ecumenical	œcuménique
a flock	un troupeau
the fold	le bercail
Lent	le Carême
to baptise, to christen	baptiser
a christening	un baptême
Communion	la communion
the Eucharist	l'Eucharistie
to redeem	racheter
redemption	le rachat, la rédemption
absolution	l'absolution
penance	la pénitence
the last rites	les derniers sacrements
your neighbour	votre prochain

The servants — Les serviteurs

lay	laïque
a layman	un laïc
secular	séculier
the Pontiff	le souverain pontife
a primate	un primat
a curate	un vicaire
a dog collar	un col ecclésiastique
the vicarage, the rectory	le presbytère
a churchwarden	un conseiller paroissial
a missionary	un missionnaire
a chaplain	un aumônier
a monk	un moine
a monastery	un monastère
a nun	une religieuse
a religious order	un ordre religieux
theology	la théologie
a theologian	un théologien
a theocracy	une théocratie

Mohammed knocks at classroom door

Fran Abrams

Yusuf Islam, formerly the pop star Cat Stevens, has been trying for more than 10 years to get state funding* for the Muslim school he founded. Now, at last, he glimpses* success. Tomorrow, architects from the official Funding Agency for Schools visit the Islamia school in north London, to check whether its buildings and facilities make it worthy of state support.

If the school is successful – the final decision rests with Gillian Shephard, the Secretary of State for Education – Islamia, with 300 pupils and a waiting list of 1,000, will be the first state supported Muslim school, enjoying similar status to hundreds of Church of England and Roman Catholic schools. For many Muslim parents, the day when their right to such schools is accepted cannot come soon enough. their growing assertiveness* over how their children are educated has stretched their relations with secular*schools to breaking point.

As the new year began, 1,500 Muslims in West Yorkshire refused to send their children to the Christian assemblies* which the law demands. A few weeks later it was revealed that a Birmingham primary school was offering Muslim religious education after the withdrawal of most of its pupils from the Christian-dominated lessons.

Conflicts such as these are bound to multiply. Britain has about 400,000 Muslim children of school age and, according to some estimates, there could be a million by 2000. Today's Muslim parents are demanding that schools adapt to accommodate their beliefs, and they are doing so with a force and a confidence that their own parents lacked.

The Independent,
February 11, 1996

1. Choose the right explanation for each of the following words (with asterisks in the passage).

1. *to fund*
A. to discover
B. to finance
C. to create

2. *to glimpse*
A. to see the possibility of
B. to see the end of
C. to see the worst of

3. *assertive*
A. remaining silent
B. showing no interest
C. speaking out with force

4. *secular*
A. not of a religious order   B. happening frequently
C. long-established

5. *an assembly*
A. a political meeting   B. a teachers' meeting
C. a gathering of pupils for prayer

2. Say whether the following statements are true (T) or false (F).

1. Yusuf Islam is a convert.

2. It was his first attempt to get state support.

3. Schools have to meet certain standards to receive state funds.

4. Islamia could be the first religious school to be state supported.

5. Some Muslim parents are getting impatient.

6. There is no religious education in British state schools.

7. Schools refuse to make any concessions to Muslims.

8. Initiatives such as Yusuf Islam's reduce segregation.

3. Three sentences have been cut up into parts and the parts scrambled. Put them back into the right order. (Punctuation and the capital letters at the beginning of the sentences have been removed whenever possible.)

1. their congregations/Church of Scotland ministers/the dangers of boring/ have been warned of

2. of poor communication and presentation/says the television age/a report to be discussed/of the Church next month/has made people more critical/at the general assembly

3. to ensure that churchgoers/as a lethal sin/rather than apathetic spectators/it describes boredom at worship/are active participants/and stresses the need

4. Fill in each blank with a word from the following list. Use each word only once.

strangers   separation   religious   areas   decades
accommodation   alarming   living   analysis

An ...(1)... picture of a society heading towards ever starker ...(2)... segregation is revealed by new research into ...(3)... patterns in Northern Ireland.

A detailed ...(4)... of population trends, disclosed for the first time by The Independent on Sunday, shows that the degree of physical ...(5)... between Protestants and Catholics is increasing year by year, with the number of segregated ...(6)... more than doubling in the last two ...(7)... .

Increasingly, large sections of the population are literally ...(8)... to one another, a fact with ominous implications for the Government's hopes of finding political ...(9)... .

The Independent on Sunday, March 21, 1993

Flooding out, trickling* in

It's impossible to under-estimate the explosive impact within the Jewish community of the survey this week showing that nearly half of British Jewish men under 40 are marrying non-Jews. This is the statistical evidence which proves the predictions of pro-minent Jewish academics such as Bernard Wassertein and Norman Cantor that the Orthodox Jewish diaspora will be reduced to a few pockets of Amish-style believers over the next century. (...)

The male intermarriage rate is the crucial statistic because the Orthodox Jewish identity is passed exclusively through the maternal line. For the ultra-Orthodox, it doesn't matter how Jewish your father or his family are, only one thing counts, the blood of your mother; if a male Jew marries out, his children are "lost".

These grim figures from the Institute of Church affairs will force the mainstream* Orthodox Jewish community to focus on something they have stubbornly ducked*: whe-ther they want to draw back into the fold* any of the "lost Jews", and do they want to convert the non-Jewish wives?

While Christians and Muslims have celebrated dramatic sto-ries of conversion with before and after comparisons, Jews never discuss the subject. It is considered tactless to mention that someone has converted; as Ruth, a convert, put it, it is like "reminding someone they used to be an alcoholic." In Islam, the process is simple, one statement and you're a Muslim, but to become a Jew takes years of examination by religious judges.

The Guardian, February 17, 1996

1. Choose the right explanation for each of the following words (with asterisks in the passage).

1. *to trickle*
A. to make a sound
B. to give out a light
C. to pour slowly

2. *mainstream*
A. difficult   B. dominant   C. marginal

3. *to duck*
A. to contradict   B. to avoid   C. to deny

4. *the fold*
A. the world   B. the crowd   C. the group

2. Choose the appropriate endings for the following sentences.

1. According to the article, after reading the survey the Jewish community would be
A. really pleased.   B. badly shaken.   C. quite indifferent.

2. For Orthodox Jews, transmission of identity is
A. out of line with common practice.
B. in accordance with common practice.
C. totally non-restrictive.

3. The survey was carried out by
A. a newspaper.
B. a university department.
C. a religious body.

4. According to the article, the Orthodox Jewish community has
A. readily faced reality.
B. never faced the situation.
C. tried to remedy the situation.

5. It may be concluded that the Orthodox Jewish community in Britain is likely to
A. increase significantly.
B. dwindle rapidly.
C. stay at the same level.

6. A biblical image is used in the article for
A. non-Jewish wives.
B. "lost Jews".
C. both "lost" Jews and non-Jewish wives.

3. *"Tactless" is the opposite of "tactful", but which of the adjectives ending in "-less" and "-ful" do not have their opposites constructed in this way?*

1. painless   2. successful   3. pitiful   4. heartless
5. godless   6. joyless   7. plentiful   8. dutiful
9. shameful   10. eventful   11. jobless   12. spotless
13. powerful   14. defenceless   15. merciful   16. countless
17. fearless

Entertainment and the Mass Media

12

Les spectacles et les mass média

The World of Entertainment	Le monde des spectacles
to entertain	divertir, amuser
to act	jouer
an actor	un acteur
an actress	une actrice
to interpret [ɪnˈtɜːprɪt]	interpréter
an interpretation	une interprétation
to play (a part, a role)	jouer (un rôle)
a part, a role	un rôle
the leading part, the lead	le rôle principal
a supporting role	un rôle secondaire
a character	un personnage
a character part	un rôle de composition
an artist	un artiste
a plot	une intrigue
a director	un metteur en scène, un réalisateur
to cast	choisir comme interprète
a cast	une distribution
to produce	produire
a production	une production
a performance	une représentation
the setting, the scenery	le décor
a designer	un décorateur
to design [dɪˈzaɪn]	dessiner, concevoir
to release	sortir, publier
a release	une sortie, une parution
a blockbuster	un film (un livre, etc.) à succès

a comedian	un comédien, un comique
a conjuror	un prestidigitateur
a trick	un tour
an act	un numéro
a circus	un cirque
a show	une revue, un spectacle
ballet	le ballet
ballet dancing	la danse classique
a ballerina	une ballerine
a pantomime	un spectacle musical de Noël

Success and failure — Le succès et l'échec

fame	la célébrité
the box office	le guichet, la caisse
a hit	un succès, un tube
a flop	un four
a fanatic, a fan	un admirateur
an idol ['aɪdl]	une idole
a masterpiece	un chef-d'œuvre
a review	une critique
a reviewer, a critic	un critique
an award	une récompense
a prize	un prix
to nominate	nommer
a nominee	un nominé, un nommé
an Oscar winner	un lauréat des Oscars

The Theatre — Le théâtre

a play	une pièce de théâtre
a playwright	un auteur dramatique
a tragedy	une tragédie
a comedy	une comédie
a drama	un drame
to stage	monter (une pièce)
the stage	la scène
to rehearse [rɪ'hɜːs]	répéter
a rehearsal	une répétition
an act	un acte
act two	le deuxième acte
the interval	l'entracte
a curtain call	un rappel

Cinema and Television — Le cinéma et la télévision

Cinema and Television	Le cinéma et la télévision
a screen	un écran
to screen	projeter
a film, a movie, a motion picture (US)	un film
a silent movie	un film muet
the feature film	le film principal
an animated cartoon	un dessin animé
a filmmaker	un cinéaste
to shoot	tourner
shooting	le tournage
a shot	un plan
a cameraman	un opérateur
to edit	monter
an editor	un monteur
editing	le montage
a sequence	une séquence
the soundtrack	la bande sonore
a scenario [sɪˈnɑːrɪəu]	un scénario
a script, a screenplay	un scénario détaillé
a screenwriter, a scenarist	un scénariste
to star	avoir pour vedette
a star	une vedette
a studio	un studio
pornography [pɔːˈnɒgrəfɪ]	la pornographie
pornographic [pɔːnəˈgræfɪk]	pornographique
a documentary	un documentaire
a detective film	un film policier
a thriller	un film à suspense
a horror movie	un film d'horreur
to dub	doubler
an undubbed film	un film en version originale
subtitles	les sous-titres

Music — La musique

Music	La musique
a concert	un concert
an orchestra [ˈɔːkɪstrə]	un orchestre
to conduct	diriger (un orchestre)
a conductor	un chef d'orchestre
a concerto [kənˈtʃɜːtəu]	un concerto
a symphony	une symphonie
a sonata [səˈnɑːtə]	une sonate

a piece	un morceau
a score	une partition
classical	classique
a bar	une mesure
a tune	un air
an instrument	un instrument
a band	une formation, un groupe
lyrics	les paroles
a musical (comedy)	une comédie musicale
to record [rɪˈkɔːd]	enregistrer
a tape/cassette recorder	un magnétophone
a record [ˈrekɔːd]	un disque
a single	un 45 tours
a maxi single	un super 45 tours
an album	un album
a compact disc	un disque compact
a CD	un CD
a CD player	un lecteur de CD
a record shop	un magasin de disques
a record company	une maison de disques
a cassette	une cassette
the charts	le hit-parade

Journalism / Le journalisme

a journalist, a newspaperman	un journaliste
a news agency	une agence de presse
to report	signaler, faire savoir
a report	un reportage
an account	un compte-rendu
reporting	le reportage
an article	un article
the *Times* editor	le directeur du *Times*
the sports editor	le rédacteur sportif
a correspondent	un correspondant
a freelance	un journaliste indépendant
a column	une chronique
a columnist	un chroniqueur
the leading article, the leader	l'éditorial principal
an editorial	un éditorial
to publish	éditer
a publisher	un éditeur
a proprietor, an owner	un propriétaire
to investigate	enquêter

an investigation	une enquête
to reveal	révéler
a revelation	une révélation
the popular press	la presse à sensation
a tabloid	un journal de petit format
the quality papers	les journaux sérieux
a copy	un exemplaire
an issue	un numéro (publication)
a headline	un titre
a banner headline	une manchette
the front-page	la une
advertisements	les publicités
classified advertisements	les petites annonces
circulation	le tirage

Radio and Television — La radio et la télévision

a radio set, a TV set	un poste de radio, de télé
a transmission	un programme, une retransmission
to broadcast	émettre
a broadcast, a programme	une émission
to listen in to	écouter (la radio)
a listener	un auditeur
a frequency	une fréquence
a wavelength	une longueur d'ondes
a waveband	une gamme d'ondes
to watch TV, to view	regarder la télé
digital TV	la télévision numérique
a viewer	un téléspectateur
a video	un enregistrement vidéo
a video recorder	un magnétoscope
a station	une station
a channel	une chaîne, un canal
a network	un réseau, une chaîne
the news	les informations
a news bulletin, a newscast	un bulletin d'information
a newsreader, a newscaster	un présentateur de journal
to announce	annoncer, présenter
an announcer	un présentateur
to comment	commenter
a commentator	un commentateur
to present	présenter
a presenter	un présentateur

a TV crew	une équipe de télé
peak time, prime time	les heures de grande écoute
the ratings	l'indice d'écoute
audience	l'audience
a schedule	une grille
a slot	une tranche horaire
a commercial	une annonce publicitaire
a spot	une coupure publicitaire
a series	une série
a serial	un feuilleton
a soap opera	un feuilleton mélo

Events — Les événements

to cover	couvrir
coverage	la couverture
live	en direct
a summary	un résumé
to highlight	mettre en valeur
the highlights	les moments forts
a source	une source
a leak	une fuite
a topic	un sujet, un thème
current affairs	l'actualité
sensational	sensationnel
sensationalism	recherche du sensationnel
off the record	hors antenne, en privé
to distort	déformer
distortion	la déformation
bias ['baɪəs]	le préjugé, le parti pris
biased, one-sided	partial, partisan
unbiased, objective	impartial, objectif
a news conference	une conférence de presse
a statement	une déclaration
a communiqué [kə'mjuːnɪkeɪ]	un communiqué

/// EXPRESSIONS

to be a sell-out	se jouer à guichets fermés
an award-winning film	un film primé
to be presented with an award	recevoir une distinction
to be in the limelight	être sous les projecteurs
to be cast against type	jouer à contre-emploi

to bring to the screen	porter à l'écran
a box-office attraction	un spectade à grand succès
to play the piano	jouer du piano
to sing out of tune	chanter faux
What's on tonight?	Que peut-on voir ce soir ?
the top of the ratings	la tête du classement
to top the bill	être en tête d'affiche
to give top billing to	donner la vedette à
to hit the headlines	faire les gros titres
to be given front-page treatment	faire la une des journaux
to give prominence to	mettre en vedette
to fuel rumours	alimenter la rumeur
to carry an exclusive tag	porter la mention "en exclusivité"
to appear on television	paraître à la télévision
to go on television	se montrer à la télévision
to be glued to the TV set	être rivé devant la télé
to be on the air	être à l'antenne
to go off the air	quitter, rendre l'antenne
to name sources	révéler ses sources
contempt of court	outrage à magistrat
letters to the editor	le courrier des lecteurs

//VOCABULAIRE COMPLÉMENTAIRE

The World of Entertainment	Le monde des spectacles
characterisation	la peinture des caractères
costumes	les costumes
make-up	le maquillage
to impersonate [ɪmˈpɜːsəneɪt]	imiter
an impersonator	un imitateur
a stand-up comedian	un comique (en solo)
to audition	auditionner
an audition	une séance d'essai
a spoof	une parodie
a theatre buff	un mordu, un cinglé de théâtre
a slapstick comedy	une comédie bouffonne
a role model	un modèle exemplaire
an icon [ˈaɪkɒn]	une figure emblématique
glamour	l'éclat, la séduction

a festival	un festival
a rerun	une reprise
a preview	une avant-première

The Theatre — Le théâtre

a cue	une réplique
a dress rehearsal	une répétition générale
the first night	la première
limelight	les feux de la rampe
stagecraft	l'art de la scène
stage fright	le trac
a stage manager	un régisseur
a repertory company	une troupe du répertoire
an understudy	une doublure
in the wings, backstage	dans les coulisses

Radio and Television — La radio et la télévision

a press review	une revue de presse
a rerun, a repeat	une rediffusion
a plug	une publicité clandestine
the tube, the box (fam.)	la téloche
a newsflash	un flash d'information
a news update	un dernier point
a news round-up	un tour d'horizon
an anchorman	un présentateur
a host	un animateur
a signature tune	un indicatif sonore
on the line	en ligne (téléphone)
airtime	le temps d'antenne
a phone-in	un programme à ligne ouverte
a quiz	un jeu avec questions
a quizmaster	un meneur de jeu
a radio car	une voiture émettrice
an aerial ['ɛərɪəl]	une antenne
a dish (aerial)	une parabole
pay per view	paiement à la séance
a descrambler box, a decoder	un décodeur
a remote control	une télécommande
cable	le câble
to tune in to	se brancher sur
to zap	zapper

Cinema and Television

Le cinéma et la télévision

an animated feature	un dessin animé de long métrage
a full-length film	un long métrage
a short film	un court métrage
a filmgoer, a cinemagoer	un cinéphile
a television film, a made-for-TV movie	un téléfilm
to adapt	adapter
an adaptation	une adaptation
a take	une prise de vue
a close-up	un gros plan
location	les extérieurs
an extra	un figurant
a cameo part	un mini rôle (pour vedette)
a set	un plateau
a stunt	une cascade
a stuntman	un cascadeur
the props	les accessoires
a propman	un accessoiriste
an X-rated film	un film classé X
a U-rated film	un film pour tous
the flicks	le cinoche
footage	une bande filmée
in slow motion	au ralenti
to replay	faire revoir
(action) replay	un retour sur l'action
a reel	une bobine
a trailer	une bande annonce
the credits	le générique
an episode, an instalment	un épisode
a sequel	une suite
an impresario [ɪmprə'sɑːrɪəu]	un imprésario
gore	l'hémoglobine
a video nasty	une cassette porno et/ou très violente
a camcorder	un caméscope
to videotape	enregistrer sur cassette

Journalism

Le journalisme

a tycoon	un magnat
a newshound	un reporter
to feature	figurer, faire figurer

133

a feature	un article de fond
a dispatch	une dépêche
a note	un billet
obituaries	la rubrique nécrologique
the agony column	le courrier du cœur
the agony aunt	le journaliste du courrier du cœur
the gossip column	les commérages
a gossip columnist	un chroniqueur mondain
a chief editor	un rédacteur en chef
readership	le lectorat
to contribute to	collaborer à
a contributor	un collaborateur
a broadsheet	un journal grand format
a rag	une feuille de chou
the gutter press	la presse à scandales
a hack	un pisse-copie
a box	un encadré
a cartoon	un dessin humoristique
a cartoonist	un dessinateur humoristique
a caption	une légende
a comic strip	une bande dessinée
the lay-out	la mise en page
a press cutting	une coupure de journal
an excerpt	un extrait
a pull-out supplement	un supplément détachable
news in brief	les nouvelles brèves
miscellaneous news	les faits divers
newsprint	le papier journal

Events — Les événements

a development	une évolution de situation
to hype	matraquer
media hype	le matraquage des médias
to fabricate	inventer, fabriquer
a news blackout	un refus d'informer
to gag	bâillonner
a gag	un bâillon
to censor	censurer
censorship	la censure
propaganda [prɒpə'gændə]	la propagande
disinformation	la désinformation
an authoritative source	une source autorisée
a reliable source	une source sûre

a press release	un avis à la presse
to brief	mettre au courant
a press briefing	un point de presse
lurid reporting	reportage à sensation
muckraking	la recherche du sordide
to pander to sb.	flatter bassement les goûts de qn.
slanted	tendancieux, partial
slant	le parti pris
libel ['laɪbəl]	la diffamation écrite
defamatory	diffamatoire
to slander	calomnier
slander	la calomnie
to sue [sjuː, suː]	poursuivre en justice
a breach of, an intrusion of	une atteinte à
privacy	l'intimité, la vie privée
damages	des dommages-intérêts

Press told to put a cap on long lenses

Andrew Culf, Media correspondent

Complaints from Prince Edward that long-lens* photographs of him kissing his girl friend were an intrusion of privacy were upheld* by the Press Complaints Commission yesterday.

The commission rejected arguments from three editors that the pictures of the prince and Sophie Rhys-Jones, taken on the Queen's estate at Balmoral, were in the public interest.

Charles Anson, the Queen's press secretary, had complained on the prince's behalf against the *Daily Express, Daily Mirror, Daily Star, Sun* and *Today.*

He argued that the pictures breached clauses of the industry's code outlawing photography of individuals on private property taken without their consent, unless in the public interest.

Stuart Higgins, the editor of the *Sun*, said he failed to see "how the public being shown that Prince Edward found happiness with Sophie could have been in any way upsetting for him" and saw no reason for apologising.

He added: "After intense speculation about the possible length of the prince's bachelorhood, the first photograph of him kissing a girl cannot be anything other than newsworthy."

Sir Nicholas Lloyd, editor of the *Daily Express*, and Brian Hitchen, editor of the *Daily Star* and member of the commission, apologised and said action had been taken to prevent further breaches.

The Guardian,
May 26, 1994

1. Choose the right explanation for each of the following words (with asterisks in the passage).

1. *a lens*
A. forms images in a camera
B. controls speed
C. adds colour to pictures

2. *to uphold*
A. to dismiss as groundless
B. to declare insufficient
C. to admit as well-founded

3. *adjudications*
A. sales of goods
B. decisions
C. contradictions

2. Say whether the following statements are true (T) or false (F).

1. The photos were taken within a short distance of the couple.

2. The reasons given to justify publication of the photos were unusual.

3. All the newspapers involved were tabloids.

4. Only one point in the code of conduct for the press leaves some room for interpretation.

5. According to the *Sun*, curiosity was aroused because of the prince's marital status.

6. All the newspaper editors reacted in the same way.

3. "Bachelorhood is made up of the noun bachelor and the suffix "-hood", signifying a period of time or a state. Use the definitions below to find more words ending in "-hood".

1. The period before you reach maturity.   C☐☐☐☐HOOD

2. Having and taking care of a baby
(for a woman).   M☐☐☐☐☐HOOD

3. The area surrounding your home. N☐☐☐☐☐☐(☐)☐HOOD

4. Those who have this title have
"Sir" before their first name.   K☐☐☐☐☐HOOD

5. The state of being a minister
(usually in the Christian religion).   P☐☐☐☐☐HOOD

4. "Newsworthy" is made up of the noun "news" and the adjective "worthy". Find three adjectives constructed in the same way and give the noun corresponding to each adjective.

1. R☐☐☐WORTHY: applies to cars and lorries.

2. A☐☐WORTHY: applies to aircraft.

3. S☐☐WORTHY: applies to ships.

Cannes Triumph for Mike Leigh

Derek Malcolm in Cannes

The British film director Mike Leigh won the Golden Palm at the Cannes Festival last night for his film *Secrets and Lies*.

A tragicomic family drama, it also won the International Critics' Prize, and Brenda Blethyn completed the triumph as best actress for her part as the white mother of an illegitimate black girl.

The film, the only British contender*, beat heavyweight Hollywood competition. Collecting his prize, Leigh said: "This is quite overwhelming. Thank you everyone." The film will be released in Britain on Friday.

Leigh said the prize would not only encourage him, but all those independent spirits "who made films about people and relationships, real life and all the things that really matter."

Secrets and Lies tells the story of a black adopted optometrist[1], Hortense, who sets out to find her real mother. To her surprise, she turns out to be a white unmarried mother called Cynthia, played by Blethyn. A family reunion leads to more revelations and emotional chaos, but in the end "everybody is changed for the better". (...)

There was a standing ovation for the recipients of the Best Actor award – the French star Daniel Auteuil and Pascal Duquenne. Duquenne is the first professional actor with Down's syndrome[2] to receive a big film festival prize. He stars as a Down's syndrome man, in *The Eighth Day*, by the Belgian director Jaco Van Dormael, whose brother also suffers from Down's syndrome.

[1] an optician
[2] a genetic disorder which results in mental handicap

The Guardian, May 21, 1996

1. Say whether the following statements are true (T) or false (F).

1. Mike Leigh did not receive the major award.

2. His film won three prizes.

3. The odds were against any British film winning the competition.

4. In his comment, Mike Leigh did not reveal what he was interested in.

5. The summary of the plot gives the impressions that the director took some risks.

6. *The Eighth Day* lacked any bearing on real-life experience.

2. "Relationships" is made up of the noun "relation" and the suffix "-ship". Find seven other nouns constructed in the same way.

1. Two or more people in business together. P□□□□□□SHIP

2. A political regime in which the leader has absolute power. D□□□□□□□SHIP

3. The state of being in possession of something.   O☐☐☐☐SHIP

4. It limits the freedom of expression.   C☐☐☐☐☐SHIP

5. A quality essential to anyone at the head of a political party for example.   L☐☐☐☐☐SHIP

6. There is no reason to feel lonely when you have this.   C☐☐☐☐☐☐☐☐SHIP

7. Clubs taking part in this competition hope to finish at the top.   C☐☐☐☐☐☐☐SHIP

3. Fill in each blank with a word from the following list. Use each word only once.

spot	charging	high-profile	nominees	appeal
missing	high	watch	suffer	

Newcomers flex their muscles in the battle to lift an Oscar

British hopes are ...(1)... for tonight's Oscars ceremony, but US television executives fear this year's lack of big name ...(2)... may lead to fewer viewers tuning in to ...(3)... the show.

With stars such as Robert Redford, Paul Newman, Clint Eastwood and Jack Nicholson ...(4)... from the line-up, analysts believe the ceremony will ...(5)... from not having the star ...(6)... of previous years.

Sources at the ABC network, which is ...(7)... a record $525,000 for a 30-second advertising ...(8)... , say they would have been happier with more ...(9)... nominations.

The Daily Telegraph, March 25, 1996

Introduction to chapters 13-20 / Introduction aux chapitres 13-20

Crime	La criminalité
Drugs	La drogue
Demonstrations	Les manifestations
Revolutions	Les révolutions
War	La guerre
Miscellaneous Topics	Centres d'intérêt divers
Accidents	Les accidents
Natural Disasters	Les catastrophes naturelles

/// VOCABULAIRE À HAUTE FRÉQUENCE

Physical Damage — Les dégats mâtériels

to blast	faire sauter, détruire
to explode	exploser, faire exploser
a blast, an explosion	une explosion
an explosive	un explosif
to set off	déclencher
to go off	se déclencher, exploser
to damage	endommager, abîmer
damage	les dégâts
to wreck	saccager, détruire
a wreck	une carcasse, une épave
wreckage	les débris, les décombres
to destroy	détruire
destruction	la destruction
to happen	se produire
to occur	survenir
to scatter	disperser
to devastate	ravager, dévaster
devastation	la dévastation, les ravages
devastating	dévastateur, catastrophique
to collapse	s'effondrer

rubble	les décombres, les gravats
debris	les débris
ruins	les ruines
to demolish	démolir
demolition	la démolition
to assess	évaluer
an assessment	une évaluation
scope, extent	l'étendue
a scale	une échelle de grandeur
the scene	les lieux
a disaster	un désastre
a catastrophe [kə'tæsrəfɪ]	une catastrophe
the aftermath	les conséquences, la suite

Casualties — Les victimes

to injure, to hurt	blesser
to wound	blesser (attaque)
slight, minor ['maɪnə]	léger
serious, major	grave
an injury	une blessure
a wound	une blessure (attaque)
to bury	ensevelir
to trap	coincer, bloquer
a shock	une commotion
unhurt	indemne
to escape	s'en sortir
alive	vivant
to shelter	abriter
a shelter	un abri, un refuge
a death toll	un bilan des morts

Rescue Work — Intervention des secours

alarm	l'alarme, l'alerte
to survive	survivre
a survivor	un rescapé
to attempt	tenter
an attempt, a bid	une tentative
to rescue	secourir
a rescue operation	une opération de secours
relief	l'aide, le secours
first aid	les premiers soins
to save	sauver

an emergency	une urgence
a refugee	un réfugié
to clear	déblayer
to pull clear	dégager
a heap	un tas
a pile	un amas
to recover	retrouver, récupérer
recovery	la récupération
to name	communiquer les noms
a helpline	un numéro spécial
a stretcher	une civière
to take to	transporter à
an ambulance	une ambulance
to identify	identifier
to name	nommer
to loot	piller
to evacuate	évacuer
evacuation	l'évacuation

Weapons — Les armes

to shoot	tirer
a shot	un coup de feu
to fire	tirer (un coup de feu)
a firearm	une arme à feu
to arm	armer
a pistol	un pistolet
a handgun	une arme de poing
a gun, a rifle	un fusil
gunfire	une fusillade
a shotgun	un fusil de chasse
a gunman	un homme armé
a bullet	une balle
a grenade	une grenade
automatic	automatique
a bomb	une bombe
to bomb	bombarder (avion)
a bombing	un bombardement
to machine gun	mitrailler
a machine gun	une mitrailleuse
a gun	un canon
a mortar	un mortier
a mortar bomb	un obus de mortier
a rocket	une roquette

to shell	bombarder (obus)
a shell	un obus
artillery	l'artillerie
ammunition	les munitions
to mine	miner
a mine	une mine
an armoured car	un véhicule blindé
a tank	un char d'assaut
a missile	un missile

Violent Actions — Les actions violentes

to threaten ['θretn]	menacer
a threat [θret]	une menace
to blackmail	faire du chantage
blackmail	le chantage
to kidnap, to abduct	kidnapper, enlever
an abduction, kidnapping	un enlèvement, un rapt
to attack	attaquer
an attack	une attaque
to clash with	se heurter à, affronter
a clash	un affrontement
to raid	attaquer
a bank raid	une attaque de banque
to burst into	faire irruption dans
to demand	exiger
a demand	une exigence
a ransom	une rançon
to take over	s'emparer de
to mask	masquer
a mask	un masque
to blow up	faire sauter
a target	une cible
to assassinate	assassiner
an assassination	un assassinat
to gun down	abattre
a network, a ring	un réseau
to fight	lutter, combattre
a fight	un combat, une lutte
a battle	une bataille
a gunfight	un échange de coups de feu
a siege [si:dʒ]	un siège
to besiege	assiéger

Security — La sécurité

Security	La sécurité
to crack down on sth.	réprimer qch.
a crackdown on	une répression de
to clamp down on sth.	donner un coup d'arrêt à, durcir la lutte contre
a clampdown on sth.	un durcissement de la lutte contre qch., un tour de vis
to combat sth.	mener une lutte contre qch.
a measure	une mesure
to look for, to search for	rechercher
a search	une recherche, une fouille
to enquire	enquêter, se renseigner
an enquiry	une enquête
to investigate	examiner, enquêter
an investigation	une enquête, une investigation
a detective constable	un inspecteur de police
a detective inspector	un inspecteur principal
a detective superintendent	un commissaire de police
a detective chief superintendent	un commissaire divisionnaire
the security forces	les forces de sécurité
a security guard	un vigile, un convoyeur de fonds
a bodyguard	un garde du corps
to patrol	patrouiller
a patrol	une patrouille
to block	bloquer
a road block	un barrage routier
to flee	fuir, s'enfuir
to surround	cerner, entourer
to overpower	maîtriser
to arrest	arrêter
an arrest	une arrestation
to hold	interpeller
to detain	garder à vue
to outlaw	mettre hors la loi
to ban	interdire
a ban	une interdiction
a raid	une descente
to curb	juguler
to quell	étouffer, réprimer
to storm	donner l'assaut
to dismantle	démanteler
to impose	imposer
a curfew	un couvre-feu

a truce	une trève
a ceasefire	un cessez-le-feu
a peacekeeping force	une force d'interposition
to give oneself in/up, to turn oneself in	se rendre, se livrer
to surrender	se rendre, capituler
a surrender	une reddition
to prevent	empêcher, prévenir
prevention	la prévention
to free, to set free, to release	relâcher, libérer
a release	une libération

/// EXPRESSIONS

to set fire to sth., to set sth. on fire	mettre le feu à qch.
to set sth. alight, ablaze	embraser qch.
to raise the alarm	donner l'alarme
to lift a ban	lever une interdiction
to make a getaway	prendre la fuite
to be in hiding	se cacher
to be on the loose, to be on the run, to be at large	ne pas avoir été arrêté, être dans la nature, être en cavale
to take refuge	prendre refuge
to keep an open mind	ne rejeter aucune piste
to pose a threat	constituer une menace
tit for tat	la loi du talion
to be under arrest	être en état d'arrestation
to raise a ransom	réunir une rançon
at point-blank range	à bout portant
to level a gun at sb., to take aim at sb.	pointer une arme sur qn., diriger une arme contre qn.
to be caught in crossfire	être pris entre deux feux
to hold sb. at gunpoint	braquer une arme sur qn.
to take up arms	prendre les armes
to be up in arms against	s'insurger contre
to lay down (one's) arms	déposer les armes
riddled with bullets	criblé de balles
to lay siege to	faire le siège de
a surface to air missile	un missile sol-air
to take one's toll	prélever son tribut
to claim 20 lives, to leave 20 people dead	faire 20 morts

to lose one's life	trouver la mort
to die instantly	mourir tout de suite
to be killed outright	être tué sur le coup
to be in a coma	être dans le coma
to lose consciousness	perdre connaissance
the kiss of life, mouth to mouth resuscitation	le bouche à bouche
to recover consciousness	reprendre connaissance
to be unaccounted for	ne pas avoir été retrouvé
to be missing	être porté disparu
flags at half mast	les drapeaux en berne
to offer condolences	présenter des condoléances

/// VOCABULAIRE COMPLÉMENTAIRE

Physical Damage — Les dégâts matériels

to rip through	souffler
to shatter	fracasser
to gut	éventrer
a tangle	un enchevêtrement
remains	les restes, les dépouilles
to cave in, to subside	s'affaisser
catastrophic	catastrophique

Casualties and Rescue work — Les victimes et l'intervention des secours

to dial 999, to dial 911 (US)	appeler police-secours
unscathed [ʌn'skeɪðd]	indemne
a cut	une coupure
to bruise [bru:z]	meurtrir, tuméfier
a bruise	une meurtrissure, un hématome
to mutilate, to maim	mutiler
belongings	les possessions
to pass out	s'évanouir
to come to	revenir à soi
to resuscitate	réanimer
resuscitation	la réanimation
survival	la survie
a theory	une hypothèse

a corpse	un cadavre
an autopsy	une autopsie
a tally of deaths	un décompte des morts
a coffin	un cercueil
a shroud	un linceul
a mortuary	une morgue, une chapelle ardente
a memorial service	une cérémonie commémorative
relatives	la famille
to shed blood	répandre le sang
bloodshed, bloodletting	l'effusion de sang
a bloodbath	un bain de sang
to mourn sb.	porter le deuil de qn.
mourning	le deuil

Violent Actions and Security / Les actions violentes et la sécurité

on the alert	en état d'alerte
to outlaw	mettre hors la loi
captive	captif
captivity	la captivité
to occupy	occuper
an occupation	une occupation
a skirmish	une escarmouche, un accrochage
to ambush	tendre une embuscade, tomber dans une embuscade
to erupt, to flare up	se déclencher brusquement
an eruption	un déclenchement brusque
a flare-up	une flambée
an upsurge, a surge	une recrudescence
a spate, a rash	(toute) une série
to trigger, to spark	déclencher, provoquer
to mastermind	organiser
a mastermind	un cerveau
a scheme [ski:m]	un stratagème, un projet
a ploy	un stratagème
to avenge	venger
revenge	une revanche
to respond	répliquer
a response	une réplique
retribution	le châtiment, la vengeance
to retaliate	riposter

retaliation	la riposte
reprisals	les représailles
a carbon copy	une réplique exacte
an assumed name	un nom d'emprunt
the whereabouts	l'endroit où est qn.
to vanish	disparaître
to conceal	dissimuler
a hideaway, a hide-out	une cachette, une planque
an arms cache [kæʃ]	une cache d'armes
a haul	une prise, un butin
a hood	une cagoule
a wig	une perruque
a sniper	un tireur isolé
a ringleader	un meneur
an accomplice	un complice
complicity	la complicité
an informant, an informer	un informateur
a repentant informer	un repenti
a tip, a tip-off	un renseignement
surveillance	la surveillance
to thwart, to foil	contrecarrer, déjouer
to stalk	traquer, filer
to move in	intervenir
to trap, to entrap	piéger
a trap	un piège, une souricière
a sting operation	une opération piège
a strike	un coup de main, un raid
to rage	faire rage
to bombard	bombarder (obus, bombes)
bombardment	le bombardement
headquarters	le quartier général
a deadline	une limite de temps, une date butoir
to cordon off to seal off	boucler, interdire l'accès
to barricade oneself	se barricader
a police cordon	un cordon de police
to handcuff	passer les menottes à
handcuffs	les menottes
to regain (control)	reprendre (le contrôle)
to extradite	extrader
an extradition	une extradition
beleaguered	assiégé, investi
a shoot-out	une fusillade
a bulletproof vest	un gilet pare-balles

a marksman, a sharpshooter	un tireur d'élite
a stray bullet	une balle perdue
a state of emergency	un état d'urgence
a state of siege	un état de siège
martial law	la loi martiale
to swoop	faire une descente
a swoop	un coup de filet
to round up	effectuer une rafle
a round-up	un regroupement, une rafle
to sweep	ratisser
a sweep	un ratissage
to sift through	passer au crible
to comb	fouiller, ratisser
to massacre, to slaughter	massacrer
a massacre, a slaughter	un massacre
to exterminate	exterminer
an extermination	une extermination
to execute	exécuter
a summary execution	une exécution sommaire
a mass grave	une fosse commune
genocide	le génocide

Weapons · Les armes

an arms dealer	un marchand d'armes
gun running	le trafic d'armes
a battery	une batterie
the butt	la crosse
a gun barrel	un canon de fusil
a silencer	un silencieux
the trigger	la détente
to pull the trigger	presser la détente
a sawn-off shotgun	un fusil à canon scié
a pump action shotgun	un fusil à pompe
a submachine gun	une mitraillette
an arms dump	un dépôt d'armes
ammunition	les munitions
a round of ammunition	une balle, une cartouche
a cartridge	une cartouche
a blank shot	un tir à blanc
a live bullet	une balle réelle
a volley	une rafale
to strafe	mitrailler, bombarder
gunshot	le plomb de chasse

a rubber bullet	une balle de caoutchouc
a limpet mine	une mine ventouse
a fire bomb	une bombe incendiaire
shrapnel	les éclats
a time bomb	une bombe à retardement
a cluster bomb	une bombe à fragmentation

Crime and Punishment **13** Délits et sanctions

(voir Introduction p. 139)

/// VOCABULAIRE À HAUTE FRÉQUENCE

General Background | Contexte général

an offence	un délit, une infraction
a crime	un délit, un crime
to commit	commettre
to break	transgresser, violer
to uphold the law	faire respecter, maintenir la loi
a criminal	un criminel
an offender	un délinquant
a law-breaker	un contrevenant
crime	la délinquance
petty crime	la petite délinquance
the crime rate	le taux de criminalité
law-abiding	respectueux de la loi
security	la sécurité
insecurity	l'insécurité

Non-Violent Crime | Les délits sans violence

shoplifting	le vol à l'étalage
a shoplifter	un voleur à l'étalage
to smuggle	passer en fraude
smuggling	la contrebande
to forge	contrefaire
forgery	la contrefaçon
to deceive [dɪ'siːv]	tromper
deception	la tromperie
confidence	la confiance
to con sb.	escroquer, duper qn.
a con	une supercherie, escroquerie
a conman	un escroc, un imposteur
to pose as	se faire passer pour
to pretend to be	affirmer être

a bogus repairman	un faux dépanneur
to trust sb.	avoir confiance en qn.
libel ['laɪbəl]	la diffamation écrite
to steal	dérober
a thief	un voleur
a theft	un vol

Violent Crime

Les délits avec violence

to rob	voler
a robbery	un vol qualifié
an armed robbery	un vol à main armée
to hold up	braquer, neutraliser
a hold-up	un braquage
to burgle	cambrioler
a burglary	un cambriolage
a burglar	un cambrioleur
to break-in	entrer par effraction
a break-in	une effraction
a hooligan	un casseur
to vandalise	vandaliser
a vandal	un vandale
vandalism	le vandalisme
a thug	un loubard
to mug, to assault	agresser
a mugging, an assault	une agression
to rape	violer
a rape	un viol
a rapist	un violeur
child abuse	les sévices aux enfants
a pædophile ['piːdəufaɪl]	un pédophile
manslaughter	homicide involontaire/ par imprudence
to murder	assassiner
a murder	un meurtre
attempted murder, a murder attempt	tentative de meurtre
to stab	poignarder
to strangle	étrangler

Enquiries and Arrests

Enquêtes et arrestations

a constable, an officer	un agent, un gendarme
a cop, a copper	un flic
to suspect	soupçonner

a suspect	un suspect
suspicion	les soupçons
suspicious	soupçonneux, suspect
a description	un signalement
a clue	un indice
a lead [liːd]	une piste
to give away	dénoncer
evidence	témoignage, preuve
to question	interroger
to accuse	accuser
an accusation	une accusation
alleged	présumé
to charge	inculper, accuser
a charge	une inculpation, une accusation

Justice | La justice

a court	un tribunal
a magistrate	un magistrat, un juge d'instance
to judge	juger
a judge	un juge
a judg(e)ment	un jugement
a trial	un procès
a case	une affaire, un procès
to prosecute	poursuivre
prosecution	des poursuites, l'accusation
a prosecutor	un procureur
to witness sth.	être témoin de qch.
a witness	un témoin
to testify	témoigner, déposer
a testimony	un témoignage
to admit, to own up	reconnaître
to confess	avouer
to deny	nier
a denial	un démenti, une dénégation
guilt	la culpabilité
guilty	coupable
not guilty	non coupable
innocent	innocent
to plead	plaider
to sentence	condamner
a sentence	une peine, une condamnation

tough, harsh, stiff	dur, rigoureux
lenient	indulgent
leniency	l'indulgence
punishment	le châtiment
to fine	donner une amende
a fine	une amende
a prison	une prison
a jail, a gaol [dʒeɪl]	une prison
to jail, to gaol	emprisonner
life imprisonment	la réclusion à vie
a life sentence	une condamnation à perpétuité
a warder, a prison officer	un gardien, un surveillant
to escape, to break out	s'évader
an escape, a break-out	une évasion
the death penalty	la peine de mort
capital punishment	la peine capitale
to abolish	abolir
abolition	l'abolition
to restore	rétablir
restoration	le rétablissement

EXPRESSIONS

to be taken in	être dupé
to steal a car	voler une voiture
to rob a passenger	voler un passager
the mail train robbery	l'attaque du train postal
to force one's way into	s'introduire de force dans
to be set upon	se faire attaquer
to produce a weapon	sortir une arme
grievous bodily harm	coups et blessures
to appear before magistrates, to appear in court	être présenté au juge
to help with enquiries	être entendu par la police
to be placed under investigation	être mis en examen
to act suspiciously	avoir une attitude suspecte
to arouse suspicion	éveiller les soupçons
to be caught red-handed	être pris sur le fait
to issue a photofit picture, to release an identikit picture	publier un portrait robot
the Serious Crime Squad	la Brigade de répression du banditisme

to be remanded on bail	être laissé en liberté sous caution, sous contrôle
to be remanded in custody	être placé en détention, être incarcéré
under house arrest	assigné à résidence
to bring to court	poursuivre en justice
to bring to trial	assigner en justice
to bring an action against, to serve a writ on	intenter une action en justice contre
to be tried in one's absence	être jugé par contumace
to settle out of court	régler à l'amiable
to drop a charge	rendre un non-lieu
to dismiss a case	prononcer la relaxe
to serve a sentence	purger une peine
to uphold a judg(e)ment	confirmer un jugement
to quash a conviction	casser une condamnation
a miscarriage of justice	une erreur judiciaire
a travesty of justice	une parodie de justice
to speak under duress	parler sous la contrainte
to take the law into one's own hands	se faire justice soi-même
to be jailed for three months	être condamné à trois mois de prison
to receive a jail sentence	être condamné à une peine d'emprisonnement
a non-custodial sentence	une peine autre que la prison
to commute a sentence	commuer une peine
to run into trouble	avoir des ennuis
to stay out of trouble	ne plus avoir d'ennuis

/// VOCABULAIRE COMPLÉMENTAIRE

General Background	Contexte général
wrongdoing	indélicatesse, méfait
a wrongdoer	un malfaiteur
a misdemeanour [mɪsdɪˈmiːnə]	un méfait, un délit
lawful	légal
unlawful	illégal
illicit	illicite

an infringement	une infraction
a first offender	un délinquant primaire
a hardened criminal	un repris de justice

Non-Violent Crime — Les délits sans violence

misconduct	l'indélicatesse
to trespass	s'introduire sans permission
a trespasser	un intrus
trespassing	l'intrusion illégale
to poach	braconner
joyriding	«emprunt» de voiture, rodéo
contraband	la contrebande
to fake	falsifier
a counterfeit note, a fake note	un faux billet
a fence	un receleur
a breach	une violation
a breach of trust	un abus de confiance
to trick sb.	tromper qn.
a trick	un tour, une supercherie
a trickster	un filou
a confidence trick	un abus de confiance
a crook	un escroc, un filou
to swindle	escroquer, estamper
a swindle	une escroquerie
to rip off	arnaquer
a rip-off	une arnaque
to defraud	spolier, gruger
to bribe	corrompre, soudoyer
a bribe	un pot de vin
bribery	la corruption
fraud	la fraude
a fraudster	un fraudeur
to defraud	escroquer, frustrer
to defame	diffamer
defamation [defə'meɪʃən]	la diffamation
defamatory [dɪ'fæmətrɪ]	diffamatoire
to slander	calomnier
slander	la diffamation orale
to solicit [se'lɪsɪt]	racoler
a prostitute	une prostituée
a pimp	un souteneur
indecent exposure	outrage public à la pudeur
gross indecency	outrage aux bonnes mœurs

Violent Crime — Les délits avec violence

a felony	un forfait, un crime
arson	l'incendie criminel
an arsonist	un incendiaire
a firebug	un pyromane
an affray	une rixe
a brawl	une bagarre
indecent assault	attentat à la pudeur
gang rape	le viol collectif
a serial killer	un tueur en série
a highwayman	un bandit de grand chemin
to tie (up), to bind	attacher
to blindfold	bander les yeux
to gag	bâillonner
a safe	un coffre-fort
a vault	une chambre forte
to get away	se sauver
a getaway	une fuite
the mob, the mafia	la mafia
a gangster, a mobster	un truand, un gangster
a godfather	un parrain
a hired gunman	un tueur à gages
a contract	un contrat
organised crime	le crime organisé, le grand banditisme
the underworld	le milieu
to racketeer [rækɪ'tɪə]	racketter
conspiracy	association de malfaiteurs

Enquiries and Arrests — Enquêtes et arrestations

an eye witness	un témoin oculaire
a statement	une déclaration, une déposition
a reward	une récompense
a beat	une ronde, un îlot
a trail	une piste
a fingerprint	une empreinte digitale
a riddle	une énigme
an alibi ['ælɪbaɪ]	un alibi
a warrant	un mandat
a manhut	une chasse à l'homme
to hound, to track down	traquer
to come forward	se présenter à la police

a jailbreak	une évasion
to recapture	reprendre (évadé)
to be involved in	être mêlé à
a motive	un mobile
to prove	prouver
a proof	une preuve
to substantiate	fournir des preuves à l'appui de
hard evidence	preuves réelles, matérielles
incriminating evidence	une pièce à conviction
an inquest	une enquête après mort
a post-mortem	une autopsie
forensic evidence	expertise médico-légale
a coroner	un chargé d'enquête après mort suspecte
the culprit	l'auteur, le coupable
a put-up job, a set-up, a frame-up	une machination, un coup monté
to frame sb.	monter un coup contre qn.
trumped up, fabricated	fabriqué
an allegation	une allégation
to lock up	mettre sous les verrous
remand	la détention préventive

Justice — La justice

a youth court	un tribunal pour mineurs
a criminal record	un casier judiciaire
previous convictions	condamnations antérieures
a jury	un jury
a juror	un juré
to sue [sjuː, suː]	intenter une action contre
to try sb.	faire passer qn. en jugement
a lawsuit	un procès
the defendant	le prévenu
the plaintiff	le plaignant
in camera	à huis-clos
a lawyer	un homme de loi
a solicitor	un notaire, un avocat-conseil
a counsel, a barrister	un avocat à la cour
a defence attorney (US)	un avocat
a district attorney (US)	un procureur
prosecution	le ministère public
the dock	le banc des accusés
the witness stand	la barre des témoins

Crime and Punishment

a hearing	une audience, une audition
an account	une déclaration
an affidavit	une déposition sous serment
a confession	un aveu
to indict [ɪnˈdaɪt]	mettre en accusation
an indictment	un acte d'accusation
a count	un chef d'accusation
to cross-examine	interroger un témoin de la partie adverse
a cross-examination	un contre-interrogatoire
to recant	se rétracter
a recantation	une rétractation
to sum up	conclure
summing-up	les conclusions
to rule	décider, ordonner
a ruling	une décision, un jugement
a verdict	un verdict
in absentia	par défaut
to acquit	acquitter
an acquittal	un acquittement
to discharge	relaxer
a discharge	une relaxe
to caution	mettre en garde
a caution	un avertissement
extenuating/mitigating circumstances	circonstances atténuantes
to exonerate	disculper, innocenter
to convict	déclarer coupable
a conviction	une condamnation
a suspended sentence	une peine avec sursis
to appeal	faire appel
mercy	la clémence
to pardon	grâcier, amnistier
pardon	la grâce
amnesty	l'amnistie
remission	remise de peine
on parole	en liberté conditionnelle
a bar	un barreau
a cell	une cellule
an inmate, a detainee	un détenu
solitary confinement	l'isolement carcéral
a prison governor	un directeur de prison
a remand centre, a detention centre	un centre de détention
exercise	la promenade (en prison)

community work	les travaux d'intérêt général
electronic tagging	le bracelet électronique
alternative punishment	peine de substitution
probation	mise à l'épreuve
a probation officer	un agent de tutelle
death row [rəu]	le couloir de la mort
a stay of execution	un sursis à exécution
an executioner	un bourreau
to deter	dissuader
deterrent	dissuasif
to prevent	prévenir, empêcher
prevention	la prévention
a neighbourhood watch	un comité de vigilance
scheme	de quartier

Man shot as he tackled post office raiders

by Paul Stokes

A retired council official was shot and a pensioner struck in the face with a crowbar* as members of the public tackled two robbers yesterday.

The robbers, who had a sawn-off shotgun, burst into a sub-post office in Poole, Dorset, and attacked a 69-year-old woman customer before demanding cash.

Passers-by moved in* as they tried to get away on a motor-cycle with £10,000 at 12.40pm.

Mr David Scovell, 53, who was the only other customer in the shop in Blandford Road, Hamworthy, tried to tackle the men. He was thrown to the ground and shot in the chest and knee at point-blank range*.

He had emergency surgery in Southampton General Hospital. As the pair tried to escape on the motorcycle, they were rammed* by a Ford Fiesta driven by Mr Fred Viegler and knocked through the shop window. Their second attempt to ride away was foiled* when the driver of a pick-up truck reversed into them, pinning* the Yamaha motorcycle to the ground.

The raiders then ran up an alley chased by two Royal Marines who had been in the Red Lion public house opposite the shop.

One of the men was caught hiding under a shed* by Inspector Rick Isaacs and Pc[1] Matt Gardener after a chase through gardens and woodland.

[1] Police constable

The Daily Telegraph, August 13, 1993

Crime and Punishment

1. **Choose the right explanation for each of the following words (with asterisks in the passage).**

1. *a crowbar*
A. a tool for forcing something open.
B. a device for firing a shot.
C. something for carrying things.

2. *to move in*
A. to go away   B. to watch   C. to intervene

3. *at point blank range*
A. within a short distance
B. at some distance
C. far away

4. *to ram*
A. to arrest   B. to collide with   C. to warn

5. *to foil*
A. to make more difficult   B. to cause to fail
C. to make easier

6. *to pin*
A. to block   B. to gather   C. to let go

7. *a shed*
A. a blanket   B. an outbuilding   C. a clump of trees

2. **Say whether the following statements are true (T) or false (F).**

1. The pensioner struck in the face was Mr David Scovell.
2. The two robbers acted brutally from the start.
3. The two robbers didn't get any cash.
4. Mr David Scovell could have been killed.
5. No damage was caused to the shop.
6. The motorcycle was partially under the truck.
7. It is usual for members of the public to act in such a way.
8. The fact that members of the public intervened served no useful purpose.

3. **Read the article again carefully. Then, without looking at it, put the events in the right order, as they actually happened.**

A. They tried to escape on a motorcycle.
B. The robbers were chased by two Royal Marines.
C. The driver of a truck reversed into the motorcycle.
D. Mr Scovell was thrown to the ground and shot in the chest.
E. They were rammed by a Ford Fiesta.
F. One of the men was caught in a shed.
G. One customer tried to tackle the robbers.
H. They attacked a woman customer.
I. They demanded some cash.

4. Read the article again and find the following:

1. A verb showing that the robbers' entry into the post office did not go unnoticed.

2. A phrase describing a weapon often used in armed robberies.

3. A verb more often used in rugby or football to mean an attempt to stop someone by physical means.

Armed police free Greek shipping agent held by kidnappers

Duncan Campbell and Helena Smith in Athens

A kidnap victim who was held masked and tranquillised in a cupboard for nine days was recovering yesterday after being freed by a complex armed police operation.

News of the kidnapping and the ransom demand, reported to be for around £20 million, was kept secret through a police information blackout.

George Fraghistas, a London-based shipping agent from a wealthy Greek shipping family, was grabbed at gunpoint by four men shortly after dark on March 24.

He was walking down a street near his home in Maida Vale, west London, when he was bundled* into the boot* of a car. One of the kidnappers got into the boot with him and handcuffed* and gagged him. He was driven to a three-storey house in Hogan Mews in Paddington, west London, where his spectacles were removed. He was forced to put earplugs* in his ears and was effectively suffering from sensory deprivation, said Commander Roy Ramm, head of the Organised Crime Group at Scotland Yard.

The kidnappers also made Mr Fraghistas take tranquillising drugs although he was not physically harmed. He was kept in a walk-in cupboard 6ft by 3ft while around 50 calls were made in an attempt to extract a ransom from his family in Greece. No money was paid.

---

1. Choose the right explanation for each of the following words (with asterisks in the passage).

1. *to bundle*
A. to cover with a blanket   B. to push roughly
C. to make room for

2. *the boot* (of a car)
A. the back seat   B. the bottom of the car
C. the luggage compartment

3. *to handcuff*
A. to immobilise the hands   B. to strike with the hand
C. to give a hand to

4. *earplugs*
A. they pinch the ears   B. they block the ears
C. they cover the ears

2. Say whether the following statements are true (T) or false (F).

1. The British police do not always carry weapons.
2. The police had asked the public for help
3. The approximate time of the kidnapping is easy to guess.
4. The kidnappers used a small car.
5. Mr Fraghistas was not likely to give a description of his kidnappers.
6. The kidnappers did not take their victim very far.
7. It is possible to imagine why their scheme went wrong.
8. The affair was concluded satisfactorily.

3. Fill in the blanks with words from the article.

1. He was down with flu for a few days , but he soon ...... and was back at work the next Monday.
2. The kidnappers ...... their victim once the ransom had been paid.
3. No freedom of expression was allowed under the military regime and the press was tightly ....
4. An agreement could be reached soon although there are still a few obstacles to be ....
5. They did not succeed the first time, but they tried again and their third ...... was successful.

4. Fill in the twelve lines across the grid with translations of the corresponding French words. This will give you the answer to number 13 in column D.

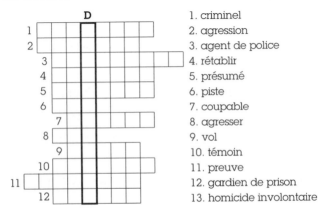

1. criminel
2. agression
3. agent de police
4. rétablir
5. présumé
6. piste
7. coupable
8. agresser
9. vol
10. témoin
11. preuve
12. gardien de prison
13. homicide involontaire

Chain attack

A woman from Portsmouth was taken to hospital after intervening in a dog fight and being beaten with a chain by the other dog's owner.

The Times, November 9, 1993

Hole in one

A would-be burglar who picked up a manhole cover to smash a store window in Sunderland, Tyne and Wear, stepped back and fell down the hole.

The Weekly Telegraph, April 20, 1994

In an honesty test set up by *Reader's Digest* magazine, which dropped 80 wallets containing £30 in towns and cities, Glasgow and Leamington Spa in Warwickshire tied as the most honest communities, while people in Cardiff were more likely to take the money and run. Overall, 65 per cent of the wallets were handed in, eight out of ten in Glasgow and Leamington Spa and only four in Cardiff. Women were more honest then men – of 32 who found wallets, 23 handed them in, while only 29 out of 48 men did so.

The Independent, June 17, 1996

Drugs **14** La drogue

(voir Introduction p. 139)

/// VOCABULAIRE À HAUTE FRÉQUENCE

Drugs

dope
narcotics [nɑː'kɒtɪks]
glue
glue sniffing
a solvent
hemp
marijuana [mærɪ'wɑːnə]
cannabis
hashish
LSD
cocaine [kə'keɪn]
crack
opium
heroin
powder
a soft drug
a hard drug

La drogue

la drogue
les stupéfiants
la colle
l'inhalation de solvants
un solvant
le chanvre
la marijuana
le cannabis
le haschish
le LSD
la cocaïne
le crack
l'opium
l'héroïne
la poudre
une drogue douce
une drogue dure

Addiction

a joint
to inhale, to sniff
to inject
an injection
a syringe [sɪ'rɪndʒ]
a needle
a fix
a dose
an overdose
high
a kick

La dépendance

un joint
inhaler, respirer
injecter
une injection
une seringue
une aiguille
une piqûre, une injection
une dose
une overdose
défoncé
une sensation

a trip	un trip
to take to	se mettre à
to use	utiliser
a user	un usager
an abuser, an addict	un toxicomane
a habit	habitude, accoutumance
abuse, addiction	la toxicomanie
dependence	la dépendance

Drug Traffic — Le trafic de drogue

to consume	consommer
consumption	la consommation
a smuggler, a courier	un passeur, un convoyeur
to traffic	faire le trafic de
a trafficker	un trafiquant
a dealer	un pourvoyeur
to deal in	faire le trafic de
trafficking	le trafic
a pusher	un revendeur
a connection	une filière
to supply	fournir
supply	l'approvisionnement
available	disponible
to launder money	blanchir l'argent
laundering	le blanchiment

Processing — La fabrication

poppy	le pavot
raw	brut
to refine	raffiner
a refinery	une raffinerie
a laboratory	un laboratoire
a chemist	un chimiste
to process	traiter
a process	un traitement
powder	poudre

The Fight against Drugs — La lutte contre la drogue

to possess	détenir
possession	la détention
to seize	saisir

a seizure ['siːʒə]	une saisie
a haul	une prise, une saisie
a street value	une valeur marchande
customs	la douane
a customs officer	un douanier
a drugs test	un contrôle anti-dopage
to detoxify	désintoxiquer
detoxification	la désintoxication
to rehabilitate	réadapter, réhabiliter
rehabilitation	la réhabilitation
to wean	sevrer
to wean oneself off	se détacher de
to get off drugs	abandonner la drogue
to give up sth.	renoncer à qch.
to relapse	rechuter
a relapse	une rechute

EXPRESSIONS

to be on drugs	se droguer
to experiment with drugs	toucher à la drogue
to dabble with drugs	tâter de la drogue
to stay clear of drugs	ne pas toucher à la drogue
to fail a drugs test	subir un contrôle positif
to get high	s'éclater
to get stoned	se défoncer
to be hooked on	être intoxiqué, être accro
to be dependent on	être en état de dépendance
to be strung out on drugs	être sous l'effet de la drogue
to go cold turkey	être en manque
to develop a habit	contracter une habitude
to kick drugs	renoncer à la drogue
to go back on drugs	se remettre à la drogue

VOCABULAIRE COMPLÉMENTAIRE

Drugs	La drogue
acid	le LSD
pot, grass	l'herbe, la marijuana
hash	le hasch

a reefer	un joint, un pétard
coke	la coca
stuff	la came
amphetamines	les amphétamines
barbiturates	les barbituriques
hallucinogen [hælu:'sɪnədʒən]	hallucinogène
paste	la pâte
resin	la résine
a tablet	une plaquette
base	la base

Addiction — La dépendance

hypodermic	hypodermique
a disposable syringe	une seringue jetable
a jab, a shot	une piqûre
intravenous	intraveineux
to snort	renifler
withdrawal symptoms	des symptômes de manque
a junkie	un drogué

Drug Traffic — Le trafic de drogue

a baron	un baron
a runner	un passeur
a peddler	un revendeur
to ship, to consign	expédier
a shipment, a consignment	une expédition

Processing — La fabrication

coca	la coca
a substitute	un produit de remplacement
a derivative	un dérivé
a chemical	un produit chimique
a lab	un labo

The Fight against Drugs — La lutte contre la drogue

to legalise	légaliser
legalisation	la légalisation
to confiscate	confisquer
confiscation	la confiscation
a drug bust	une opération anti-drogue
a bigwig, a kingpin	un gros bonnet

a kingfish	un gros poisson
small fry, minnows	le menu fretin
alternative crops	les cultures de substitution
a drugs clinic	un centre de soins aux toxicomanes
a drugs squad	une brigade des stupéfiants

Customes team seizes £50 m cocaine cargo

by Stewart Tendle

Customs and police investigators yesterday seized 250kg of cocaine worth £50 million which was hidden in a consignment of fresh flowers.

In a classic «sting»* operation, undercover officers posed as British buyers for the drug and travelled to Colombia. The Colombians also sent negotiators to meet them in Britain. According to one report, Greater Manchester police borrowed £2 million to show the Colombians that the undercover men were acting in good faith.

The cocaine arrived from Amsterdam last week and is the largest single importation of the drug by air. Its seizure at Manchester airport marked the end of a four-month customs operation codenamed Begonia.

The haul* was found in six boxes among a cargo of flowers. Neither the exporter nor the importer of the flowers knew what they concealed. Once the consignment landed, armed police and customs officers moved in to a warehouse* and arrested two Colombians.

A national intelligence drive* is currently monitoring possible Colombian drug infiltration. The national criminal intelligence service in London has established a database of suspicious sightings in Britain with the help of local police forces, immigration officials and customs officials.

Pat Cadogan, an assistant chief investigator, said yesterday: «We have broken an attempt by a major cocaine importer to set up a distribution network in the North West of England. We must have destroyed their credibility in the UK and a seizure of this kind must be a major setback for them.»

The Times, January 18, 1994

1. *Choose the right explanation for each of the following words (with asterisks in the passage).*

1. *sting*
A. very aggressive   B. meant to deceive   C. very costly

2. *the haul*
A. the amount paid   B.   the amount seen
C. the amount seized

3. *a warehouse*
A. a place for storing goods   B. a place for lodging people
C. a place for growing flowers

4. *a drive*
A. a journey by car   B. a united effort, a campaign
C. a private road

2. Say whether the following statements are true (T) or false (F).

1. The police and customs had simply waited for the drugs to arrive.
2. The traffickers were suspicious at first.
3. The drugs were sent straight from Colombia to Britain.
4. The codename for the operation was well chosen.
5. The exporter and the importer were in league with the traffickers.
6. The fight against drugs involves close cooperation between different organisations.
7. Only the representatives of the traffickers were arrested.
8. Mr Pat Cadogan was pleased with the result.

3. Read the article again and find the following.

1. Two synonyms for «shipment».
2. An adjective showing there was nothing unusual about the operation.
3. A word revealing that part of the investigations involved computers.
4. A synonym for «to establish».
5. A common way of expressing near certainty.

4. Fill in the blanks with the words corresponding to the explanation in brackets.

1. The drug had a .... value of 50 million. (value when sold)

2. The Greater Manchester police didn't have £2 million, so they had to get a .... (money lent against payment of interest)

3. With the help of the national criminal intelligence service, the police kept ...... on Colombians suspected of drug trafficking. (a close watch)

4. The exporter and the importer of the flowers had ...... been part of a scheme to smuggle drugs. (without their knowing about it)

Prescription for a fall in crime

In Merseyside, he is a folk hero, respected by police, revered by businessmen and worshipped by the men on the street. To the rest of the nation he is less admired: Dr John Marks is Britain's notorious «heroin doctor», who prescribes the drug to his patients on the NHS[1].

There is nothing illegal in what he does. But in providing addicts with heroin, rather than a Government-preferred substitute, he is seen as going against the ethos of the «war on drugs».

He argues that patients should be given more or less what they want, because otherwise they will get their fixes from the black market and enter the world of dirty needles, impure drugs and crime-funded deals. His policy claims to reduce crime, reduce the risk of Aids and other diseases to the user, and reduce the amount of money ending up in the hands of drug dealers.

Critics believed his clinic in Widnes, Cheshire, would effectively turn into a supermarket for junkies. But in the nine years he has been there this has not happened. His 400 patients attend regular counselling sessions, where they are encouraged to reduce their dosage, move to non-injected substitutes, and eventually come off the drugs. «We want to reduce the number of heroin addicts. But it is better to keep them on their dose rather than push them towards risky behaviour,» he says.

Dr Marks's success in reducing crime is indisputable. A survey showed that his patients were 15 times less likely to commit an offence in the year after they were registered with his clinic than in the year before.

[1] National Health Service

The Weekly Telegraph, October 13, 1993

1. Choose the appropriate endings for the following sentences.

1. Dr John Marks is looked upon favourably
A. by everybody.
B. by police, businessmen and the men on the street in Merseyside.
C. by the rest of the nation.

2. Through Dr Marks, addicts
A. get heroin very cheaply.
B. get a heroin substitute.
C. pay a high price for heroin.

3. Dr Marks thinks that his scheme brings about a reduction
A. in crime.
B. in crime and disease.
C. in crime, disease and the profits of dealers.

4. Critics thought his way of doing things would be
A. too harsh.   B. too expensive.   C. counterproductive

5. With Dr Marks's method, drug addicts come off drugs
A. immediately.
B. progressively.
C. entirely on their own.

6. Dr Marks
A. resorts to substitutes in the second stage.
B. is against substitutes.
C. uses substitutes right from the beginning.

2. The adjective «black» sometimes gives a pejorative meaning to the word it qualifies, as in «black market». Use the definitions below to find 6 more expressions with «black» (either two words or a compound word).

1. A place where car crashes often happen.
2. A ceremony in which the devil is worshipped.
3. A non-striker.
4. It contains the names of people that are to be avoided.
5. Forcing people to do something by using threats.
6. A person who is considered a disgrace to the group he belongs to.

3. Fill in the ten lines across the grid with translations of the corresponding French words. This will give you the answer to number 11 in column D.

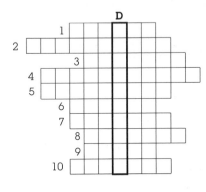

1. poudre
2. blanchiment
3. passeur
4. envoi
5. disponible
6. aiguille
7. revendeur
8. saisie
9. sensations
10. douane
11. toxicomane
(nom composé)

4. «Merseyside» refers to the area along the lower part of the River Mersey. What are the rivers that give their names to the following areas of Britain?

1. The area near Newcastle.   T☐☐☐SIDE
2. The area near Glasgow.   C☐☐☐☐SIDE
3. The area near London.   T☐☐☐☐SIDE
4. The area in Scotland with a famous   S☐☐☐SIDE
whisky trail.

Demonstrations and Riots

15 Les manifestations et les émeutes

(voir Introduction p. 139)

/// VOCABULAIRE À HAUTE FRÉQUENCE

Gatherings	Les rassemblements
to campaign for	faire campagne pour
a campaign	une campagne
a campaigner, an activist	un militant
to gather	(se) rassembler
a crowd	une foule
to organise	organiser
to stage, to hold	tenir, organiser
a meeting	une réunion
to demonstrate	manifester
a demonstration	une manifestation
to protest [prə'test]	protester
a protest ['prəutest]	une protestation, une manifestation
to march	défiler
to chant	scander
a march	une marche, un défilé
a slogan	un slogan
a placard ['plækɑːd]	une pancarte
a banner	une banderole
a mob	une foule agitée

Security	La sécurité
a precaution	une précaution
a measure	une mesure
security forces	les forces de sécurité
riot police	la police anti-émeutes
to call in	faire appel à
to contain	contenir
to maintain, to keep	maintenir

order	l'ordre
to restore	rétablir
calm	le calme
a helmet	un casque
a shield	un bouclier
a baton	une courte matraque
to wield	brandir, manier

Tension and Clashes

La tension et les affrontements

an incident	un incident
trouble	des ennuis, des incidents
unrest	l'agitation
to disturb	troubler
a disturbance	des troubles
to surge	déferler
a surge	un déferlement
to flare up, to erupt	se déclencher brusquement
a flare-up, an eruption	une flambée, un accès
to degenerate	dégénérer
to clash with	se heurter à, affronter
a clash	un affrontement
a scuffle	une échauffourée
fierce [fɪəs]	farouche
to drive back, to drive off	repousser
to break up, to disperse	(se) disperser

Riots

Les émeutes

to riot	manifester avec violence
to throw	jeter
to pelt	bombarder (projectiles)
to hurl	balancer
a missile	un projectile
a petrol bomb	un cocktail Molotov
to overturn	retourner
chaos ['keɪɒs], mayhem	la pagaille, la confusion
to use force	utiliser la force
tear gas	les gaz lacrymogènes
a water cannon	un canon à eau
to charge	charger
a charge	une charge
to ransack	saccager

/// EXPRESSIONS

a peaceful demonstration	une manifestation dans le calme
to pass off peacefully	se dérouler sans incident
to call a demonstration	appeler à manifester
to take to the street	descendre dans la rue
law and order	l'ordre public
to keep at bay	tenir en respect
to keep in hand	maîtriser, contrôler
to get out of hand	dégénérer
to be marred by	être gâché par
to force one's way	se frayer un passage
a breach of the peace	une atteinte à la
a public order offence	tranquillité publique
violence erupted again	la violence a de nouveau éclaté
an outbreak of violence	une explosion de violence
an outburst of violence	une éruption de violence
fighting broke out	des bagarres ont éclaté
to go on the rampage	se déchaîner
to bring to a standstill	paralyser
to bring chaos	semer la confusion
to open fire	ouvrir le feu
to condone violence	admettre la violence

/// VOCABULAIRE COMPLÉMENTAIRE

Gatherings	Les rassemblements
a sit-in	un sit-in
a demo	une manif
a counter demonstration	une contre-manifestation
to parade	défiler
a parade	un défilé, une parade
a route	un parcours, un itinéraire
a steward, a marshal	un membre du service d'ordre des manifestants
a loud hailer	un mégaphone
to muster	rassembler
to hand out	distribuer
a leaflet	un tract

Security

	La sécurité
a set-up	un dispositif
a police cordon	un cordon de police
to don	revêtir
gear	une tenue
clad in	revêtu de
a visor ['vaɪzə]	une visière
a truncheon ['trʌntʃən], a club	une longue matraque
to stem	endiguer
to hold off	tenir à distance
to restrain	maîtriser, contenir

Tension and Clashes

	La tension et les affrontements
a troublemaker	un perturbateur
an agitator	un agitateur
to provoke	provoquer
unprovoked	sans provocation
provocative	provocateur
provocation	la provocation
an agent provocateur	un agent provocateur
to daub	barbouiller
to dent	cabosser
to prohibit	interdire
an unlawful assembly, an illegal gathering	un rassemblement interdit
public disorder	trouble de l'ordre public
criminal damage	dégradations volontaires
assault	violences (délit)
to outnumber	déborder
to obstruct	entraver
an obstruction	une entrave
a smoke grenade	une grenade fumigène
a stun grenade	une grenade assourdissante
a tear gas canister	une grenade lacrymogène
a bystander, an onlooker	un badaud

Riots

	Les émeutes
to defy	braver
in defiance of	sans tenir compte de
a catapult	un lance-pierres

to stone	lapider
a hail	une grêle
a Balaclava helmet	un passe-montagne
a pitched battle	une bataille rangée
a running battle	des affrontements incessants
a warning shot	un coup de semonce
to block	bloquer
to tear up	arracher, desceller
to set up	dresser
to erect [ɪˈrekt]	ériger
a barricade [bærɪˈkeɪd]	une barricade

Battle rages as nuclear cargo arrives

A 40-tonne shipment of French-processed atomic waste reached a German storage depot yesterday after pitched battles between an army of riot-clad police and about 3,000 anti-nuclear protesters.

The normally peaceful farmland around Gorleben in north Germany looked like it was hit by a civil war as the controversial shipment arrived. Several thousand helmeted police lined country lanes near the medium-term storage depot, 75 miles east of Hanover, and used water cannon, tear gas and clubs to clear away waves of anti-nuclear protesters.

Eighteen policemen and two demonstrators were injured and several protesters detained when the crowds tried to block the radioactive cargo from moving some 12 miles on a giant flatbed truck from the Dannenberg railway station to Gorleben. (...)

Barricades and bonfires blocked roads and, in some villages, farmers dumped piles of manure* in the streets in a last-ditch* effort to stop the truck.

A thick wedge* of riot police, backed up by water-cannon trucks trying to hose away sit-down demonstrators, headed up a long procession of police vehicles protecting the waste shipment.

The radioactive waste which had crossed into Germany from a French reprocessing plant by rail at midday on Tuesday, had made its way through most of the country practically unhindered. It was the first of around 110 shipments set to carry nuclear waste and fuel back to German reactors over the next eight years.

Reuter, May 9, 1996

1. Choose the right explanation for each of the following words (with asterisks in the passage).

1. *manure*
A. firewood   B. fruit and vegetables   C. animal excretions

2. *last-ditch*
A. ultimate   B. early   C. fresh

3. *a wedge*
A. forming a circle
B. forming a square
C. forming a triangle

2. Say whether the following statements are true (T) or false (F).

1. It appears from the beginning that it was a victory for protesters.
2. The police expected trouble.
3. The shipment had a long journey by road.
4. The police reacted in the usual way.
5. Farmers didn't side with the demonstrators.
6. The convoy had already met with a lot of trouble.
7. Such a situation is not likely to be seen in the future.
8. The storage of nuclear waste is still a major issue.

3. The suffixes «-er» (e.g. «protester»)or «-or» (e.g. «demonstrator») indicate a person who carries out an action. Use the definitions to find 8 words ending in «-or».

1. An orchestra leader.	C □□□□□OR
2. A person who gives an organ for a transplant operation.	D□OR
3. The person in a plane or a ship who plots the course.	N□□□□□OR
4. A financial backer.	S□□□OR
5. A person who imitates another, usually to entertain others.	I□□□□□□□OR
6. A sort of gambler whose aim is to make a profit, usually on the stock exchange.	S□□□□□□OR
7. A person who holds a university chair.	P□□□□□OR
8. A person who tells a story.	N□□□□OR

4. The first word in each list is taken from the article. Which of the other three should not be associated with it?

1. waste, rubbish, paste, refuse.
2. protesters, demonstrators, activists, on-lookers.
3. to detain, to arrest, to hold, to suspect.
4. controversial, beneficial, questionable, divisive.
5. manure, muck, slurry, dust.

White marchers force Dehaene to reform law

by Toby Helm in Brussels

The Belgian Prime Minister, Jean-Luc Dehaene, bowed* last night to public pressure to reform the judicial system after more than 325,000 people marched through Brussels to protest against corruption in public life.

Mr Dehaene announced that the 166-year-old constitution would be reformed as soon as possible to end political promotions in the judicial system.

His announcement followed a massive demonstration held because of the murder of four young girls by a paedophile ring.

The protesters blamed incompetence and corruption for the failure of police to track down* sooner the alleged leader of the paedophile ring, Marc Dutroux.

They converged on the capital from all over the country. Many were dressed entirely in white or carried white lilies, white roses and white balloons to symbolise the purity of children (...)

Mr Dehaene's announcement followed meetings with the parents of victims of the paedophile network before the march started.

It will do much to reassure Belgians who believe the appointment of judges and magistrates by political parties is a root cause of corruption and the failure to solve many crimes.

A sense of outrage has spread through Belgium since Dutroux's arrest in August. The bodies of four girls aged between 8 and 19 have been found buried at houses owned by him.

Fears grew that yesterday's demonstration could become violent amid mounting public disquiet at revelations of bungling* by police and magistrates and rumours of a cover-up to protect rich paedophiles. But the march was solemn and peaceful.

The Daily Telegraph,
October 21, 1996

1. **Choose the right explanation for each of the following words (with asterisks in the passage).**

1. *to bow* (to pressure)
A. to accept immediately
B. to accept after resisting
C. to accept with pleasure

2. *to track down*
A. to abandon   B. to listen to   C. to find

3. *to bungle*
A. to do something badly
B. to do something carefully
C. to usually do something

2. Say whether the following statements are true (T) or false (F).

1. The demonstration did not lead to any results.
2. The Belgian judiciary is totally independent from political parties.
3. The protesters thought the police had taken too long to arrest Dutroux.
4. The Prime Minister's announcement was not likely to defuse the situation.
5. The demonstration did not go off as well as expected.
6. Information about each aspect of the subject is given progressively.

3. Read the article again and find the following.

1. Two verbs which are synonyms for «to demonstrate».
2. A noun used twice to underline the inefficiency of the police.
3. An adjective (a past participle), showing that the journalist took some precautions when accusing Dutroux.
4. A noun used to express something fundamental.
5. A verb explaining the fact that outrage was felt all over the country.

4. Fill in the ten lines across the grid with translations of the corresponding French words. This will give you the answer to number 11 in column D.

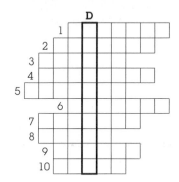

1. échauffourée
2. gaz lacrymogène (*deux mots*)
3. casque
4. flambée
5. pancarte
6. projectile
7. déclencher
8. scander
9. acharné
10. déferlement
11. militant

Terrorism and Revolutions

(voir Introduction p. 139)

16 Le terrorisme et les révolutions

/// VOCABULAIRE À HAUTE FRÉQUENCE

Terrorism / Le terrorisme

Terrorism	Le terrorisme
a terrorist	un terroriste
a target	une cible
to plant	poser, déposer
a car bomb	une voiture piégée
a letter bomb	une lettre piégée
an explosive device	un engin explosif
a bombing	un attentat à la bombe
a bomber	un poseur de bombe

Hijackings / Les détournements

Hijackings	Les détournements
to hijack	détourner un véhicule
to skyjack, to hijack	détourner un avion
a hijacker	un pirate
a skyjacker, a hijacker	un pirate de l'air
to divert	dérouter
to refuel	refaire le plein

Revolutionary Movements / Les mouvements révolutionnaires

Revolutionary Movements	Les mouvements révolutionnaires
a faction	une faction, une fraction
to rise	se soulever
an uprising	un soulèvement
to rebel [rɪˈbel]	se rebeller
a rebellion	une rébellion
a rebel [ˈrebəl]	un rebelle
the armed wing	le bras armé
the political wing	la branche politique
underground	clandestin

an insurrection	une insurrection
a guerrilla	un guérillero
to revolt	se révolter
a revolt	une révolte
to struggle	lutter
an armed struggle	une lutte armée
a civil war	une guerre civile
a homeland	une patrie

Seizing Power — La prise du pouvoir

to plot	comploter
a plot	un complot
to foment	fomenter
a conspiracy	une conspiration
a separatist	un séparatiste
a coup, a putsch	un coup d'État, un putsch
to topple	faire tomber
to overthrow	renverser
to set up, to establish	établir

EXPRESSIONS

to resort to violence	avoir recours à la violence
to prime a bomb	amorcer une bombe
to carry out a bombing	perpétrer un attentat
to admit responsibility	reconnaître, revendiquer
to claim responsibility	la responsabilité
it was the work of …	c'était l'œuvre de …
to be behind sth.	être l'auteur de qch.
to bear the hallmark of	porter le sceau de
to make safe	rendre inoffensif
to meet a demand	satisfaire une exigence
to deal with terrorists	négocier avec les terroristes
to do a deal	passer un marché
to have dealings with	avoir des tractations avec
to condone terrorism	admettre le terrorisme
to sponsor terrorism	cautionner le terrorisme
to keep tabs on sb.	surveiller étroitement qn.
to nip in the bud	étouffer dans l'œuf
to be in league with	être de mèche avec
a show of strength	une démonstration de force
a test of strength	une épreuve de force
to mount an operation	monter une opération

/// VOCABULAIRE COMPLÉMENTAIRE

Terrorism — Le terrorisme

Terrorism	Le terrorisme
a commando	un commando
a prime target	une cible de choix
a hit man	un homme de main
a hostage taker	un preneur d'otages
a captor	un ravisseur
a warlord	un chef de guerre
a reunion	des retrouvailles
debriefing	le déconditionnement psychologique
to harbour	abriter
a sanctuary	un sanctuaire
a haven	un havre, un refuge
to sabotage	saboter
a saboteur	un saboteur
a sabotage	un sabotage
an atrocity	une atrocité, une horreur
a death squad	un escadron de la mort
an anti-terrorist squad	une brigade anti-terroriste
to break away from	se séparer de
a breakaway group, a splinter group	un groupe dissident
a fringe movement	un groupuscule
an offshoot	une ramification

Bombings — Les attentats à la bombe

Bombings	Les attentats à la bombe
to perpetrate	perpétrer
an outrage	un attentat
to booby trap	piéger à l'explosif
a booby trap	un dispositif piégé
a home-made bomb	une bombe artisanale
a detonator	un détonateur
a primer, a priming device	un dispositif de mise à feu
a timer	une minuterie
a hoax	un canular
remote control	le contrôle à distance
indiscriminate	aveugle
at random	au hasard
to defuse	désamorcer

to detonate	faire exploser
a bomb disposal expert	un artificier

Revolutionary Movements — Les mouvements révolutionnaires

to stand up	se dresser
an upheaval [ʌp'hiːvəl]	un bouleversement
an insurgent	un insurgé
insurgent	insurrectionnel
turmoil	les turbulences
a feud	une lutte interne
the hard core	les irréductibles
intercommunal clashes	les affrontements entre communautés
a mutiny	une mutinerie
a mutineer [mjuːtɪ'nɪə]	un mutin
guerrilla warfare	la lutte de guérilla
a militia [mə'lɪʃə]	une milice
a militiaman	un milicien
a vigilante	une barbouze, un membre d'une milice privée
to secede, to break away	se séparer, faire sécession
to break up	éclater, se désintégrer
a break-up	un éclatement, une désintégration
secession	la sécession
partition	la partition
motherland	la mère-patrie
self-determination	l'auto-détermination
self-rule, autonomy	l'autonomie
to disband	renvoyer dans les foyers
to grant	accorder
a status	un statut
independent	indépendant
independence	l'indépendance
sovereignty ['sɒvrɪntɪ]	la souveraineté

Combating Rebellion and Terrorism — La lutte contre la rébellion et le terrorisme

to frisk	fouiller corporellement
repression	la répression
a supergrass (Ulster)	un inculpé indicateur

covert	en sous-main, clandestin
undercover	clandestin, occulte
a no-go area	une zone de non-droit
to quash, to put down	réprimer, étouffer
to foil	déjouer
to crush	écraser
to mop up	nettoyer, ratisser
a mop-up operation	une opération de nettoyage/ratissage
a firing squad	un peloton d'exécution
bloodless	sans effusion de sang
bloody	sanglant

Seizing Power — La prise du pouvoir

to depose	déposer
to oust	évincer
an attempted coup	une tentative de
a coup attempt	coup d'État
to destabilise	déstabiliser
destabilisation	la déstabilisation
to undermine	saper, amoindrir

Suicide bomb attacks kill 24 Israelis

by Anton La Guardia in Jerusalem

Islamic suicide bombers killed at least 24 Israelis and wounded about 80 others yesterday in separate attacks in Jerusalem and the port city of Ashkelon, ending a six-month lull* in attacks within Israel.

It was the bloodiest day for the country since it signed the 1993 autonomy accords with the Palestine Liberation Organisation. The attacks will undermine support for Shimon Peres, the prime minister, in May's general elections.

Police said that 22 passengers were killed and about 50 hurt when a Palestinian, thought to be from Hebron, blew himself up on a bus in the centre of Jerusalem just before 7am.

Less than an hour later a Palestinian, probably from Gaza, blew himself up at a bus stop on the outskirts* of Ashkelon, killing two others and injuring about 30.

The Islamic fundamentalist Hamas movement admitted responsibility, saying that it aimed to avenge the killing last month of the movement's chief bomb-maker, Yihya Ayyash, widely assumed to have been assassinated by Israel.

The attacks coincided with the second anniversary of the massacre of 29 Palestinian worshippers* in Hebron by a Jewish settler*.

A leaflet attributed to Hamas proclaimed: «This is holy war. Victory or martyrdom.» It also seemed to contain an offer of a ceasefire.

It said that if Israeli leaders released prisoners and halted «terrorism» against Hamas, the group would adopt a «historic position where we will be the party most keen on not having one drop of blood shed in the land of Palestine».

The Daily Telegraph, February 26, 1996

1. **Choose the right explanation for each of the following words (with asterisks in the passage).**

1. *a lull*
A. a quiet period   B. an increase
C. greater violence

2. *the outskirts*
A. the centre   B. the main streets
C. the area at the edge

3. *worshippers*
A. passers-by   B. demonstrators
C. people in a religious building

4. *settlers*
A. people who live where they were born
B. people who come to live in a new country
C. eople who live on camping sites

2. Choose the appropriate endings for the following sentences.

1. Apart from killing the suicide bombers, the bomb attacks killed
A. 24 people.   B. 26 people.   C. 24 Palestinians.

2. As a result, Shimon Peres's chances of electoral success were likely to be
A. more difficult.   B. a lot easier.   C. unaffected.

3. Suicide bombers usually
A pay no attention to the place where they carry out the attack.
B. choose deserted places.
C. select crowded places.

4. In this part of the world, violence seems to
A. intimidate people.
B. leave people indifferent.
C. lead to more violence.

5. It may be concluded that Hamas
A. would never accept to have talks with Israel.
B. might accept to have talks with Israel.
C. never mentioned talks with Israel.

3. Read the article again and find the following.

1. A compound noun referring to agreements giving a certain degree of independence.
2. A verb showing that the attacks were retaliatory.
3. A noun showing a symbolic coincidence.
4. An adjective showing a religious motivation.

4. Find words in the article which are similar in meaning to these.

1. a let-up   2. inside
3. self-rule   4. claimed
5. intended   6. slaughter

5. «Martyrdom» is made up of the noun «martyr» and the suffix «-dom». Use the explanations to find five nouns ending in the same way.

1. A country ruled by a monarch.   K◻◻DOM
2. The state of being extremely famous.   S◻◻DOM
3. A synonym for liberty.   F◻◻DOM
4. Having a lot of common sense.   W◻DOM
5. A state of mind in which you certainly
do not enjoy yourself.   B◻◻DOM

IRA blitz on gas and water plants foiled

by Stewart Tendler and Bill Frost

An IRA plot to blast gas, water and power installations and cause massive disruption to London and the south east was foiled* by Scotland Yard detectives yesterday.

Hours before the first bomb was due to be primed*, armed police raided houses in south London and discovered 36 devices under construction. Seven men were arrested and last night police were hunting for a cache of up to 180lbs of Semtex. The head of the Anti-Terrorist branch said that the bombers had been stopped «in the nick of time»*.

The targets would have included electricity switching centres, pumping stations and gas plants. Bombs may also have been destined for the rail network and police are studying several lists of other potential targets.

Police believe small but powerful bombs would have been used and the devices were similar to a new design first seen in a huge explosives find at Clonaslee, Co Laois[1], two weeks ago.

The bombings would have been the most ambitious campaign mounted by the IRA in mainland Britain. The terrorist high command abandoned the use of young, unknown recruits and is believed to have gathered some of its most experienced hands. At least one of the men held is suspected of operating on the mainland before.

[1] County Laois in the Irish Republic

The Times, July 7, 1996

1. Choose the right explanation for each of the following words (with asterisks in the passage).

1. *to foil*
A. to make something known
B. to make something impossible
C. to make something possible

2. *to prime*
A. to make ready to explode
B. to render useless
C. to make safe

3. *in the nick of time*
A. very early
B. too late
C. at the last possible moment

2. Say whether the following statements are true (T) or false (F).

1. The bombers' aim was only to cause structural damage to buildings.
2. The police had either kept a close watch or been tipped off about the bombers.

3. The police found everything they were looking for.
4. The police thought they had been unlucky.
5. New devices make the bombers' job easier.
6. The IRA's change of tactics also presented problems.

3. Fill in each blank with a word from the following list. Use each word only once. Verbs are given in the infinitive.

underground	citizen	forms	bombing	to arrest
to name	to kill	to hire	fundamentalist	

A man said to be a ...(1)... Muslim from New Jersey was ...(2)... by the FBI yesterday and charged with last Friday's ...(3)... of the World Trade Centre. Five people were ...(4)... and more than 1,000 injured in the blast.

Unofficial FBI reports ...(5)... the suspect as Salama Mohammed, a 26-year-old United States ...(6)... . He was apparently traced through the ...(7)... used to ...(8)... the van that was packed with explosive and driven into the ...(9)... car park.

The Independent, March 5, 1993

4. The name of a place can actually mean the people living or working there. For example, «Scotland Yard» is synonymous with the London police force. Match the place names (1-5 and 6-12) with their synonyms (A-E and F-J).

1. The City
2. Westminster
3. N° 10 Downing Street
4. Whitehall
5. Fleet Street

A. British journalists or national newspapers[1]
B. the Prime Minister and the Cabinet
C. British members of Parliament
D. the financial world in central London
E. the central administration of the British Government

6. The White House
7. Capitol Hill
8. Madison Avenue
9. The Pentagon
10. The Oval Office

F. the US Congress in Washington
G. the US Defense Department
H. the US President and Administration
I. the US President and his closest aides
J. advertising and public relations firms in New York

[1] although most newspaper offices have moved elsewhere

War and Espionage 17 La guerre et l'espionnage

(voir Introduction p. 139)

(voir Introduction p. 139)

/// VOCABULAIRE À HAUTE FRÉQUENCE

General background

Contexte général

military	militaire
a serviceman	un militaire
a civilian	un civil
a soldier ['səuldʒə]	un soldat
a sailor	un marin
an airman	un aviateur
the army	l'armée
the navy	la Marine nationale
the air force	l'armée de l'air
the armed forces	les forces armées
a rapid reaction force	une force de réaction rapide
an officer	un officier
a captain	un capitaine
a veteran	un ancien combattant
a base	une base

Weapons

Les armes

conventional	conventionnel, classique
nuclear	nucléaire
the atom bomb	la bombe atomique
the H-bomb	la bombe H
deadly	mortel, meurtrier
to test	essayer
a test	un essai
proliferation	la prolifération
to deter	dissuader
a deterrent	une force de dissuasion
deterrence	la dissuasion
a ballistic missile	un missile balistique
intercontinental	intercontinental

strategic	stratégique
range	la portée
medium-range	de moyenne portée
intermediate-range	de portée intermédiaire
a warhead	une ogive, une tête
to site, to install	installer
a site, an installation	un site, une installation
to deploy	déployer
deployment	le déploiement
to launch	lancer
Star Wars	la guerre des étoiles
offensive	offensif
defensive	défensif
an arsenal	un arsenal
an arms race	une course aux armements
to build up	renforcer, accumuler
arms build-up	accumulation des armements, le surarmement
to stockpile	constituer des stocks
a stockpile	un stock
a vessel	un vaisseau
a submarine	un sous-marin
a torpedo [tɔ:'pi:dəu]	une torpille
chemical ['kemɪkl]	chimique
a nerve gas	un gaz neuro-toxique
germ warfare	la guerre bactériologique

Espionage — L'espionnage

to spy	espionner
a spy	un espion
intelligence	les renseignements
secret	secret
covert	en sous-main, clandestin
undercover	clandestin, occulte
an agent	un agent
to infiltrate	infiltrer
an infiltration	une infiltration
to defect	passer dans l'autre camp
a defector	un transfuge
to pass	transmettre, divulguer
classified	classé secret
a file	un dossier
to uncover	mettre à jour, révéler

to expose	démasquer
to betray	trahir
a betrayal	une trahison
a traitor	un traître
treason	la trahison

Starting a War — L'entrée en guerre

an ally	un allié
to ally with	allier à
a coalition	une coalition
an enemy	un ennemi
a conflict	un conflit
to break out	éclater
to invade	envahir
an invasion	une invasion
a border, a frontier	une frontière
to land	débarquer
a landing	un débarquement
an offensive	une offensive

Combat — Les combats

to drop a bomb	jeter une bombe
to shoot down, to down	abattre (un avion)
to sink	couler
to torpedo	torpiller
to intercept	intercepter
a battle	une bataille
a battlefield	un champ de bataille
a front	un front
to repel	repousser
to overwhelm	submerger
to inflict	infliger
a loss	une perte
a prisoner	un prisonnier
to defeat	vaincre
a defeat	une défaite
a victory	une victoire
to liberate	libérer (un territoire)
liberation	la libération
to pull out, to withdraw	se retirer
a withdrawal, a pull-out	un retrait
to sign	signer
an armistice	un armistice

a treaty	un traité
peace	la paix

/// EXPRESSIONS

to join the army	s'engager dans l'armée
a chief of staff	un chef d'état-major
to be in command of	avoir le commandement de
the Star Spangled Banner	la Bannière étoilée
the Union Flag/Jack	le drapeau britannique
a shot across the bows	un coup de semonce
to declare war on	déclarer la guerre à
to be at war with	être en guerre avec
a weapon of last resort	une arme de dernier recours
weapons of mass destruction	les armes de destruction massive
Strategic Defense Initiative (SDI)	l'Initiative de défense stratégique
to inflict heavy losses	infliger de lourdes pertes
to sustain heavy losses	subir de lourdes pertes
to strike a mine	heurter une mine
to die in action	mourir au combat
to put out of action	mettre hors de combat
a war of attrition	une guerre d'usure
a scorched earth policy	une politique de la terre brûlée
to decommission weapons	mettre des armes hors service, désarmer
to have access to	avoir accès à
to crack, to break a code	trouver la clé d'un code

/// VOCABULAIRE COMPLÉMENTAIRE

General background	Contexte général
the Admiralty	le ministère de la Marine
a battalion	un bataillon
a platoon	une section
a squadron	un escadron, une escadrille
a seaman	un marin
a convoy	un convoi

a paratrooper	un parachutiste
airborne	aéroporté
marines	l'infanterie de marine
a sentry	une sentinelle
conscription	la conscription
a conscript	un conscrit
to draft (US)	appeler
draft (US)	la conscription
a draftee (US)	un appelé
a draft dodger (US)	un insoumis
a pacifist	un pacifiste
a peace movement	un mouvement pacifiste
cannon fodder	la chair à canon
a conscientious objector	un objecteur de conscience
a reservist	un réserviste
to enlist	s'engager
the barracks	la caserne
a garrison	une garnison
a war memorial	un monument aux morts
the national anthem	l'hymne national
a patriot ['peɪtrɪət, 'pætrɪət]	un patriote
patriotic [peɪtrɪ'ɒtɪk, pætrɪ'ɒtɪk]	patriotique
patriotism	le patriotisme
jingoism	le chauvinisme national
jingoistic	chauvin
a graduated/ flexible response	une riposte graduée
a task force	une force d'intervention
a no-fly zone	une zone interdite de survol
a buffer zone	une zone tampon
a peacekeeping force	une force d'interposition
combat troops	les troupes de combat
crack troops, elite troops	les troupes d'élite
battle dress	tenue de combat
fatigues	un treillis
logistics	la logistique
a prisoner of war	un prisonnier de guerre

Military Personel   Le personnel militaire

an admiral	un amiral
a commander	un chef militaire
a commander-in-chief	un commandant en chef
a general	un général
a brigadier-general	un général de brigade

a major-general	un général de division
a lieutenant-general	un général de corps d'armée
a colonel ['kɜːnl]	un colonel
a major	un commandant
a lieutenant [lef'tenənt, luː'tenənt]	un lieutenant
a non-commissioned officer	un sous-officier
a sergeant ['sɑːdʒənt]	un sergent
a private	un simple soldat
a chaplain	un aumônier
a standard bearer	un porte-drapeau

Weapons | Les armes

a fleet	une flotte
a destroyer	un contre-torpilleur
a frigate	une frégate
an aircraft carrier	un porte-avions
a minesweeper	un dragueur de mines
a flagship	un navire amiral
amphibious	amphibie
anti-aircraft	anti-aérien
a chopper	un hélico
a fighter	un chasseur
a bomber	un bombardier
a stealth bomber	un bombardier furtif
a strike helicopter, a helicopter gunship	un hélicoptère d'attaque
a personnel carrier	un transport de troupes
a first-strike weapon	arme de première frappe
a laser-guided bomb	une bombe guidée au laser
to step up	intensifier
to escalate	(s') intensifier
escalation	l'escalade
to wipe out	anéantir
a neutron bomb	une bombe à neutrons
a fuel air bomb	bombe à effet de souffle
to train on	orienter sur
anti-ballistic, anti-missile	anti-missile
a shield	un bouclier
a laser	un laser
a beam	un rayon
a sensor	un capteur
smart weapons	les armes intelligentes
bacteriological	bactériologique

mustard	la moutarde
to scrap	mettre au rebut
armament, weaponry	l'armement
overkill	la surcapacité de destruction
a balance	un équilibre
to disarm	désarmer
disarmament	le désarmement
unilateral	unilatéral
multilateral	multilatéral
a moratorium	un moratoire

Espionage — L'espionnage

counter espionage, counter intelligence	le contre-espionnage
hush-hush	archi-secret
a mole	une taupe
a cipher	un chiffre, un code
to decipher	déchiffrer
to tap	mettre sur écoute
to bug	installer un micro
to lure	persuader par la ruse
a bait	un appât
to expel	expulser
an expulsion	une expulsion

Starting a War — L'entrée en guerre

to manœuvre [məˈnuːvə]	manœuvrer
a manœuvre	une manœuvre
to concentrate	concentrer
a concentration	une concentration
to reinforce, to beef up	renforcer
a reinforcement	un renforcement
to call up	appeler, rappeler
a call-up	un appel, un rappel
an alliance	une alliance
neutral	neutre
neutrality	la neutralité
a warrior	un guerrier
a warmonger	un va-t-en guerre
a hawk	un faucon
a dove	une colombe
to blockade	faire le blocus de
a blockade	un blocus

to intervene [ɪntəˈviːn]	intervenir
an intervention	une intervention
an aggression	une agression
an aggressor	un agresseur
a pre-emptive strike	une attaque préventive

Combat — Les combats

a ground/land offensive	une offensive terrestre
a beachhead, a bridgehead	une tête de pont
to overrun	envahir
a counterattack	une contre-attaque
to strike back	répliquer
an onslaught, an assault	un assaut
a stronghold	un bastion
a bulwark	un rempart, une fortification
to pound	pilonner
to airdrop	parachuter
an airdrop	un parachutage
a dogfight	un combat aérien
to bail/bale out, to eject	s'éjecter
to withstand sth.	résister à qch.
to hold out	tenir bon
to fight off, to repulse	repousser
a trench	une tranchée
to entrench	retrancher
to dig in	se retrancher
a foxhole	un abri individuel
to close in	cerner
to encircle	encercler
to advance	avancer
an advance	une avancée
to scuttle	saborder
to retreat	battre en retraite
a retreat	une retraite
to fall back	se replier
a setback	un revers
to rout [raut]	mettre en déroute
a rout	une déroute
to desert	déserter
to capture	capturer
a capture	une capture
unconditional	sans condition
to capitulate	capituler
a capitulation	une capitulation

an armistice	un armistice
peace talks	des pourparlers de paix
an olive branch	un rameau d'olivier
a safe haven,	une enclave de sécurité,
a security zone	une zone de protection

Nato threatens air strikes and demands Sarajevo siege guns be put under UN control

by Andrew Marshall in Brussels, Robert Block in Belgrade and Tony Barber in London

NATO last night drafted* a plan to break the siege of Sarajevo, which included the threat of air strikes to persuade the Bosnian Serbs besieging the city to pull back their guns, and the demilitarisation of the Bosnian capital.

The draft agreement threatened immediate retaliation for any further Serbian artillery attacks on the city. It also laid down a 10-day deadline for placing artillery under UN control within a 20-kilometre radius. Any artillery in this area not placed under UN control would be subject to attack.

Differences over the timing and distances kept NATO ambassadors arguing late into the night. But the basic thrust* of the plan, a Franco-American initiative, seemed to have overcome long-entrenched British objections.

NATO's decision followed the mortar attack which killed 68 in the Bosnian capital on Saturday, and finally galvanised the West to turn its rhetoric on intervention into action. In Sarajevo, the United Nations Force commander in Bosnia-Herzegovina, Lieutenant-General Sir Michael Rose, brokered* an agreement with Bosnian Serbs and Muslim army commanders to begin withdrawing Serbian guns from the hills around Sarajevo at about noon today. But within minutes of General Rose's dramatic announcement of the deal, Bosnian Serb leaders threw the whole undertaking* into disarray. «We agreed to an immediate ceasefire. But there is no precise agreement on demilitarisation,» said a senior Bosnian Serb official.

The Independent,
February 10, 1994

1. *Choose the right explanation for each of the following words (with asterisks in the passage).*

1. *to draft*
A. to finance   B. to accept   C. to prepare

2. *the thrust*
A. the aim, the direction   B. the length of time
C. the total cost

197

3. *to broker*
A. to refuse to take part
B. to bring to an end
C. to act as an intermediary

4. *an undertaking*
A. an assembly   B. a project   C. a population

2. Say whether the following statements are true (T) or false (F).

1. The Bosnian Muslims were inside Sarajevo.

2. NATO was ready to use ground troops against the Serbs.

3. The whole Serbian artillery would be under UN control.

4. The European countries involved had the same viewpoint.

5. The Bosnian Serbs occupied strategic positions around Sarajevo.

6. According to the Bosnian Serb official, his side was ready to surrender its guns.

3. The first word in each list is taken from the article. Find which of the other three is not synonymous with it.

1. to include, to contain, to involve, to accept.

2. a strike, an attack, a stoppage, a raid.

3. to pull back, to abstain, to withdraw, to disengage.

4. retaliation, reprisal, resumption, retribution.

5. an area, a closure, a district, a sector.

4. Two sentences have been cut into parts and the parts scrambled. Put them back into the right order. (Punctuation and the capital letters at the beginning of the sentences have been removed whenever possible.)

1. a turning-point in the civil war / have reached a wide-ranging / which could prove to be / Bosnia's Muslims and Croats / peace agreement in Washington

2. which closely links / after almost a year / they have reached an accord / in Central Bosnia and in the city of Mostar / of bloody fighting / the political future of their communities / between the two sides

198

400,000 flee as Israel steps up raids

by Ohad Gozani in Tel Aviv

Israel is to step up* its air and artillery attacks in Lebanon against Hizbollah guerrillas, it said yesterday. As 400,000 Lebanese fled north to avoid the bombardment, Israel called for a further six miles of southern Lebanon to be evacuated.

But it also offered to halt the campaign if the Iranian-backed Islamic militants stopped rocketing towns and villages in northern Israel (...)

There was panic in the port city of Tyre yesterday after Israel ordered thousands of people out of their homes in southern Lebanon. Lebanese civilians in an area up to 20 miles north of the Israeli border were ordered to leave by 3pm GMT[1]. The ultimatum was calculated to raise the pressure on the Beirut government to turn against Hizbollah.

An Israeli helicopter gunship also knocked out the electricity supply to sections of Beirut, in the fourth attack on the capital.

The White House last night pinned the blame* for the escalation of the conflict on «provocative acts» by Hizbollah. A statement said: «We call upon Hizbollah to cease their acts which have provoked these actions by Israel.» An official said the State Department was in contact with «those parties that might have influence over Hizbollah». This was taken to mean Syria.

Thousands of Israelis, mostly children and elderly people, have been evacuated from areas within guerrilla rocket range*.

[1] Greenwich Mean Time

The Daily Telegraph, April 15, 1996

1. Choose the right explanation for each of the following words (with asterisks in the passage).

1. *to step up*
A. to cease   B. to reduce   C. to intensify

2. *to pin the blame on*
A. to say it is the fault of
B. to show sympathy for
C. to regret the absence of

3. *within range*
A. that can be seen
B. that cannot resist
C. that can be hit

2. Choose the appropriate endings for the following sentences.

1. Hizbollah guerrillas had their bases in
A. northern Lebanon.
B. northern Israel.
C. southern Lebanon.

2. Bringing Israeli attacks to an end depended on
A. Israel and Hizbollah.
B. Israel, Hizbollah and Beirut.
C. Israel only.

3. Israeli attacks affected
A. people in southern Lebanon only.
B. people inside and outside southern Lebanon.
C. Hizbollah members only.

4. The American President sided with
A. Lebanon.
B. Hizbollah.
C. Israel.

5. Because of Israeli actions, the security zone was
A. reduced.
B. maintained.
C. enlarged.

6. As future events were to show for Israel, hitting civilian targets can lead to
A. more support.
B. general indifference.
C. deep outrage.

3. Fill in each blank with a word from the following list. Use each word once only. Verbs are given in the infinitive.

shots	fire	to wound
to search	to attack	machine-guns

US marines and Nigerian soldiers ...(1)... snipers in central Mogadishu with grenades, ...(2)... and rifles in a five-hour battle yesterday. At least one Somali was killed and three marines and two Nigerians were ...(3)... .
Several hundred marines ...(4)... house-to-house for weapons after the battle. ...(5)... were also fired at the UN offices in the capital, and a relief agency, International medical Corps, about half a mile from the fighting reported that it came under ...(6)... .

Associated Press, February 26, 1993

Miscellaneous topics **18** Sujets divers

VOCABULAIRE À HAUTE FRÉQUENCE

Sexuality	La sexualité
morals	la moralité
sex	le sexe
sexual intercourse	rapport sexuel
a partner	un partenaire
an affair	une liaison
permissive	permissif
permissiveness	la permissivité
contraception	la contraception
contraceptive	contraceptif
a pill	une pilule
a condom	un préservatif
family planning	le planning familial
birth control	la régulation des naissances
a homosexual, a gay	un homosexuel
a lesbian	une lesbienne
heterosexual, straight	hétérosexuel

Abortion and Euthanasia	L'avortement et l'euthanasie
pregnant	enceinte
a pregnancy	une grossesse
a single mother	une mère célibataire
unborn	pas encore né
to terminate	interrompre
a termination	une interruption
to abort	avorter
an abortion	un avortement
an embryo ['embrɪəu]	un embryon
a foetus ['fi:təs]	un foetus
a human being	un être humain

euthanasia [juːθəˈneɪzjə]	l'euthanasie
to legalise	légaliser
legalisation	la légalisation

Women's Liberation — La libération de la femme

male	masculin
female	féminin
to dominate	dominer
dominance	la dominance
an object	un objet
sexism	le sexisme
a sexist	un sexiste
a male chauvinist	un phallocrate
male chauvinism	la phallocratie
equality	l'égalité
an opportunity	une chance
to liberate	libérer
to emancipate	émanciper
emancipation	l'émancipation
to stereotype ['steriətaɪp]	stéréotyper
a stereotype	un stéréotype
housekeeping	les travaux du ménage

Immigration — L'immigration

a foreigner, an alien ['eiliən]	un étranger
foreign, alien	étranger
to emigrate	émigrer
emigration	l'émigration
an emigrant	un émigrant
immigration	l'immigration
an immigrant	un immigrant
to migrate [maɪˈgreɪt]	migrer
a migration	une migration
a migrant	un migrant
to settle	s'installer
a settlement	une installation, une colonie de peuplement
a permit	un permis
legal	en situation régulière
illegal	clandestin
a citizen	un citoyen
citizenship	la citoyenneté
to naturalise	naturaliser

naturalisation	la naturalisation
to melt	fondre
a melting-pot	un creuset
to adapt	s'adapter
adaptation	l'adaptation
to integrate	(s')intégrer
integration	l'intégration
a quota ['kwəutə]	un contingent
ethnic	ethnique
a minority	un minorité
a prejudice	un préjugé
racial	racial
tension	la tension
a racist	un raciste
racism	le racisme
to discriminate	faire de la discrimination
discrimination	la discrimination
to segregate	faire de la ségrégation
segregation	la ségrégation
a ghetto	un ghetto

Human Rights — Les droits de l'homme

to oppress	opprimer
oppression	l'oppression
free	libre
freedom	la liberté
to move	se déplacer
movement	le déplacement
to banish	exiler, bannir
to deport	déporter
deportation	la déportation
ethnic cleansing ['klenzɪŋ]	la purification ethnique
a right	un droit
a charter	une charte
a convention	une convention
to abuse sth. [ə'bjuːz]	attenter à qch.
an abuse [ə'bjuːs]	une atteinte, un non-respect
to violate	violer
a violation	une violation
a case	un cas
to persecute	persécuter
persecution	la persécution
to harass	harceler
harassment	le harcèlement

to pick on sb.	harceler qn.
a dissident	un dissident
to torture	torturer
an ordeal [ɔːˈdiːəl]	une épreuve, un calvaire
to disappear, to vanish	disparaître
a disappearance	une disparition
missing	disparu
to grant	accorder
to deny	refuser
an exit visa	un visa de sortie
political asylum	l'asile politique
a concentration camp	un camp de concentration
a labour camp	un camp de travail
a mass grave	un charnier, une fosse commune

Electronics and Computers

L'électronique et les ordinateurs

a component	un composant
a transistor	un transistor
silicon	le silicium
a chip	une puce
data [ˈdeɪtə, ˈdætə]	les données
a data base	une base de données
to process	traiter
processing	le traitement
a processor	un processeur
word processing	le traitement de textes
computing	l'informatique
to computerise	informatiser
computerisation	l'informatisation
a bar code	un code barres
a (floppy) disk, a diskette	une disquette
a key	une touche
a keyboard	un clavier
a CD-Rom	un CD-Rom
multimedia [mʌltɪˈmiːdɪə]	multimédia
a monitor	un moniteur
a central processing unit	une unité centrale
a laptop (computer)	un (ordinateur) portable
a desktop computer	un ordinateur de bureau
to store	mettre en mémoire
storage capacity	la capacité de mémoire

a memory	une mémoire
to erase [ɪˈreɪz, ɪˈreɪs], **to delete** [dɪˈliːt]	effacer
to download	télédécharger
to upload	télécharger
a program	un programme
software	le logiciel
hardware	le matériel
to hack	pirater
a hacker	un pirate informatique
a password	un mot de passe
upgradable	évolutif
e-mail	le courrier électronique
information superhighways	les autoroutes de l'information

/// EXPRESSIONS

to have sex	avoir des rapports sexuels
a red-light district	un quartier réservé/chaud
to have an abortion	se faire avorter
to be born out of wedlock	être né hors mariage
a single parent family	une famille monoparentale
to go out to work	prendre un emploi
the right of abode	le droit de s'établir
to be prejudiced against	avoir des préjugés contre
to be detained without trial	être détenu sans jugement
a prisoner of conscience	un prisonnier d'opinion
crime against humanity	crime contre l'humanité
the Data Protection Registrar	la Commission informatique et liberté
computer aided design	la conception assistée par ordinateur
computer aided manufacture	la fabrication assistée par ordinateur
to gain access to	obtenir l'accès à

/// VOCABULAIRE COMPLÉMENTAIRE

Sexuality	La sexualité
promiscuous	de moeurs légères
promiscuity	la promiscuité sexuelle

extra-marital	extra conjugal
to womanise	courir les femmes
casual sex	les rapports sexuels de rencontre
sexual harassment	le harcèlement sexuel
a brothel	une maison close
a clinic	un centre médico-social
a French letter	une capote anglaise
a sheath	un préservatif
a diaphragm	un diaphragme
a coil	un stérilet
a jelly	une gelée
to sterilise	stériliser
sterilisation	la stérilisation

Abortion and Euthanasia
L'avortement et l'euthanasie

unwanted	non souhaité
legitimate	légitime
illegitimate	illégitime
a bastard	un bâtard
a right-to-lifer	un opposant à l'avortement
pro-choice	partisan de l'avortement
mercy killing	l'euthanasie

Women's Liberation
La libération de la femme

motherhood	la maternité
to bring up children	élever des enfants
a day-care centre (US)	une halte-garderie
a creche, a day nursery	une crèche
domestic/household appliances	les appareils ménagers
to break up	se briser (mariage)
to divorce	divorcer
a divorce	un divorce
alimony	une pension alimentaire

Immigration
L'immigration

a native	un autochtone
a fellow citizen	un concitoyen

a resident	un habitant
a national	un ressortissant
an expatriate [eks'pætriət]	un expatrié
to adjust	(s')adapter
an adjustment	une adaptation
to assimilate	assimiler
an assimilation	une assimilation
a root	une racine
to uproot	déraciner
a way of life	un mode de vie
a lifestyle	un style de vie
an inner city area	un quartier urbain défavorisé
a menial job	un emploi subalterne
to exploit	exploiter
exploitation	l'exploitation
a sweatshop	un atelier clandestin, ou à main-d'oeuvre sous-payée
positive discrimination (UK), affirmative action (US)	quotas pour minorités, discrimination positive
xenophobia [zenə'fəubiə]	la xénophobie
to repatriate	rapatrier
repatriation	le rapatriement

Human Rights — Les droits de l'homme

a resolution	une résolution
to comply with sth.	se conformer à qch.
to guarantee [gærən'ti:]	garantir
a guarantee	une garantie
to safeguard	sauvegarder
a safeguard	une sauvegarde
a breach	une infraction, un manquement
to flout	bafouer
to intimidate	intimider
intimidation	l'intimidation
to muzzle	museler
a witch hunt	une chasse aux sorcières
a hunger strike	une grève de la faim
to forcefeed	alimenter de force
to exile ['ekzaıl]	exiler
exile	l'exil
an exile	un exilé
an exodus	un exode
an influx	un afflux

Miscellaneous topics

Electronics and computers	L'électronique et les ordinateurs
a circuit ['sɜːkɪt]	un circuit
input	l'entrée
output	la sortie
a sensor	un capteur
to display	afficher
a display	un affichage
to print	imprimer
a printer	une imprimante
ink jet	jet d'encre
bubble jet	à bulle d'encre
to transmit	transmettre
transmission	la transmission
to connect	relier
connection	la liaison
a network	un réseau
compatible	compatible
a spreadsheet	un tableur
a mainframe computer	un gros ordinateur

1. Choose the right explanation for the following words (with asterisks in the passage).

1. *forensic (experts)*
A. who represent a foreign country
B. who study the cause of death
C. who negotiate a deal

2. *to survey*
A. to keep watch over
B. to make a detailed study of
C. to take a quick look at

2. Say whether the following statements are true (T) or false (F).

1. The three warring parties in the conflict are mentioned in the first paragraph.
2. The team of experts was on a preliminary mission.
3. There were no risks involved in their mission.
4. It is understandable why «safe area» is placed between inverted commas.
5. The Serbs in Bosnia supported the Bosnian government.
6. The article contains no example of ethnic cleansing.
7. We are made aware of the details that spy satellites can pick out.

UN hunts mass graves in Bosnia

Julian Borger in Zagreb

United Nations war crime investigators began examining suspected mass grave sites in eastern Bosnia yesterday, in search of the remains of up to 8,000 Muslims missing since the Serb capture of Srebrenica last year.

A six-man team of forensic* experts from the UN's war crimes tribunal based in The Hague set out under American protection to mark and survey* sites north and west of Srebrenica, a former UN «safe area», where most of the missing are thought to lie buried. Exhumation of the suspected graves is expected to begin within the next month.

The US 2nd brigade based in nearby Vlasenica has provided a team of about 100 men, eight armoured cars, artillery and attack helicopters, which will intervene if the forensic team comes under threat while working on Serb-held territory. (...)

Bosnian Serb forces overran the government-controlled enclave around Srebrenica in July 1995, sweeping aside Dutch UN troops who were supposed to help secure the safety of local Muslims in a UN-declared «safe area». Most of the women and children were bused to government territory, but almost all the men were rounded up and few have been seen since.

Survivors have told investigators of mass executions and the use of bulldozers to bury thousands of bodies. Days after the fall of Srebrenica, US spy satellites photographed areas of freshly dug earth in six locations north and west of Srebrenica.

The Guardian, April 4, 1996

3. Look at the verbs taken from the article and give the corresponding nouns.

1. to hunt
2. to suspect
3. to survey
4. to think
5. to bury
6. to expect
7. to intervene

4. Fill in the blanks with the appropriate words from the following list. Use each word only once.

rate	pregnancies	failing	Health
provision	condoms	to reduce	pupils

School condoms

Tom Sackville, Under-Secretary of State for ...(1)..., advocated the ...(2)... of free ...(3)... in schools for ...(4)... aged 16 and over in an effort ...(5)... the number of teenage ...(6).... He said Britain's teenage pregnancy ...(7)... – the highest in Europe – was an «appalling national ...(8)...».

The Independent, March 25, 1993

The battle for Cyberspace

Will future generations look back on yesterday as the day when a death warrant was signed for the hitherto* omni-potent personal computer and with it the dominance of Bill Gates and his Microsoft group? Oracle corporation, the world's second largest software company clearly hopes so. Larry Ellison, Oracle's chair-man regards personal compu-ters as much too expensive and far too complicated for most people. In order to open up a truly mass market, Oracle has stripped the PC of most of its expensive clothes like hard disk drives and expensive inter-nal chips. Instead he is plan-ning to introduce a «network computer» (or NC) which wouldn't even need today's pricey shop-purchased compu-ter programmes. The NC links up to the worldwide Internet network of computers through a modem and will receive all its software – from games to spreadsheets* – from the Net. Nothing needs to be loaded in. Already an army of software developers is working on glo-bally mobile software (called «applets») which can be called down from anywhere in the world where there is an NC.

To prove he means business, Mr Ellison yesterday announ-ced a dizzy array* of the world's most powerful electro-nic manufacturers who have agreed common standards for the new generation of $500 computers including IBM, Motorola, Nokia, Digital, and Sun Systems, manufacturer of Java software (which is predic-ted to dominate the software of Cyberspace just as Microsoft dominated the PC).

The Guardian, May 5, 1996

1. Choose the right explanation for each of the following words (with asterisks in the passage).

1. *hitherto*
A. until now   B. in the future   C. from time to time

2. *a spreadsheet*
A. a word-checking program
B. a program for printing documents
C. a program for making calculations and tables

3. *an array*
A. a small number   B. a stoppage   C. a collection

2. Choose the appropriate endings for the following sentences.

1. According to the journalist, the threat to Microsoft
A. can be ignored.
B. should be taken seriously.
C. can be taken lightly.

2. Oracle aims to sell more computers by making them
A. more powerful.   B. more reliable.
C. cheaper and simpler.

3. Larry Ellison thinks that, with network computers, individual needs will be
A. better provided for.
B. taken less into account.
C. totally ignored.

4. The agreement reached by the manufacturers developing the system came
A. too early.
B. too late.
C. at the right time.

5. With such keen competition, the customer is likely to be
A. the winner.
B. unaffected.
C. the loser.

3. A chairman is the head of a company. Match the people (1-6) with what they are at the head of (A-F).

1. an editor   A. a sports team
2. a conductor   B. a group of workers
3. a skipper   C. an orchestra
4. a foreman   D. a cast of actors
5. a shop steward   E. a newspaper
6. a director   F. trade union members in one factory

Accidents 19 Les accidents

(voir Introduction p. 139)

/// VOCABULAIRE À HAUTE FRÉQUENCE

Road Crashes	Les accidents de la route
a moped	un cyclomoteur
a vehicle	un véhicule
a lorry, a truck (US)	un camion
a tanker	un camion-citerne
a coach	un car
a caravan	une caravane
a camper	un camping car
a seat belt	une ceinture de sécurité
a pedestrian	un piéton
a motorist	un automobiliste
a crash helmet	un casque
a bend, a corner	un virage, un tournant
to overtake	doubler
to brake	freiner
a brake	un frein
to slow down	ralentir
to pull up	s'arrêter
to pull out	déboîter
a pile-up	un carambolage
to skid	déraper

Rail Crashes	Les accidents de chemin de fer
a station	une gare
the railway, the railroad (US)	le chemin de fer
the locomotive, the engine	la locomotive
a carriage	un wagon
a passenger train	un train de voyageurs

a goods train, a freight train	un train de marchandises
a commuter train	un train de banlieue
a level crossing	un passage à niveau
a track	une voie
a line	une ligne
a rail	un rail
to derail	dérailler

Plane Crashes / Les accidents d'avion

an aircraft	un appareil
an airliner	un avion de ligne
a jumbo jet	un gros porteur
a jet engine	un réacteur
a flight	un vol
to land	atterrir
to take off	décoller
take-off	le décollage
an airport	un aéroport
a runway	une piste
a control tower	une tour de contrôle
a pilot	un pilote
a hostess, a stewardess	une hôtesse
to crash	s'abîmer, s'écraser
the flight recorder	l'enregistreur de vol
the black box	la boîte noire

Shipwrecks / Les naufrages

a vessel	un vaisseau
a trawler	un chalutier
a cargo ship, a freighter	un cargo
a merchant vessel	un navire marchand
an oil tanker	un pétrolier
a captain	un commandant
to sail	naviguer
a sailor	un marin
a fisherman	un marin-pêcheur
shipping	la navigation
to register	immatriculer
to run aground	s'échouer
a hull	une coque
a hold	une soute, une cale
to sink	sombrer
to abandon	évacuer

to drift	dériver
a lifeboat	un canot de sauvetage
to pick up	recueillir
a tug	un remorqueur
to tow	remorquer
a wreck	une épave
to drown	se noyer

Mining Accidents — Les accidents de mine

a coal-mine, a coalpit, a colliery	une mine de charbon
a miner	un mineur
a pitman, a colliery worker	un mineur de charbon
a shaft	un puits
a gallery	une galerie
fire damp	le grisou
dust	la poussière
to drill, to bore	creuser, forer

Fires — Les incendies

a blaze	un incendie, un brasier
ablaze	en flammes
to catch fire	prendre feu
to burn, to blaze	brûler
a burn	une brûlure
overcome	intoxiqué
to inhale	respirer, aspirer
a firefighter, a fireman	un pompier
a fire engine, a firetruck (US)	une pompe à incendie
to pour	déverser
a ladder	une échelle
to put out, to extinguish	éteindre
to char	calciner
ashes	les cendres

Climbing Accidents — Les accidents de montagne

a peak	un pic
to climb, to scale	grimper, escalader
ascent	l'ascension
a rope	une corde

| a cliff | une falaise |
| an avalanche | une avalanche |

Common Vocabulary / Vocabulaire commun

safety	la sécurité
a passenger	un passager
a crew	un équipage
to carry, to transport	transporter
on board, aboard	à bord
an engine failure	une panne de moteur
to overturn	se retourner
to hit	heurter
to bump into, to run into, to crash into	percuter
to knock down	renverser
to run over	écraser
to collide with	entrer en collision avec
a collision	une collision
a head-on collision	une collision de front
to involve	impliquer, comprendre
a shock	un choc, une commotion
to bruise [bru:z]	meurtrir
a bruise	une meurtrissure
a stitch	un point de suture
a distress signal	un signal de détresse
May Day, an SOS message	un SOS
to locate	localiser

EXPRESSIONS

in the opposite direction	en sens inverse
a hit-and-run driver	un chauffard (avec délit de fuite)
to ride pillion	être le passager d'un deux roues
to come off the rails	quitter les rails
an unmanned level crossing	un passage à niveau non gardé
to be bound for	être à destination de
to be on one's way to, to be en route to	faire route vers
to be due to land at	dont l'atterrissage est prévu à
to ditch in the sea	faire un amerrissage forcé

to lose control	perdre le contrôle
to bring under control	maîtriser, circonscrire
to go out of control	échapper au contrôle
to winch to safety	hélitreuiller
to be detained in hospital	être hospitalisé

VOCABULAIRE COMPLÉMENTAIRE

Road Crashes / Les accidents de la route

an estate car, a station wagon (US)	un break
to slew round	faire un tête à queue
a roadworthy car	une voiture en bon état
an articulated lorry	un semi-remorque
a trailer	une remorque
to jacknife	se mettre en travers
a juggernaut	un mastodonte
winding	sinueux
to swerve	faire une embardée
an MOT (= Ministry of Transport) test	un contrôle obligatoire

Rail Crashes / Les accidents de chemin de fer

rolling stock	le matériel roulant
a truck, a wagon	un wagon de marchandises
a derailment	un déraillement
an embankment	une levée de terre, un remblai
a driver	un mécanicien
a guard	un chef de train
a buffer	un butoir
points	un aiguillage

Air crashes / Les accidents aériens

a freight plane	un avion cargo
a wide-body jet	un avion gros-porteur
the body	la carlingue

to pressurise	pressuriser
pressurisation	la pressurisation
the fuselage	le fuselage
the landing gear, the undercarriage	le train d'atterrissage
an escape chute	un toboggan
an airstrip	une piste sommaire
airworthy	en état de vol
to ground	clouer au sol
a balloon [bəˈluːn]	un ballon
an airship	un dirigeable
a microlight	un ultra léger
a glider	un planeur
a hang glider	un deltaplane
a paraglider	un parapente
a descent	une descente
to disintegrate	se désintégrer
disintegration	la désintégration
to scatter	(se) disperser
a mid-air collision	une collision en vol

Shipwrecks · Les naufrages

a flag of convenience	un pavillon de complaisance
a trawl net	un chalut
a shipping lane	un couloir de navigation
a sailing ship	un voilier
a sailing dinghy	un dériveur
a bulk carrier	un vraquier
a container vessel	un porte-conteneurs
crippled	désemparé
stricken	en détresse
the bridge	la passerelle
the deck	le pont
a rudder	un gouvernail
a line	un câble
to list	gîter
to capsize	chavirer
to bail out	écoper
a distress beacon	une balise de détresse
a flare	une fusée de détresse
a coastguard	un garde-côte
a life-raft	un radeau de survie
adrift	à la dérive
to refloat	renflouer

Accidents

Fires	Les incendies
a fire brigade	un corps de pompiers
a breathing apparatus	un appareil respiratoire
an inferno	une fournaise
a conflagration	un sinistre
a seat of fire	un foyer d'incendie
to ignite	(s')allumer
embers	des braises
a short-circuit	un court-circuit
fumes	les émanations
asphyxiated	asphyxié
to smoulder	couver
to fan	attiser
to douse	noyer en arrosant
foam	la mousse
to spray	pulvériser
to smother	étouffer
remains	les restes
a brushfire	un feu de broussailles

Climbing Accidents	Les accidents de montagne
a mountaineer [maʊntɪˈnɪə]	un alpiniste
a potholer	un spéléologue
an expedition	une expédition
a ledge	une corniche
a gully	un couloir
a crevasse [krɪˈvæs]	une crevasse
exposure	le refroidissement
frostbite	des gelures

Common Vocabulary	Vocabulaire commun
to career	aller à toute vitesse
hypothermia [haɪpəˈθɜːmɪə]	l'hypothermie
to topple	(se) renverser
to ram	emboutir
to plough into	s'encastrer dans
concussion	commotion
to hamper, to hinder	gêner, entraver
a near miss	une quasi collision
to maintain, to service	entretenir
maintenance, servicing	l'entretien

to overhaul	réviser
an overhaul	une révision
negligence, carelessness	la négligence

Pensioners killed on Legion day trip

by Paul Stokes, Colin Randall and Sean O'Neill

Ten elderly people were killed when a coach taking them home from a Royal British Legion* outing careered off* the M4 motorway near the Severn Bridge, plunged 20ft down an embankment and landed on its roof in a ditch*.

Two more died in hospital from their injuries and seven others were seriously hurt. One couple drowned underneath the coach, which was returning to Christchurch in Dorset from a trip to a brewery in Cardiff.

Rescuers had to wade chest deep in water covered in a four-inch film of oil which had leaked from the coach. The front four passengers, who had seat belts, were cut free as they hung strapped in upside down. A crane* was brought in to hoist the coach and an emer-

gency treatment centre was set up in an inflatable tent.

All 19 surviving passengers, many in their 70s, were taken to hospital. The driver, Stephen Brown, 39, was given a routine breath test, which proved negative.

He told police he swerved to avoid an object in the motorway seconds before the crash. Other witnesses said cars were crashing into pieces of wooden pallets.(...)

It is understood most of the deaths resulted from the roof of the 52-seater coach being crushed. Many of the injured had to be brought out through an 18-inch gap between the collapsed roof and the body of the vehicle.

The Daily Telegraph, May 31, 1995

1. *Choose the right explanation for each of the following words (with asterisks in the passage).*

1. *the British legion*
A. a military unit   B. an association of war veterans
C. a tour operator

2. *to career off*
A. to overturn   B. to take the wrong lane
C. to leave at full speed

3. *a ditch*
A. an excavation for drainage   B. a garden
C. a farm outbuilding

4. *a crane*
A. a sort of tractor   B. a repair vehicle
C. a device for lifting things

2. Say whether the following statements are true (T) or false (F).

1. The accident happened in the east of Britain.
2. The coach did not overturn.
3. Landing in a ditch made things worse for one couple.
4. The seat belts seem to have been efficient.
5. A lorry may have shed part of its load.
6. Some lives might have been saved if the coach had landed on its wheels.
7. An 18-inch gap is about 45 centimetres high.

3. «Inflatable» (= that can be inflated) is made up of the verb «inflate» and the suffix «-able». The opposite is «uninflatable» (that cannot be inflated). Make similar adjectives constructed in the same way.

that cannot be:

1. shrunk
2. forgiven
3. thought of
4. shaken
5. forgotten
6. spoken
7. drunk
8. sold (two forms)

4. The words between brackets have been scrambled. Put the letters back into the right order.

Tyre dump goes up in flames

A dump containing up to a million tyres was on (eifr) in Sheffield last night.

Dense, black (kemos) was visible up to 15 miles away from the depot, at Deepcar. The (teha) affected high-power electricity cables, causing (wopre) supplies to be cut off in some (rasea).

Eight fire appliances and more than 40 (fistherifreg) were sent to the (zebal), along with environmental officials.

The police have (nawder) residents close to the depot to keep their windows and doors (solced) and not to go (arne) the fire. They also set up road (scklob) to prevent people visiting the site.

Local residents had been opposed to the opening of the tyre depot two (syrea) ago.

The Independent on Sunday, March 21, 1993

Crew may have died before jet plunged into swamp

by Quentin Letts in New York and Harvey Elliott

The crew of an ageing DC-9 airliner may have been dead or unconscious before their jet plunged into the Florida Everglades killing all 109 on board, including two British tourists.

The pilot for the cut-price domestic airline Valujet told air traffic controllers that the cockpit was filling with smoke minutes after he took off from Miami for Atlanta.

As he turned back towards the airport, witnesses say the 27-year-old aircraft made a series of irrational manoeuvres, banking* sharply then straightening and flying at an angle of 75 degrees into the alligator-infested swamp*.

Rescuers yesterday gave up hope of finding survivors and were unable to locate anything more than fragments of the jet, which had recently suffered engine troubles. The two Britons were named as Roger and Devlin Loughney but identities of the other passengers and crew were being withheld until relatives were informed.

Teams trying to recover the aircraft's flight recorder, which had a radio beacon, were hampered by the muddy and inhospitable terrain where the jet crashed on Saturday, 30 minutes after take-off.

Attempts to build a road across the swamp were abandoned and rescuers were considering trying to drain the land to reach the site.

Investigators want to recover the bodies of the crew and passengers to establish whether they were wearing oxygen masks and if their lungs contained enough smoke to have caused them to black out*. A fire could have been caused by an electrical fault.

The Times, May 13, 1996

1. Choose the right explanation for each of the following words (with asterisks in the passage).

1. *to bank*
A. to gain height
B. to have one wing lower than the other
C. to reduce speed

2. *swamp*
A. small lake
B. large river
C. area of wet soft land

3. *to black out*
A. to lose consciousness
B. to put out the lights
C. to stop all communications

2. Choose the appropriate endings for the following sentences.

1. The journalists seemed to
A. have no idea of what caused the accident.
B. be blaming the crew for the accident.
C. have a pretty good idea of what caused the accident.

2. The pilot reported
A. no incident.
B. an incident.
C. several incidents.

3. While watching the plane, witnesses
A. were intrigued by the manoeuvres.
B. suspected nothing.
C. tried to intervene.

4. Finally, the airliner
A. disappeared into the swamp.
B. was half-sunk into the mud.
C. was scattered over the swamp.

5. The solutions rescuers came up with in order to reach the scene of the crash were
A. impossible to implement.
B. easy to implement.
C. difficult to implement.

6. The journalists seem to think the crash was caused by
A. human error
B. engine failure.
C. an incident which incapacitated the crew.

3. Read the article again and find the following.

1. equivalents for:
A. next of kin   B. retrieve   C. black box
D. hinder   E. to confirm   F. to faint

2. the opposites of:
G. international   H. released
I. flood   J. landing

4. Fill in the eleven lines across the grid with translations of the corresponding French words. This will give you the answer to number 12 in column D.

1. falaise
2. navigation (bateaux)
3. défaillance
4. chalutier
5. dériver
6. entrer en collision
7. cargo
8. puits (de mine)
9. dépasser, doubler
10. épave
11. marin-pêcheur
12. pompier

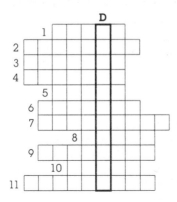

Long wait to know capsized yachtsman's fate

Rescuers searching for the British yachtsman whose boat overturned in the Southern Ocean said last night it would be two days before they knew if he had survived.

Tony Bullimore, one of Britain's most experienced sailors has been missing since his 60ft yacht, Global Exide Challenger, capsized three days ago. Air crews picked up a manually activated alarm signal from his yacht – a strong indication that he was still alive.

The Guardian, January, 8, 1996

999 car death

Simon Taupin, 15, from Ramsgate, Kent, has died after being hit by a police car answering a 999 call.

The Times, November 9, 1993

Natural Disasters | 20 | Les catastrophes naturelles

(voir Introduction p. 139)

/// VOCABULAIRE À HAUTE FRÉQUENCE

Earthquakes — Les tremblements de terre

Earthquakes	Les tremblements de terre
a tremor	une secousse (tellurique)
a shock wave	une onde de choc
a quake	un séisme
an earthquake	un tremblement de terre
to measure	mesurer
to register	enregistrer, atteindre
a scale	une échelle
magnitude	l'amplitude, la magnitude
an epicentre ['epɪsentə]	un épicentre
an aftershock	une réplique, une secousse résiduelle
to rock	ébranler
a crack	une fissure
a fault	une faille
a fault line	une ligne de fracture
a landslide, a landslip	un glissement de terrain
a landfall	un éboulement de terrain

Wind, Water and Rain — Le vent, l'eau et la pluie

Wind, Water and Rain	Le vent, l'eau et la pluie
a gale	un coup de vent, une tempête
a storm	une forte tempête
a hurricane ['hʌrɪkən]	un ouragan
a tornado [tɔː'neɪdəu]	une tornade
a cyclone ['saɪkləun]	un cyclone
the path	le trajet, la trajectoire
a typhoon [taɪ'fuːn]	un typhon
torrential	diluvien
to rip off	arracher

to blow down, to tear down	abattre
to sweep across	balayer
a flood	une inondation
to flood	inonder
to swell	(se) gonfler
swell	la houle
the tide	la marée
a tidal wave	un raz de marée
to overflow	déborder
waterlogged	détrempé, gorgé d'eau
a bank	une rive
a sandbag	un sac de sable
to sandbag	protéger avec des sacs de sable
a dyke	une digue
mud	la boue
a dam	un barrage
to burst	se rompre
to wash away	emporter
to drown	submerger, noyer
drought [draut]	la sécheresse

Volcanoes — Les volcans

a volcano [vɒl'keɪnəu]	un volcan
a crater ['kreɪtə]	un cratère
to erupt	entrer en éruption
an eruption	une éruption
to steam	dégager de la vapeur
steam	la vapeur
to spit	cracher
to spew out	vomir
lava ['lɑːvə]	la lave
ash	la cendre
a slope	une pente
a flow, an outflow	une coulée

Common Vocabulary — Vocabulaire commun

physical damage	les dégâts matériels
to hit, to strike	frapper, atteindre
to affect	toucher
to disrupt	perturber
a disruption	une perturbation
to be cut off	être coupé du reste

225

to be stranded, marooned	être bloqué, coincé
chaos ['keɪɒs]	le chaos, la pagaille
havoc	les ravages, les dégâts
homeless	sans abri
to re-house	reloger
makeshift	de fortune
a stricken area	une zone sinistrée
to warn	avertir
a warning	un avertissement, un avis
power lines	les lignes électriques
power supply	l'alimentation en courant
a power failure	une panne de courant
a power cut	une coupure de courant
to wipe out	anéantir

/// EXPRESSIONS

to overflow its banks	déborder
to burst its banks	sortir de son lit
to bring chaos	semer la confusion
to bring havoc, to leave a trail of damage, to cut a path of destruction	provoquer de gros dégâts, tout détruire sur son passage
to take shelter	s'abriter
overhead power lines	les lignes électriques aériennes
a stricken area	une zone sinistrée
to wipe off the map	rayer de la carte

/// VOCABULAIRE COMPLÉMENTAIRE

Earthquakes	Les tremblements de terre
to sway	osciller
a foundation	une fondation
concrete	le béton
to slip off	glisser
to crumble	s'effriter
seismological [saɪzmə'lɒdʒɪkəl]	sismologique
a seismologist [saɪz'mɒlədʒɪst]	un sismologue
to raze	raser

Wind and Rain

a whirlwind	un tourbillon
to roar	rugir
to batter	battre, assaillir
to lash	fouetter, cingler
a groundswell	une lame de fond
to swamp	submerger
to whip up	soulever, faire monter
to flatten	aplatir
to toss	ballotter
to board up	obstruer avec des planches
a levee	une levée, une digue

Le vent et la pluie

Volcanoes

a volcanologist, a vulcanologist	un volcanologue, un vulcanologue
dormant	en sommeil
extinct	éteint
volcanic	volcanique
to rumble	gronder
a rumble	un grondement
a plume	un panache
molten	en fusion, liquide
a layer	une couche

Les volcans

Common Vocabulary

structural damage	dégâts aux installations
a swathe [sweɪð]	un sillage, une traînée
to engulf	engloutir
matchwood	des fétus de bois
to uproot	déraciner
to seal	colmater
a chasm ['kæzəm]	un gouffre

Vocabulaire commun

227

America's storm of the century

from Patrick Brogan in Washington

Blizzards and hurricane-force winds lashed* America's east coast during the weekend, killing at least 67 people.

Airports in Boston, New York, Washington and Atlanta were closed. Motorways were shut down, and millions left without electricity.

Emergency conditions were declared in 12 states and tens of thousands of people spent the night in shelters after being evacuated from their homes.

Blizzard conditions continued throughout yesterday in parts of the north-east as the storm pushed into Canada, leaving as much as 50 ins[1] of snow in places, paralysing much of the eastern seaboard*.

«It's not too much to say it's the storm of the century,» said Joe Friday, director of the National Weather Service.

Presidential spokesman George Stephanopoulos said Florida suffered about 50 separate tornadoes. About two million people were left without power there, and about 18 died in the storms.

A 36-year-old woman died when a tornado swept through her mobile home. She and her husband had moved to a government-sponsored trailer* park south of Miami after Hurricane Andrew destroyed their home last August.

«It took about one-and-a-half seconds and it was over,» said Mr Bob Honawitz, her husband. He had fallen asleep on the couch and she was asleep in bed when the tornado struck.

A Honduran freighter sank in the Gulf of Mexico off Florida and at least three of ten crew members were killed. Others were found in a life raft.

[1] inches

The Herald, March 15, 1993

1. Choose the right explanation for each of the following words (with asterisks in the passage).

1. *to lash*
A. to hit gently
B. to hit with force
C. to hit slowly

2. *the seaboard*
A. the area along the coast
B. an area far from the sea
C. overseas

3. *a trailer*
A. a lorry
B. a tent
C. a mobile home

2. Say whether the following statements are true (T) or false (F).

1. The state of Washington was hit by the hurricane.
2. All means of transport are mentioned in the article.
3. The hurricane took on different forms according to latitude.
4. No special measures were taken by the authorities.
5. The White House was kept informed of the situation.
6. Mr and Mrs Honawitz had always lived in a trailer.
7. Tornadoes can be very short-lived.
8. The shipwreck left no survivors.

3. Read the article again and find equivalents for the following.

1. snowstorm
2. to whip
3. refuge
4. to go on
5. to bring to a standstill
6. electricity
7. a cargo ship

4. Choose the appropriate endings (A-F) for the following sentences (1-6).

1. Rescue workers were sifting through the wreckage of
2. The death toll from an earthquake and subsequent tidal waves that struck the Indonesian
3. Aftershocks every five minutes
4. Most of the fragile mud and brick huts in the two rural townships
5. In north London a woman was killed when
6. The authorities in Los Angeles have enforced a night curfew amid concern

A. a shop-sign, dislodged by the wind, struck her on the head.

B. island of Flores on Saturday rose to 1,232 yesterday, officials said.

C. that looters may take advantage of the chaos and destruction resulting from yesterday's earthquake.

D. hampered rescue work for several hours.

E. a shopping centre with dogs trained to sniff out bodies.

F. collapsed, burying thousands of people alive as they slept.

Los Angeles ablaze* after quake strikes

by Giles Whittell in Los Angeles and our Foreign Staff

A violent earthquake shook Los Angeles yesterday, killing at least 16 people, buckling* highways, wrecking thousands of homes and sparking* hundreds of fires that left the city shrouded* in black smoke.

The quake, which struck the San Fernando Valley northwest of the city at 4.31am, was the worst in southern California for forty years, measuring 6.6 on the Richter scale. Some three million people felt its impact as it reverberated from Las Vegas to San Diego, followed by more than twenty aftershocks.

The Los Angeles mayor and the governor of California declared states of emergency and called out the National Guard, while President Clinton offered to do everything humanly possible to help. He indicated that he would declare the region a disaster area, opening the way for federal aid.

Although the quake was not as strong as some in recent years, it was unusually destructive because its epicentre was in a densely populated area. Its timing – two hours before rush hour on a national holiday honouring Martin Luther King – almost certainly saved many lives.

Those who died included at least seven people in a collapsed block of flats near the epicentre in Northridge, half a dozen heart attack victims, a police motorcyclist who drove off a freeway that split in two, and a woman who slipped in her home, hit a cot* and broke her neck.

The Times, January 18, 1994

---

1. Choose the right explanation for each of the following words (with asterisks in the passage).

1. *ablaze*
A. destroyed
B. on fire
C. quiet

2. *to buckle*
A. to divert
B. to repair
C. to bend and twist

3. *to spark*
A. to be the cause of
B. to put out
C. to make worse

4. *to shroud*
A. to asphyxiate
B. to envelop
C. to brighten

5. *a cot*
A. a bedside carpet
B. an armchair
C. a small bed for babies

2. Say whether the following statements are true (T) or false (F).

1. The damage caused by the earthquake is expressed at the beginning by one verb only.
2. The location of the quake is clearly situated.
3. The tremor was felt only in California .
4. The number of aftershocks was below normal.
5. California was to receive some outside help.
6. Emotional shock was to blame for some deaths.
7. Some accidents could be attributed to bad luck.

3. Read the article again and find the following.

1. A verb implying destruction, in the first paragraph.
2. A verb expressing the echo of a sound.
3. Two adjectives showing that, in the US, help can come from outside the state.
4. A noun which is used to mean the origin of an earthquake.
5. An American word for a major road (the equivalent of a dual carriageway in Britain).

4. The noun corresponding to «strong» is «strength». In the same way, find the nouns corresponding to the following adjectives.

1. long   2. wide   3. high
4. deep   5. broad

Nine die in Tuscan floods

The Italian village of Montepania lies partly submerged after heavy flooding devastated western Tuscany yesterday. The death toll in the region rose to nine as Italy's new Environment Minister said past governments had not done enough to prevent such disasters.

Rivers burst their banks, sweeping away cars, flooding houses and cutting off roads to several villages on the coastal plain and in foothills inland from the Mediterranean port of Massa.

Reuter, June 21, 1996

The Weather **21** Le temps

///VOCABULAIRE À HAUTE FRÉQUENCE

Common features	Traits communs
fine, fair	beau
unsettled	instable
changeable	variable
dull	maussade
clear	clair
sunny, bright	ensoleillé
to brighten up	s'éclaircir, se dégager
sunshine	l'ensoleillement
mist	la brume
fog	le brouillard
slight, light	léger
thick	épais
dense	dense
to form	se former
to lift	se lever
a patch	une nappe, une plaque
patchy	en nappes
an anticyclone	un anticyclone
a depression	une dépression
pressure	la pression
a ridge	une dorsale
a trough [trɒf]	une zone (basse pression)
a front	un front
widespread	répandu, général
a spell, a period ['pɪəriəd]	une période
to range from ... to	aller de ... à (températures)
a range	une gamme
a prospect	une perspective
an outlook	une prévision
a weather forecast	un bulletin météorologique
Celsius	Celsius, centigrade
bad weather	les intempéries
an area ['ɛərɪə]	une zone

Wind | Le vent

calm	calme
windy	avec du vent
windswept	balayé par le vent
moderate	modéré
fresh	frais
to freshen	fraîchir
strong, high, heavy	fort, violent
a breeze	une brise
to gust	souffler en rafales
a gust	une rafale
to turn	tourner
to veer	remonter (sens des aiguilles)
to back	descendre (sens inverse)
prevailing	dominant
a gale	un coup de vent, une tempête
severe [sɪ'vɪə]	fort
a storm	une forte tempête
stormy	très agité, orageux
to let up	se calmer
a let-up, a lull	une accalmie, un répit
to blow over	se calmer, s'apaiser
to die down	tomber
southerly	du sud
southwards	vers le sud

Rain | La pluie

rainfall	les précipitations
rainy	pluvieux
wet, damp	humide
cloudy	nuageux
to cloud over	se couvrir
drizzle	la bruine
light rain	le crachin
a shower	une averse
showery rain	pluie en averses
an outbreak of rain	une ondée
to pour	tomber à flots
to dry up	devenir plus sec
to clear away	se dégager
a thunderstorm	un orage
thunder	le tonnerre
thundery	orageux

to brew	couver
to break out	éclater
lightning	la foudre
hail	la grêle
a rainbow	un arc-en-ciel

Heat — La chaleur

mild	doux
warm	chaud
warmth	la chaleur modérée
hot	très chaud
a heat wave	la canicule
dry	sec
drought [draut]	la sécheresse

Cold — Le froid

cool	frais
chilly	très frais
to freeze	geler
freeze	le gel
a frost	une gelée
a sharp frost	une forte gelée
freezing-point	zéro degré centigrade
minus 6	moins 6
hoar frost, white frost	la gelée blanche
ice	la glace
icy	glacé, glacial
sleet	le grésil
to snow	neiger
snowy	neigeux
a blizzard	un blizzard
to melt	fondre

/// EXPRESSIONS

a trough of low pressure	une zone dépressionnaire
a ridge of high pressure	une ligne de hautes pressions
a breath of wind	un souffle de vent
it's pouring with rain	il pleut à verse
a clap of thunder	un coup de tonnerre
a flash/bolt of lightning	un éclair

torrents of rain	des trombes d'eau
a burst of rain	une averse
the thaw sets in	le dégel s'installe
to bask in the sun	se dorer au soleil

/// VOCABULAIRE COMPLÉMENTAIRE

Common Features — Traits communs

settled	stable
set fair	beau fixe
to break through	percer
a mixture	un mélange
haze	la brume légère
smog	le smog
to thicken (up)	s'épaissir
to hang around, to linger	traîner
to persist	persister
to prevail	l'emporter
to extend	s'étendre
to establish	s'établir
prolonged	prolongé
to wear off, to weaken	s'affaiblir
to fill	se combler
the met office	les services de la météo
a weatherman	un météorologue
a meteorologist	un météorologiste
the shipping forecast	la météo marine
a synopsis	un résumé de la situation
to predict	prévoir
overnight	pendant la nuit
coastal	côtier
inland	à l'intérieur (du pays)

Wind — Le vent

brisk	vif
an airflow, an airstream	un flux d'air
breezy	avec de la brise
to whip up	activer
to strengthen, to pick up	se renforcer
a squall	une bourrasque
a whirlwind	un tourbillon

The Weather

to ease off	s'atténuer, mollir
to abate, to subside	s'apaiser, se calmer
a shift	une saute
south-westerly	du sud-ouest

Rain — La pluie

the damp, moisture	l'humidité
overcast	couvert
to edge into	se glisser, s'introduire
a belt	une frange
a blustery shower	une giboulée
a squally shower	un grain
torrential	torrentiel, diluvien
a downpour, a deluge	un déluge
patchy rain	pluies éparses
isolated	isolé
persistent	persistant
to break up	se disperser
a bright interval	une éclaircie
to peter out	s'effilocher
to die away, to die out	s'affaiblir, cesser
a hailstone	un grêlon

Heat — La chaleur

sultry	étouffant
close	lourd
to pick up	remonter (températures)
sun-tanned	bronzé
sun-stroke	une insolation

Cold — Le froid

wintry	hivernal
frosty	glacial
groundfrost	gelée au sol
raw	rigoureux
the ice cap	la calotte glaciaire
the tip of the iceberg	la partie visible de l'iceberg
a flurry	une rafale (neige)
to thaw	dégeler
a thaw	un dégel
slush	la neige fondante
a cold snap	un coup de froid

Celsius and Fahrenheit

C = Celsius
F = Fahrenheit

0°C = 32° F
100° C = 212° F

F temperature
= 9/5 C temperature + 32

C temperature
= 5/9 F temperature - 32.

Record snowfalls as blizzards paralyse US

Ellen Wulfhorst

Blizzards buried the north-eastern United States under record snowfalls yesterday, closing businesses and schools, stranding* travellers and foiling* plans to reopen the federal government.

Thirty inches (76 cm) fell in Philadelphia, almost 28 inches (71 cm) in Newark, New Jersey, and 18 inches (46 cm) in New York's Central Park, the National Weather Service said.

Washington looked like a ghost town as the storm accomplished what the long-running budget dispute between President Bill Clinton and the Republican-led Congress had failed to do – shut down the federal government entirely.

There were reports of at least 30 weather-related deaths. Some were due to traffic accidents, including one person struck by a snow plough* in New Jersey.

A man in Maryland and two people in Delaware died while shovelling snow and one man in Delaware died after hitting his head in a snowmobile* accident.

There were two deaths in Pennsylvania, and another three people were found dead out of doors in Philadelphia, but officials said they could not be sure whether they had died from exposure.

There was no mail delivery in New York, Washington and Philadelphia, and airports in Washington, Philadelphia, New York and Boston were closed. Overseas passengers hoping to land in New York found themselves diverted to Bangor, Maine.

Reuter, January 9, 1996

The Weather

1. Choose the right explanation for each of the following words (with asterisks in the passage).

1. *to strand*
A. to prevent from travelling
B. to make it impossible to find one's way
C. to be unable to get warm

2. *to foil*
A. to make known
B. to make possible
C. to make impossible

3. *a snowplough*
A. a vehicle for cutting into the ground
B. a snow-carrying vehicle
C. a snow-clearing vehicle

4. *a snowmobile*
A. a snow-clearing vehicle
B. a vehicle for travelling on snow
C. a snow-gathering vehicle

2. Say whether the following statements are true (T) or false (F).

1. Blizzards raged all over the United States.
2. Bad weather had one unusual consequence.
3. The amount of snow seemed to increase from east to west.
4. It's clear from the article that Bill Clinton is a Democrat.
5. Only two people died in Pennsylvania.
6. Some north-eastern states seemed to have been less affected.

3. «Snow plough» and «snowmobile» are compound nouns. Use the definitions to find 6 more compound nouns beginning with «snow».

1. A white, early spring flower.	SNOW☐☐☐☐
2. Snow pressed between the hands.	SNOW☐☐☐☐
3. A frame for walking on snow.	SNOW☐☐☐☐
4. Snow driven by the wind into piles.	SNOW☐☐☐☐☐
5. The snowy top of a mountain.	SNOW☐☐☐
6. Seen fluttering in the air when it snows.	SNOW☐☐☐☐☐

European weather

High pressure over the British Isles continues to dominate the weather, keeping most of western Europe settled with areas of fog and frost. The fog is most likely over western France.

It will be generally dry in many areas today, though some showers will fall, especially over northern Germany, eastern Spain and the Balearics.

Over the weekend, most areas will stay dry, although northern Germany may have some light rain or drizzle.

It will be cloudy almost everywhere, though with some brighter intervals.

Fog, freezing in places, is most likely to persist in western Germany, Luxembourg and inland France.

Away from the fog, daytime temperatures will be mostly well up for the time of year.

The weather over Scandinavia will be less settled, with snow likely, especially in the mountains on Sunday.

Colder weather, with some snow reaching the Alps, is likely towards the middle of next week.

BRITAIN: areas of fog, especially over Northern Ireland, north-west England, the western Midlands and East Wales will mostly clear, but a few patches may persist all day.

During the evening, fog will thicken again over parts of England and Wales. Away from the fog, it will be dry nearly everywhere with a little sunshine.

Daytime temperatures will be mainly normal, but there will be frost and icy roads in places early and late.

The Guardian, January 17, 1992

Travel and Traffic 22 Les voyages et la circulation

/// VOCABULAIRE À HAUTE FRÉQUENCE

The Weather	Le temps
poor visibility	mauvaise visibilité
(black) ice	le verglas
icy	verglacé
a patch	une plaque, une nappe
treacherous ['tretʃərəs]	plein d'embûches, traître
hazardous	dangereux, risqué
slippery	glissant
a snowdrift	une congère
snowbound	enneigé
flooded	inondé
to be stranded	être bloqué
to close	barrer
a closure	une fermeture
to block	bloquer
to abandon	abandonner
to re-open	ouvrir de nouveau
care	la prudence
a crossing	une traversée
smooth	calme
choppy	légèrement agitée
rough	agitée

Incidents	Les incidents
to disrupt	perturber
a disruption	une perturbation
chaos ['keɪɒs]	la confusion, le chaos
road works	les travaux routiers
to break down	tomber en panne
a breakdown	une panne

Traffic Flow — La circulation

a trip, a journey	un voyage
to travel	voyager
busy	animé
heavy	dense
crowded	chargé
congested	encombré
congestion	encombrement
a tailback	une retenue
a jam	un embouteillage
to crawl	avancer au pas
eastbound	vers l'est
southbound	vers le sud
speed	la vitesse
a limit	une limitation
a restriction	une restriction
to avoid	éviter
to divert	dévier
a diversion	une déviation
an alternative route	un itinéraire de remplacement
rush hours, peak hours	les heures de pointe
to commute	faire la navette entre son domicile et son travail
a commuter	un banlieusard
car-sharing	le co-voiturage

Road Traffic — La circulation routière

the Highway Code	le code de la route
a driving licence	un permis de conduire
a driving test	un examen d'obtention du permis
a road hump, a sleeping policeman	un ralentisseur, une bande rugueuse
a cycle lane	une piste cyclable
a built-up area	une agglomération
a thoroughfare	une artère
main	principal
a carriageway	une chaussée
a dual carriageway	une quatre-voies
a motorway, a freeway (US)	une autoroute
a lane	un couloir, une voie
the hard shoulder	la bande d'arrêt d'urgence

a junction	une bretelle d'accès et/ou de sortie, un échangeur
a turn-off	une sortie
a bypass	une route de contournement
a ring road	une rocade
a beltway (US)	un périphérique
a rest area	une aire de repos
a service area	une aire de services
a filling station	une station-service
petrol, gasoline (US), gas (US)	l'essence
diesel (oil)	le gazole
a roundabout	un rond-point
clockwise	dans le sens des aiguilles
anticlockwise	dans les sens inverse des aiguilles
a toll	un péage
to park	garer, stationner
a car park, a parking lot (US)	un parking
drink driving	la conduite en état d'alcoolémie
careless	imprudent
reckless	dangereux
to speed	commettre un excès de vitesse

Public transport — Les transports publics

the underground, the Tube, the subway (US)	le métro
a ferry	un ferry
a ferry terminal	une gare maritime
to board, to get on board	monter à bord
to sail	naviguer, partir
a sailing	un départ de bateau
a harbour, a port	un port
to run	fonctionner
to delay	retarder
a delay	un retard
a schedule ['ʃedjuːl, 'skedjuːl]	un horaire
on schedule	à l'heure
a scheduled flight	un vol régulier
domestic	intérieur
nonstop	sans escale
to charter	affréter
a charter plane	un avion charter
an air traffic controller	un contrôleur de la navigation aérienne, un aiguilleur du ciel

to depart	partir
a departure	un départ
an arrival	une arrivée
incoming traffic	le trafic à l'arrivée
outgoing traffic	le trafic au départ
to cancel	annuler
a cancellation	une annulation
to check	vérifier
to enquire [ɪnˈkwaɪə]	se renseigner
an enquiry	une demande de renseignements
information	des renseignements

Holidays — Les vacances

a vacation (US)	un congé
a bank holiday	un jour férié
a holidaymaker	un vacancier
a package holiday	un séjour à forfait
a holiday resort	une station de vacances
to rent	louer
to book, to reserve	réserver
a reservation	une réservation
a berth	une couchette
a travel agent	un agent de voyages
a travel agency	une agence de voyages
a tour operator	un voyagiste, un organisateur de voyages
accommodation	le logement
a boarding-house, a guest-house	une pension de famille
board and lodging	la pension
to put sb. up	loger qn.
self-catering accommodation	une location meublée
an en suite bedroom	une chambre avec w.c. et salle d'eau privés
no vacancies	complet

// EXPRESSIONS

visibility down to 20 yards	visibilité réduite à 20 mètres
closed to traffic	interdit à la circulation
to drive with extra care	conduire avec une extrême prudence
to set out on a journey	se mettre en route

to go dead slow, to go at a crawl	avancer au pas
to do a ton *(fam.)*	faire du 160 à l'heure
to jump the lights	griller les feux
bumper to bumper	pare-chocs contre pare-chocs
a one-way street	une rue à sens unique
to do/make a U-turn	faire demi-tour
to ban sb. from driving	suspendre le permis de qn.
fully booked up	complet (à la réservation)
back to normal	retour à la normale
to enquire with somebody	se renseigner auprès de qn.
a high-speed train	un train à grande vitesse
a roll-on roll-off ship	un navire roulier
to be a good sailor	avoir le pied marin
to stagger holidays	étaler les vacances
to blow in the bag	souffler dans le ballon

/// VOCABULAIRE COMPLÉMENTAIRE

The weather / Le temps

fogbound	noyé dans le brouillard
to grit	sabler
grit	le gravier, le sable
to drift	accumuler
impassable	impraticable
unusable	inutilisable, impraticable
marooned	bloqué, isolé

Incidents / Les incidents

to shed	répandre
a load	un chargement
to leak	s'échapper (liquide, gaz)
a leak, a leakage	une fuite
to burst	éclater, se rompre
a burst	une rupture (canalisation)
a main	une canalisation
maintenance	l'entretien
a repair	une réparation

re-surfacing	la réfection du revêtement
a recovery vehicle	une dépanneuse

Traffic Flow — La circulation

packed	comble, bondé
to slow down	ralentir
a slow-down	un ralentissement
a bumper	un pare-chocs
a traffic warden	un contractuel
a ticket	un ticket
a fine	une amende
a clamp, a Denver boot	un sabot de blocage
a contraflow system	une mise en deux sens d'une voie à sens unique
a weekend motorist	un chauffeur du dimanche
a major road	une route principale
a minor road	une route secondaire
a country lane	un chemin rural
an access	un accès
a slip road	un voie d'accès ou de sortie
a stretch	une portion, une section
a lay-by	une bande de stationnement
an interchange	un échangeur
a turnpike (US)	une autoroute à péage
a breathaliser, a drunkometer (US)	un éthylomètre
a breath test	un passage à l'éthylomètre
intoxicated	en état d'ébriété
to disqualify	frapper d'une suspension
a disqualification	une suspension, un retrait
to take away	retirer
an endorsement	une mention sur le permis

Public Transport — Les transports publics

a wharf, a quay [kiː]	un quai
to dock	accoster
a hovercraft	un aéroglisseur
a taxiway	une piste de dégagement
jet lag	l'effet du décalage horaire

Commuters face chaos on sixth day of strikes

by David Graves

Commuters into London face travel chaos again today because of the sixth strike by Tube drivers, with the imminent prospect of more industrial action on the railways.

London Underground said last night that it expected the Tube network to be at a virtual standstill, although a spokesman said he hoped that talks could be held with the unions to resolve the dispute before the next threatened strike on Aug 7.

During the stoppage last Thursday, the Underground ran 10 trains at various times. The spokesman said the effect of today's strike was expected to be the same.

ASLEF, the driver's union, has held five 24-hour stoppages since June 27 in a dispute over working hours. The Rail, Maritime and Transport Union joined the last two strikes.

The Underground spokesman said: «We have suggested that the dispute should be referred to independent arbitration and hope the unions are able to accept this.»

The unions have accused the Underground of reneging* on a pledge* to cut an hour from the working week. The company says that any reduction is conditional on productivity gains. More strikes are planned.

Traffic has been jammed on many main roads during the strikes. A car-sharing hotline has been set up by the RAC[1] and the Freewheelers group to try to cut the number of vehicles.

Drivers who call 0191 222 0090 will be matched to people in their area who want a lift.

[1] The Royal Automobile Club, an organisation for motorists.

The Daily Telegraph, July 27, 1996

1. Choose the right explanation for each of the following words (with asterisks in the passage).

1. *to renege*
A. to repeat   B. to reduce   C. not to keep

2. *a pledge*
A. a promise   B. an obstacle   C. a refusal

2. Say whether the following statements are true (T) or false (F).

1. The strike had been on for six days in a row.

2. The spokesman sounded both optimistic and pessimistic.

3. The number of trains running was a great help to would-be passengers.

4. The RMTU played a bigger part than ASLEF in the Underground strikes.

5. This extract devotes the same space to the unions and to the Underground spokesman.

6. Such strikes often lead to greater solidarity.

7. The arguments used by both sides were unusual.

3. Read the passage again and find the following.

1. A noun meaning «paralysis».

2. A verb meaning «to bring to an end by finding a solution».

3. A noun describing a process by which two parties in a dispute put their case to an outside person, or body.

4. A noun meaning the rate of production or efficiency of a workforce.

5. A compound noun describing a practice whose aim is to reduce both traffic jams and pollution.

6. A noun meaning a ride as a passenger in a car.

4. The noun «spokesman» (now often replaced by «spokesperson») has the ending «-man». Use the explanations to find 8 other nouns ending in «-man».

1. He delivers the mail.	P□□□MAN
2. He uses nets or lines.	F□□□□□MAN
3. He acts as an intermediary.	M□□□□□MAN
4. He is good at shooting.	M□□□□MAN
5. He keeps an eye on buildings, sometimes at night.	W□□□□MAN
6. He collects litter and rubbish.	D□□□MAN
7. He plays the part of an actor, when it becomes dangerous.	S□□□□MAN
8. He is in charge of a group of workers.	F□□□MAN

Seven die in icy chaos on main roads

by Michael Durham

At least seven motorists died and scores were injured as icy conditions and freezing fog brought chaos to the motorway system in the Midlands and northern England yesterday.

Roads were closed in Derbyshire, Nottinghamshire and Yorkshire as dozens of accidents were reported in thick fog. A 19-mile tailback halted traffic on the M1 after a multiple pile-up which killed three people near Alfreton, Derbyshire.

The weather centre said freezing conditions and poor visibility would continue today and probably worsen tonight, everywhere «north of Oxfordshire». The RAC advised drivers to use extreme caution.

Police said three people died in the M1 accident on the south-bound carriageway, involving a bus, a lorry and several cars. Visibility was only 50 yards. The M1 was closed in both directions over a seven-mile stretch after a series of minor crashes.

On the M62 at Ainley Top, near Huddersfield in West Yorkshire, 60 vehicles were involved in a pile-up in which one man died and four people were seriously injured. One of the vehicles was believed to be an oil tanker which caught fire.

Visibility was down to 25 yards when the crash happened, just after midday on the westbound carriageway. There were long tailbacks and road closures from earlier accidents on both carriageways.

The Independent, December 22, 1992

1. Choose the appropriate endings for the following sentences.

1. Traffic on some motorways was disrupted by
A. a particular weather condition.
B. two different weather conditions.
C. three different weather conditions.

2. The newspaper correspondent gave a more detailed account of
A. one accident.
B. two accidents.
C. three accidents.

3. The correspondent apparently
A. witnessed the accidents.
B. drove to the scene.
C. had mainly to rely on police reports.

4. As a result, the extract is
A. somewhat patchy.
B. clearly organised.
C. extremely vague.

5. Visibility was
A. poorer on the M1.
B. poorer on the M62.
C. just as bad on both motorways.

6. After reading the extract, we realise that the seriousness of accidents depends on
A. the type of vehicles involved.
B. the type of vehicles involved and their loads.
C. the direction in which the vehicles are travelling.

2. «To worsen» means «to make worse». Similarly, what verbs would you use to express the following?

to make:
1. blacker   2. darker   3. weaker   4. softer
5. sharper   6. wider   7. deeper   8. less
9. moister   10. brighter   11. higher   12. longer
13. stronger

3. The article contains the verb «to close» and the noun «closure». Find the nouns corresponding to the following list of verbs taken from the article.
1. to report   2. to halt   3. to freeze
4. to continue   5. to advise   6. to die
7. to involve   8. to injure   9. to believe

4. Fill in the twelve lines across the grid with translations of the corresponding French words. This will give you the answer to number 13 in column D.

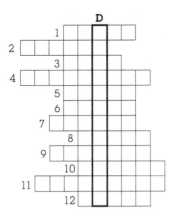

1. plaque (verglas...)
2. calme, lisse
3. réserver
4. congère
5. éviter
6. itinéraire
7. vol
8. vérifier
9. circulation
10. annuler
11. déviation
12. retard
13. artère (circulation)

Sport 23 Le sport

/// VOCABULAIRE
À HAUTE FRÉQUENCE

Sports and Sportsmen	Les sports et les sportifs
football, soccer ['sɒkə]	le football
cycling	le cyclisme
motor-racing	la course automobile
athletics [æθ'letıks]	l'athlétisme
an athlete ['æθliːt]	un athlète
a runner	un coureur
boxing	la boxe
a team	une équipe
a champion	un champion
a substitute	un remplaçant
a manager	un directeur technique
a coach, a manager (soccer)	un entraîneur
to train	s'entraîner
to practise	pratiquer
practice	la pratique
a referee [refə'riː]	un arbitre
a ball	un ballon
shape, fitness	la forme
fit	en forme

Sporting Events	Les épreuves sportives
to play	jouer, disputer
an event	une rencontre, une épreuve
a game	une partie
a tie	une rencontre éliminatoire
away	à l'extérieur
at home	à domicile
to race	participer à une course
a race	une course

horse racing	les courses de chevaux
a tournament	un tournoi
a Grand Prix	un Grand prix
Olympic	olympique
to attempt	tenter
a bid, an attempt	une tentative
to compete (in)	participer (à)
a competition	une compétition
a competitor	un concurrent
an opponent	un adversaire
a stage	une étape
a friendly match	une rencontre amicale
a championship	un championnat
a cup	une coupe
a round	un tour, une reprise
a final	une finale

Sports Results — Les résultats sportifs

to score	marquer
a goal	un but
a try	un essai
a point	un point
to serve	servir
a serve	un service
to lead	mener
a lead	une avance
a penalty	une pénalité
to win	gagner
a win, a victory	une victoire
to defeat	vaincre
a defeat	une défaite
to lose	perdre
to draw, to tie	faire match nul
a draw	un match nul
to qualify, to be through	(se) qualifier
to knock out, to eliminate	éliminer
elimination	l'élimination
to retain	conserver
a title	un titre
to set up	établir
a record	un record
a performance	une performance
to finish	terminer

Spectators and Facilities
Les spectateurs et les installations

a stadium	un stade
a ground	un terrain
the pitch	l'aire de jeu, le terrain
a stand	une tribune
the terraces	les gradins
a spectator	un spectateur
to watch	regarder
to attend sth.	assister à qch.
attendance	l'assistance
a track	une piste
a lap	un tour (de piste)
to support	encourager
support	le soutien
a supporter, a fan	un supporter
to behave	se conduire
behaviour	la conduite
to cheer	acclamer
to hiss at sb.	siffler qn.
to jeer at sb.	railler, huer
to boo	conspuer, huer
a hooligan	un casseur, un voyou
hooliganism	le vandalisme

EXPRESSIONS

short of practice	à court d'entraînement
in fine form	en bonne forme
to turn professional	devenir professionnel
Arsenal versus Chelsea	Arsenal contre Chelsea
the first round of the Cup	le premier tour de la Coupe
with one game in hand	avec un match de retard
to be held to a draw	être contraint au match nul
to clinch a title	décrocher un titre
to take a battering	subir une déroute
to drop one's serve	perdre son service
to break sb.'s serve	prendre le service de qn.
against all odds	contre toute attente
to be the odds-on favourite	être le grand favori
to cross the finishing line	franchir la ligne d'arrivée
to carry shoulder high	porter en triomphe

to play for time	jouer la montre
to score an own goal	marquer contre son camp
to disallow a goal	refuser un but
to clock under 4 minutes	être chronométré à moins de 4 minutes
top of the table	en tête du classement
bottom of the table	en queue de classement
to fail a drugs test, to test positive	subir un contrôle positif

VOCABULAIRE COMPLÉMENTAIRE

Sports and Sportsmen · Les sports et les sportifs

a tracksuit	un survêtement
swimming	la natation
freestyle	(nage) libre
breaststroke	la brasse classique
diving	le plongeon
fencing	l'escrime
wrestling	la lutte, le catch
skiing	le ski
skating	le patinage
figure skating	le patinage artistique
sailing	la voile
windsurfing, sailboarding	la planche à voile
a sailboard	une planche à voile
rowing	l'aviron
hiking, rambling	la randonnée
judo	le judo
a judoka	un judoka
a racing car	une voiture de course
a racing driver	un pilote de course
Formula One	la Formule 1
the grid	la grille (de départ)
practice	les essais
the pits	les stands
show jumping	le saut d'obstades
a side	une formation
a squad	un groupe
a team mate	un coéquipier
a runner-up	un deuxième (classement)

a skipper	un capitaine
a fitness test	un dernier essai (pour voir si le joueur peut jouer)
to substitute for sb.	remplacer qn.
an umpire	un juge, un arbitre
a linesman	un juge de touche
a post	un poteau
the crossbar	la barre transversale
amateur	amateur
professional	professionnel
to select	sélectionner
a selector	un sélectionneur
to cap (soccer, rugby...)	sélectionner
a cap (soccer, rugby...)	une sélection
a foul	une irrégularité
a free kick	un coup franc
a penalty kick	un pénalty
to book	avertir
a booking	un avertissement
a yellow card	un carton jaune
to send off	expulser
a send-off	une expulsion
to suspend	suspendre
a suspension	une suspension
to transfer	transférer
a transfer	un transfert
a transfer fee	le montant d'un transfert

Sporting Events — Les épreuves sportives

a fixture	une rencontre
the first leg	la rencontre aller
the second leg	la rencontre retour
to contest, to contend	disputer
a contest	une rencontre
a contestant, a contender	un concurrent
a heat	une éliminatoire, une série
a dead-heat	un résultat ex-æquo
to field	aligner (une équipe)
a field	l'ensemble des concurrents
kick-off	le coup d'envoi
to shoot	tirer
a shot	un tir
to wrongfoot	prendre à contrepied
to volley	reprendre de volée

a volley	une volée
half-time	la mi-temps
injury time, stoppage time	les arrêts de jeu
extra time	les prolongations
a quarter-final	un quart de finale
a semi-final	une demi-finale
play-off	la finale des premiers
on aggregate	sur l'ensemble des deux rencontres
the Grand Slam	le Grand Chelem

Soccer · Le football

a midfielder	un milieu de terrain
a striker	un avant de pointe
a sweeper	un libéro
the penalty area, the box	la surface de réparation
to save	parer, sauver
a save	une parade
a cross	un centre
a header	une tête
to clear	dégager
a clearance	un dégagement
a throw-in	une remise de la touche
a penalty shootout	la séance de tirs au but
the football pools	le loto sportif

Rugby Football · Le rugby

a scrum	une mêlée
a loose scrum	une mêlée ouverte
a scrum half	un demi de mêlée
a fly half, a stand-off (half)	un demi d'ouverture
a three-quarter (back)	un trois-quarts
a prop	un pilier
a hooker	un talonneur
a ruck	un regroupement
a line-out	une remise à la touche
a drop kick	un coup de pied tombé

Tennis · Le tennis

lawn	le gazon
clay	la terre battue
the base line	la ligne de fond

a singles match	un simple
a doubles match	un double
a forehand drive	un coup droit
a backhand drive	un revers
a net	un filet
a net approach	une montée au filet
a seeded player	une tête de série
the seeds	les têtes de série
30-love	30-zéro
an unforced error	une faute directe
deuce	égalité
advantage	avantage
a tie-break	un jeu décisif
in straight sets	sans concéder un set

Athletics / L'athlétisme

high jump	le saut en hauteur
long jump	le saut en longueur
pole vault	le saut à la perche
triple jump	le triple saut
discus	le disque
shot put	le lancer de poids
javelin	le javelot
hammer	le marteau
a hurdle	une haie
the finishing straight	la dernière ligne droite
a relay	un relais
the baton	le témoin

Miscellaneous Sports / Sports divers

multihull	multicoque
a trimaran ['traɪməræn]	un trimaran
a catamaran ['kætəməræn]	un catamaran
a single-handed race	une course en solitaire
an instructor	un moniteur
downhill	la descente (ski)
the yellow jersey	le maillot jaune
an overall leader	un leader au classement général
a time trial	une course contre la montre

256

Sports Results / Les résultats sportifs

to outplay	surclasser
to overwhelm, to crush	écraser
to thrash	battre à plate couture
to trounce	rosser
a rout, a drubbing	une déroute, une raclée
to outpoint	surclasser (boxe)
on points	aux points
to abandon	abandonner
to triumph	triompher
a triumph	un triomphe
a success	un succès
a showing	une prestation
a goalless draw	un match nul 0 à 0
two-nil	deux à zéro
the final whistle	le coup de sifflet final
a trophy	un trophée
a medal	une médaille
a podium	un podium
to dethrone	détrôner
to celebrate	fêter
celebrations	les réjouissances
to congratulate	féliciter
congratulations	les félicitations
to draw	tirer au sort
a draw	un tirage au sort
to relegate	reléguer
relegation	la relégation
a table	un classement
a division	une division
to cheat	tricher
a drugs test	un contrôle anti-dopage
anabolic steroids	les stéroïdes anabolisants
random testing	les contrôles inopinés

Spectators and Facilities / Les spectateurs et les installations

a gate	une grille, une porte, une assistance, une foule
a capacity crowd	un stade/une salle combles
a turnstile	un tourniquet
a grandstand	une tribune d'honneur
the Mexican wave	la ola

a dressing-room	un vestiaire
the venue ['venju:]	le lieu de déroulement
a ticket tout	un revendeur de billets
to gamble	jouer de l'argent
to bet	parier
a bet, a wager	un pari
a punter	un parieur

Bailey flies flag for Canada but reflects glory on Jamaica

Iain Macleod

Donovan Bailey's magnificent victory in the final of the men's 100 metres here on Saturday evening emphasized yet again the tradition of Jamaican-born sprinters and finally confirmed the vacuum* that exists in the United States, for so long the dominant force in world sprinting.

Bailey's surge* from 50 metres out was remarkable as he added Olympic gold to the world title he won in Gothenburg last year. His time of 9.84 sec was a new world record by 0.01 sec and as Canada, Bailey's adopted country, celebrated, they doubtless did not mourn* America's failure to win a medal, a repeat of Gothenburg.

Only twice this century – with the exception of the 1980 Games in Moscow which were boycotted by the Americans – have the United States not had a medallist in the 100 metres final, in 1928 and 1976. Dennis Mitchell's fourth place is an indication of how the balance of power has shifted. «This may be a wake-up call,» said Mike Marsh, the American who finished fifth.

For the third successive Games, a Jamaican-born sprinter headed the rest of the world in the Olympic final, though of course Ben Johnson in Seoul in 1988 subsequently tested positive for steroids and was stripped of the title. Four years ago, Linford Christie, at the centre of so much drama here, won for Britain. Christie, according to the American, Michael Johnson, was the catalyst for undermining the notion of the United States' invulnerability.

The Daily Telegraph, July 29, 1996

---

1. *Choose the right explanation for each of the following words (with asterisks in the passage).*

1. *a vacuum*
A. high pressure   B. an abundance   C. a lack

2. *surge*
A. falling behind   B. moving ahead   C. remaining constant

3. *to mourn*
A. to feel sad   B. to feel pleased   C. to feel indifferent

2. Say whether the following statements are true (T) or false (F).

1. Two ideas are underlined in the first paragraph.
2. Bailey's victory in the final came as a surprise.
3. It could be said that Donovan Bailey killed two birds with one stone.
4. It could also be said that Bailey's victory and the results of the final added insult to injury for the United States.
5. Mike Marsh finished first among the US finalists.
6. It could be said that Ben Johnson blotted his copybook.
7. According to Michael Johnson, Linford Christie may go down in the history of the 100 metres.

3. Test your knowledge by choosing the appropriate endings for the following sentences.

1. Linford Christie was disqualified in the final because
A. he tested positive.
B. he jumped the gun twice.
C. he arrived late.

2. Another West Indian got a medal in the 100-metre final. It was
A. Frankie Fredericks.
B. Michael Johnson.
C. Ato Boldon.

3. Canada was to upset the US team once more in the Atlanta games with its victory in the
A. 400-metre final.
B. 4 x 400 metre relay.
C. 4 x 100 metre relay.

4. «Medallist» is a noun ending with the suffix «-ist». Use the explanations to find 7 more nouns ending in «-ist».

1. A person who drives a car.   M◻◻◻◻IST
2. A person who writes books of fiction.   N◻◻◻◻IST
3. A person who plays an instrument or sings alone. S◻◻◻IST
4. A person who plays an instrument often found in churches. O◻◻◻◻IST
5. A person who writes a regular article in a newspaper. C◻◻◻◻◻IST
6. A person who does amusing or satirical drawings. C◻◻◻◻◻◻IST
7. A person who writes words for songs.   L◻◻◻◻IST

Bold Nigerians pull off another thrilling escape.

by *Richard Williams*

Terrible starters but masters of suspense, Nigeria became the first African team to win the Olympic football tournament by defeating Argentina by 3-2 in another hectic* and enthralling* match in Sanford Stadium in Athens on Saturday afternoon.

In front of 86,117 people, who filled the University of Georgia's great concrete bowl to capacity, Nigeria went behind to a goal from Argentina halfway through the second minute, or about 10 seconds earlier than they had conceded the first goal to Brazil in the semi-final. But, in just the same way, they fought back. And when they fell behind again, they fought back once more.

Against Brazil they had equalised at 3-3 with 20 seconds left on the clock and then scored their sudden-death winner in the fourth minute of extra time. In the final the winning goal came with only 90 seconds of normal time remaining. The fact that it was scored with perhaps four of their men offside did nothing to reduce the belief that justice had been served.

The Nigerians had delighted not only the hundreds of their own supporters, gathered in knots around the stadium, but the thousands of American families who had been thrilled by the Africans' speed and sense of adventure.

Little sympathy was wasted on the silver medal winners, who had tried to close up the game after going 2-1 ahead and paid the price for their caution.

The Guardian, August 8, 1996

1. Choose the right explanation for each of the following words (with asterisks in the passage).

1. *hectic*
A. at a slow pace
B. with dull moments
C. full of activity

2. *enthralling*
A. exciting
B. boring
C. painful

2. Say whether the following statements are true (T) or false (F).

1. The phrase "Terrible starters but masters of suspense" is fully justified later in the extract.
2. Argentina's scores were 1-0, 1-1, 2-1, 2-2 and 3-2.

3. The semi-final against Brazil ended in a draw after 90 minutes.

4. Nigeria played 30 minutes extra time to qualify for the final.

5. The journalist deplored the referee's mistake.

6. Both teams in the final played attacking football.

7. American spectators responded well to an unfamiliar sport.

8. European universities have no reason to envy sports facilities in American universities.

3. The prefix «off-» is to be found in the word «offside». Match the similarly-constructed words (1-8) with their explanations (A-H).

1. off-licence	A. a dangerous way of skiing
2. off the record	B. a place selling alcoholic beverages
3. off-duty	C. unprepared (of a speech, answer, etc.)
4. offshore	D. unusual and rather strange
5. off the cuff	E. not at work
6. off colour	F. not for publication or to be included in any report
7. off piste	G. outside the country of reference
8. offbeat	H. not feeling well

4. Fill each blank with a word from the list. Use each word only once. Verbs are given in the infinitive.

goal	defenders	attackers	to foul
minutes	area	free-kick	

When Javier Zanetti ...(1)... Emmanuel Amunike with two ...(2)... to go, Wilson Oruma took the ...(3)... just outside the left-hand edge of the penalty ...(4)... .

As the ball swung across, five Argentinian ...(5)... moved out with perfect syncronisation.

Four green-shirted ...(6)... were left exposed, and one of them – Amunike, appropriately enough – banged the ball past Pablo Cavallero in Argentina's ...(7)... .

The Guardian, August 8, 1996

MATT

THE MANCHESTER MAN WHO SAID FOOTBALL IS ONLY A GAME

Countries and People 24 Les pays et les gens

L'anglais utilise parfois un nom différent de l'adjectif pour désigner les habitants. Dans ce cas, il est précédé de l'article indéfini.

A-C

Afghanistan	l'Afghanistan
Afghan	afghan
an Afghan, an Afghani	un Afghan
Albania	l'Albanie
Albanian	albanais
Algeria	l'Algérie
Algerian	algérien
Angola	l'Angola
Angolan	angolais
Argentina	l'Argentine
Argentinian	argentin
Armenia	l'Arménie
Armenian	arménien
Australia	l'Australie
Australian	australien
Austria	l'Autriche
Austrian	autrichien
Azerbaijan	l'Azerbaïdjan
Azerbaidjani	azeri
an Azeri, an Azerbaijani	un Azerbaïdjanais
Bangladesh	le Bangladesh
Bangladeshi	bengalais
B(y)elarus, B(y)elorussia	le Bélarus, la Biélorussie
B(y)elorussian	biélorusse
Belgium	la Belgique
Belgian	belge
Benin	le Bénin
Beninese	béninois
Bolivia	la Bolivie
Bolivian	bolivien
Brazil	le Brésil
Brazilian	brésilien
Bosnia	la Bosnie

Bosnian	bosniaque
Bulgaria	la Bulgarie
Bulgarian	bulgare
Burma	la Birmanie
Burmese	birman
Burundi	le Burundi
Burundi	burundais
a Burundian	un Burundais
Cambodia	le Cambodge
Cambodian	cambodgien
Cameroon	le Cameroun
Cameroonian	camerounais
Canada	le Canada
Canadian	canadien
Chad	le Tchad
Chadian	tchadien
Chile	le Chili
Chilean	chilien
China	la Chine
Chinese	chinois
Colombia	la Colombie
Colombian	colombien
the Congo	le Congo
Congolese	congolais
Costa Rica	le Costa Rica
Costa Rican	costaricain
Croatia	la Croatie
Croatian	croate
a Croat	un Croate
Cuba	Cuba
Cuban	cubain
Cyprus	Chypre
a Cypriot	un Chypriote
the Czech Republic	la République tchèque
Czech	tchèque

D-I

Denmark	le Danemark
Danish	danois
a Dane	un Danois
Ecuador	l'Equateur
Ecuadorian	équatorien
Egypt	l'Egypte
Egyptian	égyptien

El Salvador	le Salvador
Salvadorian	salvadorien
England	l'Angleterre
English	anglais
an Englishman	un Anglais
Eritrea	l'Erythrée
Eritrean	érythréen
Estonia	l'Estonie
Estonian	estonien
Ethiopia	l'Ethiopie
Ethiopian	éthiopien
Finland	la Finlande
Finnish	finlandais
a Finn	un Finlandais
France	la France
French	français
Gabon	le Gabon
Gabonese	gabonais
the Gambia	la Gambie
Gambian	gambien
Germany	l'Allemagne
German	allemand
Georgia	la Géorgie
Georgian	géorgien
Ghana	le Ghana
Ghanaian	ghanéen
Great Britain	la Grande-Bretagne
British	britannique
a Briton	un Britannique
Greece	la Grèce
Greek	grec
Grenada	la Grenade
Grenadian	grenadien
Guatemala	le Guatemala
Guatemaltan	guatémaltèque
Guinea	la Guinée
Guinean	guinéen
Guyana	la Guyane
Guyanese	guyanais
Haiti	Haïti
Haitian	haïtien
Holland	la Hollande
Dutch	hollandais
a Dutchman	un Hollandais
Honduras	le Honduras

Honduran	hondurien
Hungary	la Hongrie
Hungarian	hongrois
Iceland	l'Islande
Icelandic	islandais
an Icelander	un Islandais
India	l'Inde
Indian	indien
Indonesia	l'Indonésie
Indonesian	indonésien
Iran	l'Iran
Iranian	iranien
Iraq	l'Irak
Iraqi	irakien
Ireland	l'Irlande
Irish	irlandais
an Irishman	un Irlandais
Israel	Israël
Israeli	israélien
Italy	l'Italie
Italian	italien

J-N

Jamaica	la Jamaïque
Jamaican	jamaïcain
Japan	le Japon
Japanese	japonais
Java	Java
Javanese	javanais
Jordan	la Jordanie
Jordanian	jordanien
Kazakhstan	le Kazakhstan
Kazakh	kazakh
Kenya	le Kenya
Kenyan	kenyan
Korea	la Corée
Korean	coréen
Kuwait	le Koweït
Kuwaiti	koweïtien, koweïti
Kirghizstan	le Kirghizstan
Kirghiz	kirghiz
Laos	le Laos
Laotian	laotien
Latvia	la Lettonie

Latvian	letton
Lebanon	le Liban
Lebanese	libanais
Liberia	le Libéria
Liberian	libérien
Libya	la Libye
Libyan	libyen
Lithuania	la Lituanie
Lithuanian	lituanien
Luxembourg, Luxemburg	le Luxembourg
Luxemburger	luxembourgeois
Malaysia	la Malaisie
Malaysian	malais
Mali	le Mali
Malian	malien
Malta	Malte
Maltese	maltais
Mauritania	la Mauritanie
Mauritanian	mauritanien
Mexico	le Mexique
Mexican	mexicain
Moldova	la Moldavie
Moldovan	moldave
Morocco	le Maroc
Moroccan	marocain
Mozambique	le Mozambique
Mozambican	mozambicain
Namibia	la Namibie
Namibian	namibien
the Netherlands	les Pays-Bas
New Zealand	la Nouvelle-Zélande
a New Zealander	un Néo-zélandais
Nicaragua	le Nicaragua
Nicaraguan	nicaraguayen
Niger	le Niger
Nigeria	le Nigéria
Nigerian	nigérian
Norway	la Norvège
Norwegian	norvégien

P-Z

Pakistan	le Pakistan
Pakistani	pakistanais
Palestine	la Palestine

Palestinian	palestinien
Panama	le Panama
Panamanian	panaméen
Paraguay	le Paraguay
Paraguayan	paraguayen
Peru	le Pérou
Peruvian	péruvien
the Philippines	les Philippines
Phillipine, Filipino	philippin
a Filipino	un Philippin
Poland	la Pologne
Polish	polonais
a Pole	un Polonais
Portugal	le Portugal
Portuguese	portugais
Romania, Roumania	la Roumanie
Romanian, Roumanian	roumain
Russia	la Russie
Russian	russe
Rwanda	le Rwanda
Rwandan	rwandais
Saudi Arabia	l'Arabie saoudite
Saudi	saoudien
Scotland	l'Écosse
Scottish, Scots	écossais
a Scot, a Scotsman	un Écossais
Senegal	le Sénégal
Senegalese	sénégalais
Serbia	la Serbie
Serbian	serbe
a Serb	un Serbe
Slovakia	la Slovaquie
Slovakian	slovaque
a Slovak	un Slovaque
Slovenia	la Slovénie
Slovenian	slovène
a Slovene	un Slovène
Somalia	la Somalie
Somalian, Somali	somalien
a Somali	un Somalien
South Africa	l'Afrique du Sud
South African	sud-africain
Spain	l'Espagne
Spanish	espagnol
a Spaniard	un Espagnol

Sri Lanka	le Sri Lanka
Sri Lankan	sri lankais
Sudan	le Soudan
Sudanese	soudanais
Sweden	la Suède
Swedish	suédois
a Swede	un Suédois
Switzerland	la Suisse
Swiss	suisse
Syria	la Syrie
Syrian	syrien
Taiwan	Taiwan
Taiwanese	taiwanais
Tajikistan, Tadzhikistan	le Tadjikistan
Tajiki, Tadzhiki	tadjik
a Tajik, a Tadzhik	un Tadjik
Tanzania	la Tanzanie
Tanzanian	tanzanien
Thailand	la Thaïlande
Thai	thaïlandais
Tibet	le Tibet
Tibetan	tibétain
Togo	le Togo
Togolese	togolais
Tunisia	la Tunisie
Tunisian	tunisien
Turkey	la Turquie
Turkish	turc
a Turk	un Turc
Turkmenistan	le Turkménistan
Turkmen	turkmène
Uganda	l'Ouganda
Ugandan	ougandais
The Ukraine	l'Ukraine
Ukrainian	ukrainien
Uruguay	l'Uruguay
Uruguayan	uruguayen
Uzbekistan	l'Ouzbekistan
Uzbek	ouzbek
Venezuela	le Venezuela
Venezuelan	vénézuélien
Vietnam	le Vietnam
Vietnamese	vietnamien
Wales	le Pays de Galles
Welsh	gallois

a Welshman	un Gallois
the West Indies	les Antilles
West Indian	antillais
Yemen	le Yemen
Yemeni	yéménite
Yugoslavia	la Yougoslavie
Yugoslavian	yougoslave
a Yugoslav	un Yougoslave
Zambia	la Zambie
Zambian	zambien
Zimbabwe	le Zimbabwe
Zimbabwean	du Zimbabwe

Key ▮ Corrigé

Les références de page correspondent aux pages où vous trouverez les articles sur lesquels portent les exercices.

1. The Environment

page 16

1. 1/A, 2/C, 3/B, 4/B.

2. 1/F, 2/T, 3/F, 4/F, 5/F, 6/T.

3. 1. supertanker, 2. catastrophe, 3. oil, 4. important, 5. to offload, 6. cargo, 7. crude, 8. ran.

4. 1. NATO (North Atlantic Treaty Organisation), 2. UNO (United Nations Organisation), 3. CAP (Common Agricultural Policy), 4. IMF (International Monetary Fund), 5. GDP (Gross Domestic Product), 6. WHO (World Health Organisation).

page 18

1. 1/B, 2/C, 3/A, 4/B, 5/B, 6/C.

2. 1. ballistic, 2. catastrophic, 3. domestic, 4. democratic, 5. volcanic, 6. cosmetic, 7. plastic, 8. forensic.

3. 1. standard, 2. dustbin, 3. harmless, 4. process, 5. threaten, 6. sustainable, 7. destroy, 8. storage, 9. release, 10. discharge.

2. The Economy I

page 30

1. 1/C, 2/A.

2. 1/B, 2/C, 3/B, 4/A, 5/C, 6/A.

3. 1. to manage, 2. to delay, 3. a saloon, 4. a branch.

page 32

1. 1/B, 2/A, 3/C.

2. 1/F, 2/T, 3/F, 4/T, 5/T, 6/F, 7/T.

3. 1. rigid, strict, hard, 2. once again, 3. unpopular.

4. 1. a/one twentieth, 2. a/one tenth, 3. a/one fifth, 4. a/one third, 5. two fifths, 6. a/one half, 7. three-fifths, 8. two-thirds, 9. four-fifths.

3. The Economy II

page 42

1. 1/C, 2/A, 3/C.

2. 1/T, 2/T, 3/F, 4/F, 5/T, 6/F, 7/T.

3. 1. insolvency, 2. thrashed out, 3. a co-chairman, 4. the Channel Tunnel operator, 5. (a) to totter, (b) to resume, (c) to unveil, (d) to avert.

4. 1. delinquency, 2. frequency, 3. leniency, 4. complacency, 5. fluency.

page 43

1. 1/B, 2/C, 3/B, 4/A, 5/A.

2. 1. getaway, 2. showdown, 3. cover-up, 4. pull-out, 5. turnover, 6. shake-up, 7. shoot-out, 8. set-aside.

3. 1. liabilities, 2. repayment, 3. agenda, 4. stake, 5. overdue, 6. account, 7. repay, 8. partner 9. stock, 10. buoyant 11. bankruptcy

4. The Third World

page 50

1. 1/C, 2/A, 3/C, 4/B.

2. 1/F, 2/T, 3/T, 4/F, 5/F, 6/T.

3. 1. A. threefold, B. three times, 2. A. afterward, B. outward, C. inward, D. homeward, E. wayward.

page 51

1. 1/B, 2/A,3/C, 4/B, 5/A.

2. 1. malnutrition, starving, malnourished, hunger, hungry, 2. relief, aid, 3. shuttled, evacuate, emerged, spread.

3. The UN Secretary General said that while conditions were improving for many peoples around the world, Africa was the only region where poverty was expected to increase during this decade.

5. Employment

page 58

1. 1/A, 2/B.

2. 1/F, 2/T, 3/F, 4/T, 5/T, 6/T, 7/F.

3. cutting, group, aside, costs, president, loss, necessary.

4. 1. executive, 2. bonus, 3. unemployed, 4. shipyard, 5. management, 6. retirement, 7. overtime, 8. register, 9. benefit, 10. workforce, 11. engineer, 12. competition.

page 59

1. 1/C, 2/A, 3/C, 4/A, 5/B.

2. 1. low-paid, 2. increase or rise, 3. classified, 4. rate, 5. security, 6. included, 7. minimum.

3. 1. take home, 2. almost, 3. free time, 4. large scale, 5. additional, 6. to reduce.

6. Disputes and Tensions

page 69

1. 1/T, 2/T, 3/T, 4/F, 5/F, 6/T, 7/F, 8/T, 9/F, 10/F.

2. 1. leakage, 2. storage, 3. postage, 4. wreckage, 5. drainage, 6. usage.

3. 1. breakthrough, 2. break-up, 3. break-in, 4. breakout.

page 70

1. 1/B, 2/C.

2. 1/B, 2/C, 3/B, 4/A.

3. 1. pull out, 2. breakthrough, 3. stumbling block, 4. peace process, 5. broken.

7. Medicine

page 80

1. 1/B, 2/B, 3/A.

2. 1/T, 2/F, 3/F, 4/T, 5/F, 6/T, 7/F, 8/T.

3. 1/C, 2/E, 3/A, 4/B/D.

4. 1. to contaminate, 2. to examine, 3. to fertilise, 4. to prescribe, 5. to transmit, 6. to conceive, 7. to explain, 8. to recognise, 9. to describe, 10. to produce.

5. 1. undergone, 2. breast, 3. singer, 4. surgery, 5. lump, 6. operation, 7. recuperating, 8. media, 9. alone, 10. quiet.

page 82
1. 1/A, 2/C, 3/C, 4/B.

2. 1/T, 2/F, 3/F, 4/F, 5/T.

3. 1. developed, 2. breakthrough, 3. spread, 4. food chain.

8. Space

page 88
1. 1/B, 2/C, 3/A, 4/C, 5/A.

2. 1/B, 2/C, 3/B, 4/A, 5/C, 6/C.

3. 1. cosmonaut, astronaut, 2. manufacturing, 3. vital, 4. jettison, 5. Kathy.

4. 1. to mix, 2. extreme, 3. decrease, 4. to mend, 5. to tell.

page 90
1. 1/C, 2/A.

2. 1/T, 2/F, 3/T, 4/T, 5/F, 6/F, 7/F, 8/T.

3. 1. freight, 2. bid, 3. to remain, 4. to beat.

4. 1. spacesuit, 2. flightpath, 3. laboratory, 4. device, 5. steer, 6. backpack, 7. cargo, 8. panel, 9. lifeline, 10. countdown, 11. spacecraft

9. Politics I

page 97

1. 1/C, 2/B, 3/C, 4/A.

2. 1/T, 2/F, 3/T, 4/F, 5/F, 6/T, 7/T.

3. 1/T, 2/F, 3/F, 4/F, 5/T.

4. 1. to surge, landslide, 2. recovery, 3. battleground, stronghold.

page 99

1. 1/B, 2/A.

2. 1/T, 2/T, 3/T, 4/F, 5/F, 6/F, 7/F.

3. 1. entry, 2. publication, 3. design, 4. improvement, 5. conduct, 6. consideration, 7. comparison, 8. avoidance, 9. indication, 10. adjustment.

4. 1. outcome, 2. close, 3. stand, 4. deposit, 5. counting 6. rating, 7. retain, 8. round, 9. survey, 10. join, 11. policy, 12. Tory, 13. constituency

10. Politics II

page 110

1. 1/A, 2/C, 3/C, 4/B.

2. 1/C, 2/B, 3/C, 4/A, 5/A, 6/B.

3. 1. new, 2. close, 3. polls, 4. contender, 5. neck, 6. rival.

page 112

1. 1/B, 2/C.

2. 1/F, 2/T, 3/T, 4/F, 5/F, 6/T.

3. 1. attempt, 2. small(er) calibre, 3. destruction, 4. single shot.

4. 1. investment, 2. enlargement, 3. improvement, 4. statement, 5. derailment, 6. settlement, 7. harassment, 8. impeachment.

page 121

1. 1/B, 2/A, 3/C, 4/A, 5/C.

2. 1/T, 2/F, 3/T, 4/F, 5/T, 6/F, 7/F, 8/F.

3. A. Church of Scotland ministers have been warned of the dangers of boring their congregations.

B. A report, to be discussed at the general assembly of the Church next month, says that the television age has made people more critical of poor communication and presentation.

C. It describes boredom at worship as a lethal sin and stresses the need to ensure that churchgoers are active participants rather than apathetic spectators.

4. 1. alarming, 2. religious, 3. living, 4. analysis, 5 separation, 6. area, 7. decades, 8. strangers, 9. accommodation.

page 123

1. 1/C, 2/B, 3/B, 4/C.

2. 1/B, 2/A, 3/C, 4/B, 5/B, 6/B.

3. 2. successful, 4. heartless, 5. godless, 7. plentiful, 8. dutiful, 10. eventful, 11. jobless, 12. spotless, 14. defenceless, 16. countless.

12. Entertainment and the Mass Media

page 136

1. 1/A, 2/C, 3/B.

2. 1/F, 2/F, 3/T, 4/T, 5/T, 6/F.

3. 1. childhood, 2. motherhood, 3. neighbo(u)rhood, 4. knighthood, 5. priesthood.

4. 1. roadworthy, roadworthiness, 2. airworthy, airworthiness, 3. seaworthy, seaworthiness.

page 137

1. 1/F, 2/T, 3/T, 4/F, 5/T, 6/F.

2. 1. partnership, 2. dictatorship, 3. ownership, 4. censorship, 5. leadership, 6. companionship, 7. championship.

3. 1. high, 2. nominees, 3. watch, 4. missing, 5. suffer, 6. appeal, 7. charging, 8. spot, 9. high-profile.

13. Crime and Punishment

page 160

1. 1/A, 2/C, 3/A, 4/B, 5/B, 6/A, 7/B.

2. 1/F, 2/T, 3/F, 4T, 5/F, 6/T, 7/F, 8/F.

3. 1/H, 2/I, 3/G, 4/D, 5/A, 6/E, 7/C, 8/B, 9/F.

4. 1. burst into, 2. sawn-off shotgun, 3. tackle.

page 161

1. 1/B, 2/C, 3/A, 4/B.

2. 1/T, 2/F, 3/T, 4/F, 5/T, 6/T, 7/T, 8/T.

3. 1. recovered, 2. freed, 3. gagged, 4. removed, 5. attempt.

4. 1. criminal, 2. assault, 3. constable, 4. restore, 5. alleged,
6. lead, 7. guilty, 8. mug, 9. theft, 10. witness, 11. evidence,
12. warder, 13. manslaughter

14. Drugs

page 168

1. 1/B, 2/C, 3/A, 4/B.

2. 1/F, 2/T, 3/F, 4/T, 5/F, 6/T, 7/T, 8/T.

3. 1. cargo, consignment, 2. classic, 3. database, 4. to set up,
5. must (have), must (be).

4. 1. street, 2. loan, 3. tabs, 4. unwittingly.

page 170

1. 1/B, 2/A, 3/C, 4/C, 5/B, 6/A.

2. 1. a black spot, 2. a black mass, 3. a blackleg, 4. a black-
list, 5. blackmail, 6. a black sheep.

3. 1. powder, 2. laundering, 3. courier, 4. consignment,
5. available, 6. needle, 7. peddlar, 8. seizure, 9. kicks,
10. customs, 1. drug addict

4. 1. Tyneside, 2. Clydeside, 3. Thameside, 4. Speyside.

15. Demonstrations and Riots

page 177

1. 1/C, 2/A, 3/C.

2. 1/F, 2/T, 3/F, 4/T, 5/F, 6/F, 7/F, 8/T.

3. 1. conductor, 2. donor, 3. navigator, 4. sponsor, 5. impersonator, 6. speculator, 7. professor, 8. narrator.

4. 1. paste, 2. on-lookers, 3. to suspect, 4. beneficial, 5. dust.

page 178
1. 1/B, 2/C, 3/A.

2. 1/F, 2/F, 3/T, 4/F, 5/F, 6/T.

3. 1. to march, to protest, 2. failure, 3. alleged, 4. root, 5. to spread.

4. 1. scuffle, 2. tear gas, 3. helmet, 4. eruption, 5. placard, 6. missile, 7. trigger, 8. chant, 9. fierce, 10. surge, 11. campaigner

16. Terrorism and Revolutions

page 185
1. 1/A, 2/C, 3/C, 4/B.

2. 1/A, 2/A, 3/C, 4/C, 5/B.

3. 1. autonomy accords, 2. to avenge, 3. anniversary, 4. holy.

4. 1. a lull, 2. within, 3. autonomy, 4. admitted, 5. aimed, 6. massacre.

5. 1. kingdom, 2. stardom, 3. freedom, 4. wisdom, 5. boredom.

page 187
1. 1/B, 2/A, 3/C.

2. 1/F, 2/T, 3/F, 4/F, 5/T, 6/T.

3. 1. fundamentalist, 2. arrested, 3. bombing, 4. killed, 5. named, 6. citizen, 7. forms, 8. hire, 9. underground.

4. 1/D, 2/C, 3/B, 4/E, 5/A, 6/H, 7/F, 8/J, 9/G, 10/I.

17. War and Espionage

page 197

1. 1/C, 2/A, 3/C, 4/B.

2. 1/T, 2/F, 3/F, 4/F, 5/T, 6/F.

3. 1. to accept, 2. a stoppage, 3. to abstain, 4. resumption, 5. a closure.

4. 1. Bosnia's Muslims and Croats have reached a wide-ranging peace agreement in Washington which could prove to be a turning-point in the civil war.

2. After almost a year of bloody fighting between the two sides, in Central Bosnia and in the city of Mostar, they have reached an accord which closely links the political future of their two communities.

page 199

1. 1/C, 2/A, 3/C.

2. 1/C, 2/B, 3/B, 4/C, 5/C, 6/C (Qana bombardment in April 1996).

3. 1. attacked, 2. machine-guns, 3. wounded, 4. searched, 5. shots, 6. fire.

18. Miscellaneous Topics

page 208
1. 1/B, 2/B.

2. 1/F, 2/T, 3/F, 4/T, 5/F, 6/F, 7/T.

3. 1. hunt, 2. suspicion (or a suspect), 3. survey, 4. thought, 5. burial, 6. expectation (or expectancy), 7. intervention.

4. 1. Health, 2. provision, 3. condoms, 4. pupils, 5. to reduce, 6. pregnancies, 7. rate, 8. failing.

page 210
1. 1/A, 2/C, 3/C.

2. 1/B, 2/C, 3/A, 4/C, 5/A.

3. 1/E, 2/C, 3/A, 4/B, 5/F, 6/D.

19. Accidents

page 219
1. 1/B, 2/C, 3/A, 4/C.

2. 1/F, 2/F, 3/T, 4/T, 5/T, 6/T, 7/T.

3. 1. unshrinkable, 2. unforgivable, 3. unthinkable, 4. unshak(e)able, 5. unforgettable, 6. unspeakable, 7. undrinkable, 8. unsaleable or unsellable.

4. fire, smoke, heat, power, areas, firefighters, blaze, warned, closed, near, blocks, years.

page 221
1. 1/B, 2/C, 3/A.

2. 1/C, 2/B, 3/A, 4/A, 5/C, 6/C.

3. 1. A. relatives, B. recover, C. flight recorder, D. hamper, E. establish, F. to black out

2. G. domestic, H. withheld, I. drain, J. take-off.

4. 1. cliff, 2. shipping, 3. failure, 4. trawler, 5. drift, 6. collide, 7. freighter, 8. shaft, 9. overtake, 10. wreck, 11. fisherman, 12. firefighter

20. Natural Disasters

page 228

1. 1/B, 2/A, 3/C.

2. 1/F, 2/F, 3/T, 4/F, 5/T, 6/F, 7/T, 8/F.

3. 1. blizzard, 2. to lash, 3. shelter, 4. to continue, 5. to paralyse, 6. power, 7. a freighter.

4. 1/E, 2/B, 3/D, 4/F, 5/A, 6/C.

page 230

1. 1/B, 2/C, 3/A, 4/B, 5/C.

2. 1/F, 2/T, 3/F, 4/F, 5/T, 6/T, 7/T.

3. 1. to wreck, 2. to reverberate, 3. National, federal 4. epicentre, 5. freeway.

4. 1. length, 2. width, 3. height, 4. depth, 5. breadth.

21. The Weather

page 238

1. 1/A, 2/C, 3/C, 4/B.

2. 1/F, 2/T, 3/T, 4/T, 5/F, 6/T.

3. snowdrop, snowball, snowshoe, snowdrift, snowcap, snowflake.

22. Travel and Traffic

page 246

1. 1/C, 2/A.

2. 1/F, 2/T, 3/F, 4/F, 5/F, 6/T, 7/F.

3. 1. standstill, 2. to resolve, 3. arbitration, 4. productivity, 5. car sharing, 6. a lift.

4. 1. postman, 2. fisherman, 3. middleman   4. marksman 5. watchman, 6. dustman,   7. stuntman, 8. foreman.

page 248

1. 1/B, 2/B, 3/C, 4/A, 5/B, 6/B.

2. 1. to blacken, 2. to darken, 3. to weaken, 4. to soften, 5. to sharpen, 6. to widen, 7. to deepen, 8. to lessen, 9. to moisten, 10. to brighten, 11. to heighten, 12. to lengthen, 13. to strengthen.

3. 1. report, 2. halt, 3. frost or freeze, 4. continuation (or continuance), 5. advice, 6. death, 7. involvement, 8. injury, 9. belief.

4. 1. patch, 2. smooth, 3. book, 4. snowdrift, 5. avoid, 6. route, 7. flight, 8. check, 9. traffic, 10. cancel, 11. diversion, 12. delay, 13. thoroughfare

23. Sport

page 258

1. 1/C, 2/B, 3/A.

2. 1/T, 2/F, 3/T, 4/T, 5/F, 6/T, 7/T.

3. 1/B, 2/C, 3/C.

4. 1. motorist, 2. novelist, 3. soloist, 4. organist, 5. columnist, 6. cartoonist, 7. lyricist.

page 260

1. 1/C, 2/A.

2. 1/T, 2/F, 3/T, 4/F, 5/F, 6/F, 7/T, 8/F.

3. 1/B, 2/F, 3/E, 4/G, 5/C, 6/H, 7/A, 8/D.

4. 1. fouled, 2. minutes, 3. free-kick, 4. area , 5. defenders, 6. attackers, 7. goal.

Crédits

Textes

Nous exprimons notre vive gratitude aux journaux qui nous ont permis de reproduire certains de leurs articles :

The Daily Telegraph
The Financial Times
The Guardian
The Herald (Glasgow)
The Independent
Independent on Sunday
The Sunday Telegraph
The Times
The Weekly Telegraph

et les agences de presse :
Agence France Presse
Associated Press
Reuter

Illustrations

p. 17 : Colin Wheeler *(The Independent)* ; p. 41 : Kipper Williams *(The Guardian)* ; pp. 29, 83, 111, 198, 261 : Matt *(The Daily Telegraph, The Weekly Telegraph)* ; pp. 96, 138, 211, 247 : Austin *(The Guardian)*.

Achevé d'imprimer en France par Pollina, 85400 Luçon - n° 72945
N° d'édition : 2119-01 - Dépôt légal : septembre 1997